TREASURES OF
Illinois

Illinois State Capitol in Springfield
Photo by Deepak

by Damon Neal

a part of the Morgan & Chase Treasure Series
www.treasuresof.com

MORGAN & CHASE PUBLISHING INC.

© 2008 Morgan & Chase Publishing, Inc. All rights reserved.
No portion of this book may be reproduced or utilized in any
form, or by any electronic, mechanical or other means without
the prior written permission of the publisher.

Morgan & Chase Publishing, Inc.
531 Parsons Drive, Medford, Oregon 97501
(888) 557-9328
www.treasuresof.com

Printed and bound by Taylor Specialty Books–Dallas TX
First edition 2008
ISBN: 978-1-933989-29-7

THE
TREASURE
SERIES

I gratefully acknowledge the contributions of the many
people involved in the writing and production of this book.
Their tireless dedication to this endeavour has been inspirational.
–William Faubion, Publisher

The Morgan & Chase Publishing Home Team

Operations Department:
V.P. of Operations–Cindy Tilley Faubion
Travel Writer Liaison–Anne Boydston
Shipping & Receiving–Virginia Arias
Customer Service–Elizabeth Taylor
IT Engineer–Ray Ackerman
Reception–Samara Sharp

Production Department:
Production Department:
Office Manager–Sue Buda
Editor/Writer–Robyn Sutherland
Photo Coordinator–Wendy L. Gay
Graphic Design Team–Jesse Gifford, Jacob Kristof

Administrative Department:
CFO–Emily Wilkie
Accounting Assistants–David Grundvig, Tiffany Myers
Website Designer–Molly Bermea
Website Software Developer–Ben Ford

Contributing Writers:
Mary Beth Lee, Lynda Kusick, Anne Schmidt, Bruce Stevens, Kenneth Hill, Lew Merrell, Michael Lagrimas, Randy
Gale, Richard C. Winter, Susanne Pawlikowski, Catherine Perez, Dusty Alexander, Jeanie Erwin, Jennifer Buckner, Kait
Fairchild, Karuna Glomb, Kate Zdrojewski, Laura Young, Marek Alday, Mary Knepp, Maya Moore, Nancy McClain,
Patricia Smith, Paul Hadella, Robert J. Benjamin, Sandy McLain, Todd Wels, Tamara Cornett

Special Recognition to:
Casey Faubion, April Higginbotham, Megan Glomb, Eric Molinsky, Heather Allen, Mary Murdock,
Clarice Rodriguez, C.S. Rowan, Prairie Smallwood, Vikki West, Gene Mitts

Cover Photos
Large front cover of Chicago by Michael Hicks
Back cover photo of Buckingham Fountain by Rick Aiello
Small photo of Illinois Capitol Building by Becky Pitzer
Small photo of cardinal by Mike Epp

While we have made every effort to ensure that the information contained in this book is accurate at the time of publishing, neither the authors nor Morgan & Chase Publishing shall have
any liability to any person or entity with respect to any loss or damage caused or alleged to be caused directly or indirectly by use or inclusion of the information contained in this book.
Trademarked names appear throughout this book. Rather than list the names and entities that own the trademarks or insert a trademark symbol with each mention of a trademarked
name, we state that we are using the names only for editorial purposes and to the benefit of the trademark owner with no intention of infringing upon that trademark. All trademarks or
service marks are the property of their respective owners.

To the people of Illinois.
Thank you for making this book possible.

The Cloud Gate in Chicago's Millenium Park.
Photo by John Attebury

ILLINOIS FACTS:

Admitted to the Union: 1818, the 21th state
Population (2006): 12,831,970
Largest City: Chicago, 2,833,321
Largest Metro Area: Chicago Metro, 9,505,748
Highest Elevation: Charles Mound, 1,235 feet

Animal: White-Tailed Deer
Bird: Cardinal
Fish: Bluegil
Flower: Violet
Motto: State Sovereignty, National Union
Nickname: Prairie State
Tree: White Oak

Foreword

Welcome to the Treasures of Illinois. This book is a resource that can guide you to some of the best places in Illinois, a state known for its professional sports teams and impressive agricultural production. Illinois is also home to Chicago, the metropolitan area that offers visitors unbelievable sights and sounds as well as being the birthplace of Senator Hillary Rodham Clinton. The state's mid-section is commonly called the Heart of Illinois and its eastern border is massive Lake Michigan.

During your visit you can marvel at the Museum of Science and Industry, the only remaining building from the 1893 Columbian Exposition, or you can catch a game with the 2005 World Series champions, the Chicago White Socks. Whether you choose to wander along the Trail of Tears National Historic Trail or watch the flurry of activity of O'Hare International Airport, this state has everything to make your visit memorable.

From the beginning of this project we were blessed to see incredible works of art and explore communities that were so much more than just places to visit. Whether you are a world traveler or you have spent your entire life in Illinois, you will find people and places in this book that will both inspire and interest you. The Treasure Series idea was born over 20 years ago by entrepreneurs who were raised in family-owned businesses. Today they oversee overall book quality and maintain the high selection standards for the Treasures who are featured within the Treasure Series books.

In preparing the Treasures of Illinois we talked to literally thousands of business people about their products, their services and their passion. We cheered for the Chicago Bulls on one day and visited the Lincoln Home National Historic Site the next. We slept in beds fit for royalty and we tasted traditional dishes of the region. You are holding the result of our efforts in your hands. Treasures of Illinois is a 175-page compilation of the best places in Illinois to eat, shop, play, explore, learn and relax. We will always be thankful to the friendly, intelligent people who populate Illinois. We had the privilege of seeing all the people and places this book is about. All you have to do now is enjoy.

Cindy Tilley Faubion

Illinois Map and Regions

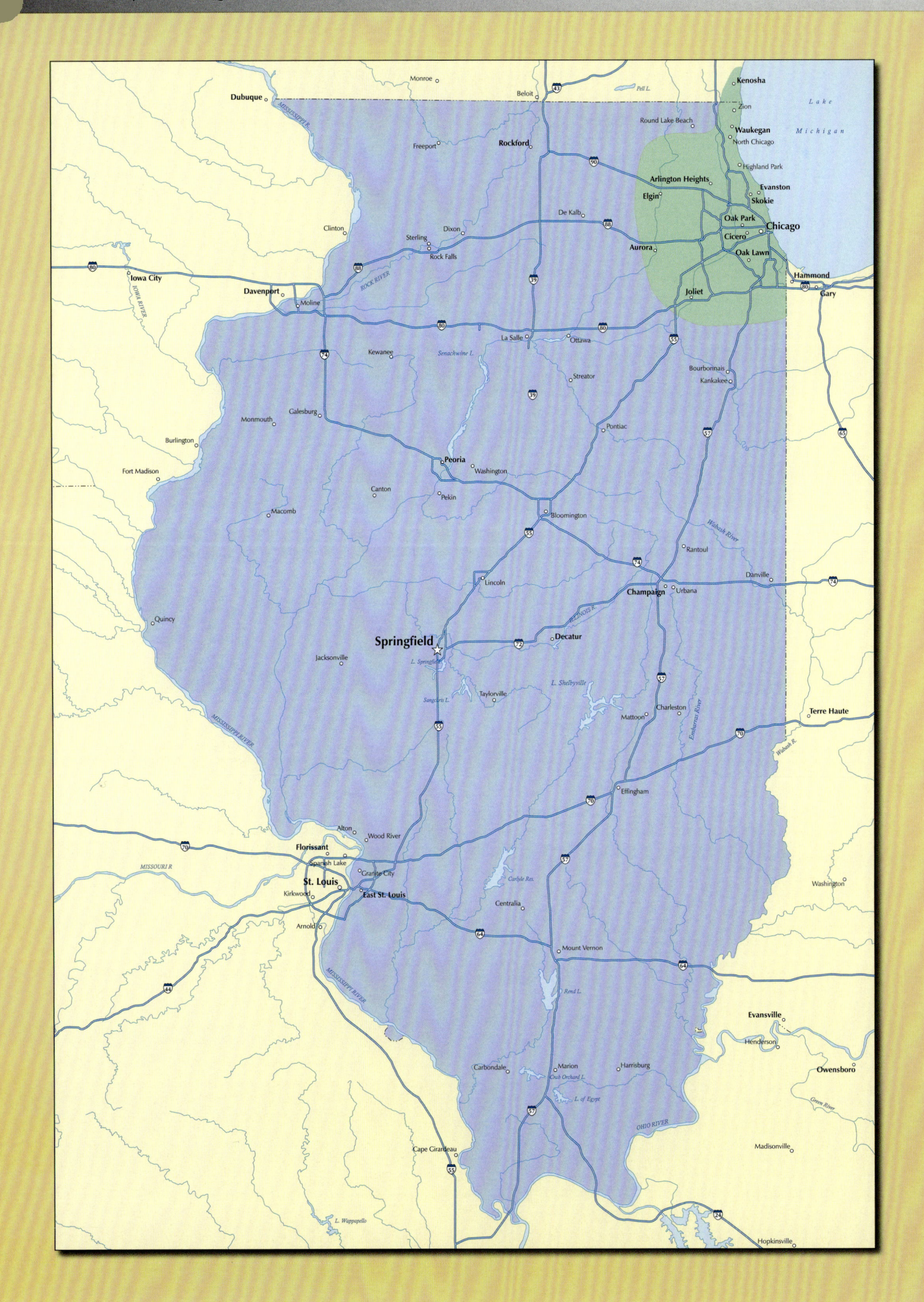

Table of Contents

2 Chicago Metro

- 4 Accommodations & Resorts
- 9 Arts & Crafts
- 14 Attractions & Recreation
- 23 Bakeries, Treats, Coffee & Tea
- 34 Farms, Markets & Delis
- 39 Fashion & Beauty
- 53 Flowers & Events
- 60 Galleries & Fine Art
- 65 Home & Garden
- 76 Restaurants & Cafés
- 88 Shopping & Gifts

2 Greater Illinois

- 104 Accommodations & Resorts
- 114 Arts & Crafts
- 118 Attractions & Recreation
- 130 Bakeries, Treats, Coffee & Tea
- 135 Farms, Markets & Delis
- 140 Fashion & Beauty
- 144 Flowers & Events
- 145 Galleries & Fine Art
- 148 Home & Garden
- 152 Restaurants & Cafés
- 167 Shopping & Gifts

174 Indices

- 174 Index by Treasure

Chicago Metro

333 Wacker Drive, Chicago.

Cloud Gate aka "The Bean" in Millennium Park, Chicago
Photo by Jonah H

Chicago Metro

- 4 **Accommodations & Resorts**
- 9 **Arts & Crafts**
- 14 **Attractions & Recreation**
- 23 **Bakeries, Treats, Coffee & Tea**
- 34 **Farms, Markets & Delis**
- 39 **Fashion & Beauty**
- 53 **Flowers & Events**
- 60 **Galleries & Fine Art**
- 65 **Home & Garden**
- 76 **Restaurants & Cafés**
- 88 **Shopping & Gifts**

Chicago Theatre at Night
Photo by Chris Metcalf

Accommodations & Resorts—Chicago Metro

TownePlace Suites Chicago Lombard

TownePlace Suites Chicago Lombard is the perfect setting for extended-stay travelers. With 126 spacious suites in three floor plans, you'll enjoy the comfort of a home away from home. The studio floor plan provides distinct living, sleeping and work areas to meet all of your needs. The one bedroom suite offers a little extra space with a full kitchen, plus separate living, sleeping and work areas. The deluxe two bedroom suite offers more privacy with a television in each bedroom. The living area has a relaxing sofa so you can kick back, just like home. Kitchens have full-size appliances so you can eat in as often as you'd like. Luxury bedding complete with thick, cozy mattresses and crisp linens lure you to sleep in after a hard day's night. Free high-speed Internet access and cable television make extended stays a little more comfortable. A complimentary continental breakfast is served daily. You can rejuvenate in a large outdoor pool and an exercise room. With a full-service business center on-site, you won't have far to go to find a copier or fax machine. Even your pet is welcome at TownPlace Suites. Whatever your lodging needs, TownePlace Suites Chicago Lombard works with you, always going above and beyond the call of duty.

455 E 22nd Street, Lombard IL
(630) 932-4400 or (800) 228-9290
www.towneplacesuiteslombard.com

Chicago Metro—Accommodations & Resorts

Hotel Baker

The stained glass peacock window over the doorway invites you into the lobby. Gaze around at the marble floor, hand stenciled woodwork and antique furnishings, and you'll understand why Hotel Baker is known as the Crown Jewel of the Fox. The hotel began as the dream of Colonel Edward Baker, who envisioned an elegant resort where friends, visitors and dignitaries could find comfort and modern conveniences. Hotel Baker opened in 1928 and made a sensation with its exotic European details, imported furnishings and modern culinary technology, including meat slicers, egg cookers and toasters. It enjoyed a stellar reputation as the place to stay in St. Charles. Now lovingly restored to its former splendor, the hotel offers the best of the past and the present. Owner Joe Salas has preserved the stately ambiance of this historic gem while continuing the tradition of modern amenities and style. Period furnishings and accents add to the feeling of timelessness in the rooms, no two of which are alike. Some rooms feature screened in balconies with private hot tubs. The Waterfront Restaurant serves prime steaks and fresh seafood, a European breakfast buffet and Champagne Brunch on Sundays. The Waterfront patio provides wonderful views of the river. The glorious two-story Rainbow Room offers a lighted dance floor that has hosted the likes of Tommy Dorsey, Guy Lombardo and Louis Armstrong in its time. Banquet and meeting facilities accommodate up to 300. Find a luxurious legacy at Hotel Baker.

100 W Main Street, St. Charles IL (630) 584-2100 or (800) 284-0110 www.hotelbaker.com

Accommodations & Resorts—Chicago Metro

Harrison House Bed & Breakfast

Lynn and Neal Harrison have turned their cozy inn into a gracious hideaway where folks arrive as guests and leave as friends. Harrison House Bed & Breakfast first opened to the public in 1987 after a five-month, in-depth renovation that restored the stately 1904 manor to its former turn-of-the-century glory. The elegant Victorian home was originally constructed as a wedding gift to Amelia Mickenbecker by her husband, Henry. The pair went on to raise eight children in the home, filling it with laughter and love. The Harrison's have brought new life to the old home by once again welcoming friends and guests. Harrison House Bed & Breakfast offers five comfortable guest rooms, three of which offer king beds and whirlpool tubs. Amenities include fresh in-room flowers, complimentary evening refreshments and both cable television and high-speed Internet service. In the morning, guests are awakened by the tempting scents of a scrumptious breakfast coming from the warm country kitchen. The inn is centrally located near Naperville's historic downtown and other exciting area attractions. Discover your new home away from home and new friends at Harrison House Bed & Breakfast.

26 N Eagle Street, Naperville IL
(630) 420-1117
www.harrisonhousebb.com

Oscar Swan Country Inn

Once you've visited Oscar Swan Country Inn, it becomes clear what Chicago financier Oscar Swan had in mind when he built the home as a country getaway in 1902. A century later, the Colonial Williamsburg Revival house and the surrounding eight-acre property continues to be a worthy getaway. Hans and Nina Heymann bought the Geneva estate in 1985 and, following three years of renovations, opened the inn to guests in 1988, a time when bed-and-breakfasts were still quite rare. Guests staying in the home's seven guest rooms get to know each other over a superb breakfast prepared in a commercial kitchen and served in the dining room or on the patio. You'll be in the middle of town with the advantage of gardens, an outdoor swimming pool, satellite television and an accommodating staff. The inn caters several on-site weddings a week, turning Nina, a former home economics professor, into a wedding planner. You can stage a wedding reception for 250 people in a permanent tent surrounded by lawns. The tent offers brick floors and three-season comfort. The inn also offers indoor reception space in the main house with its 12-over-12 window panes, wood floors and three fireplaces. A restored two-floor barn called the Gathering offering a casual setting for up to 140 people. Murder mysteries, private dinners, fundraisers, high teas and business meetings fill the Oscar Swan's calendar of events. Retreat to the comforts of Oscar Swan Country Inn.

1800 W State Street (Route 38), Geneva IL (630) 232-0173 www.oscarswan.com

Accommodations & Resorts—Chicago Metro

Sheraton Suites Elk Grove

Located in beautiful Elk Grove Village minutes from O'Hare Airport, Sheraton Suites Elk Grove Village offers 253 spacious and luxurious suites. The private bedrooms include one king or two double beds and remote control television. Enjoy a beautifully decorated separate living room for entertaining and relaxing. Guest rooms come with high-speed Internet access, in-room video games and movies. The large bathrooms provide deluxe amenities. If you are on a working vacation, you will appreciate the generously sized desk. A fax/copier/printer, data port and voicemail are available. Take some time to enjoy the whirlpool, the indoor and outdoor pools or the fitness center. After you have worked up an appetite you'll find plenty of ways to satisfy it at the casual Junipers Restaurant. Later, you can retreat to the relaxing atmosphere of the Lobby Lounge Bar, where you'll find a daily happy hour and large-screen TV. If you are planning a corporate conference or special event, the Sheraton has many rooms available, all equipped to assure your event is a success. Versatile audio-visual and dining packages fit every need. You'll enjoy the convenience of nearby attractions that include sports, shopping and museums. For an unforgettable event or a relaxing stay, rely on the Sheraton Suites Elk Grove. You are assured of finding a warm professional staff and excellent service.

121 NW Point Boulevard, Elk Grove Village IL

Chicago Metro—Arts & Crafts

Thanks for the Memories

Do you love to preserve memories? Sue Lech can help. As owner of Thanks for the Memories, she offers thousands of scrapbooking items that can make the best of times last forever. For the past eight years, Sue and her associates have been providing customers with the latest and greatest in scrapbooking, papercrafting and stamping supplies. With an inventory that includes more than 2,000 stickers, 2,500 styles of paper and hundreds of embellishments, Thanks for the Memories is definitely the scrapbooking headquarters for Northern Illinois. You'll find Creative Imaginations, Quickutz and Scrappin' Sports. Supplies to make your own party, graduation, shower or wedding invitations are featured. The shop's frequent buyer program provides an incentive to visit the store on a regular basis. Accumulate $150 in purchases and you'll received a 25-percent-off coupon on your entire next purchase. Secret Saturdays lure customers with buy-one-get-one free and surprise discounts throughout the store. A monthly newsletter provides crafters with a calendar of store events such as classes, demos and sales. It also lists the newest supplies on hand. Whether you're a seasoned stamper or a neophyte scrapper, Thanks for the Memories is one place you'll surely want to visit.

737 W IL Route 22, Lake Zurich IL
(847)-438-8322
www.thanks-4-the-memories.com

The Canvasback Ltd.

Everyone involved with the Canvasback, from the artists, instructors and staff to the owner, has one thing in common: a passion for needlepoint. Sally Volkert was an interior designer with a degree in art who developed an interest in needlepoint. She eventually chose to start a business of her own to be near her children when they were young and recruited her sister-in-law, Mary Gee Volkert, as her business partner. The needlepoint store they purchased was a fledgling operation, so they changed the format and added services, classes, hand-painted canvases and a selection of new and exciting fibers. Now the beginning classes are always full, and Camp Canvasback introduces scores of children to the world of needlepoint. The Canvasback staff members keep their expertise current with needle arts classes and seminars. Despite its growth, the Canvasback is still a reflection of Sally and Mary Gee's original goals. Unfortunately, Mary Gee passed away in 1996, due to a terminal illness. Sally has continued to build the business with the help of 10 talented staff members. You can look forward to attentive, friendly service, talented and creative staff and classes, and the best products the industry has to offer at the Canvasback.

1747 Orchard Lane, Northfield IL
(847) 446-4244
www.canvasback-needlepoint.com

Beadhive

If you're searching for an enticing array of beads and beading supplies, buzz over to the Beadhive. Owners and longtime friends Leslie Owings and Jean Narimatsu offer the finest-quality beads and an extensive supply of modern tools to help you create fashionable accessories through this ancient art form. Be dazzled by Swarovski crystal beads from Austria, semi-precious stones, Japanese delicas, Czech glass beads and exquisite glass lampwork beads. Browse handmade silver, copper and brass components created by area artists and sterling and gold-filled settings. You'll also find an array of hand-beaded jewelry to inspire your imagination, including birthstone earrings and mother bracelets. You can request custom-designed jewelry for your wedding or as a gift for someone special. You may also bring in estate beads for repair and reworking. If you want to learn beading, the owners are happy to teach you the ropes. Discover your need for beads at Beadhive.

316 Franklin Street, Geneva IL (630) 232-3866

Needle Pointe

Needle Pointe attracts needlepoint enthusiasts from throughout the Chicago area, thanks to a large inventory, trunk shows by renowned canvas painters and classes for every interest and skill level. Brothers Rick and Joel Greenman and Joel's wife, Cheryl, purchased the Palatine shop in 2004 and promptly quadrupled the inventory. The store makes shopping a breeze with a wall of color for comparing fibers, many of which are hand-spun and hand-dyed. The Greenmans also display colorful hand-painted canvases on the walls. They can create custom-painted canvases from your photos and offer custom finishing and framing of your completed pieces. Leading artists give demonstrations and teach specialized classes. Rick and Joel have extensive retail experience, and Cheryl is a needlepoint enthusiast who won an honorable mention the first time she entered an American Needlepoint Association contest. After opening the shop, Rick took needlepoint lessons to be able to answer customer questions and soon became hooked on the activity. The store offers an open stitch night for working on your project in the company of fellow needle fans. For a stimulating shopping environment and owners who understand your needs, visit Needle Pointe.

122 W Northwest Highway, Palatine IL (847) 963-0794
www.needlepointeltd.com

Craftique and Never Enough Knitting

Proving that creativity knows no bounds, the same people who stock up on supplies at Never Enough Knitting are often regular customers at the quilting shop Craftique, too. These two stores are located at the same address in downtown Wheaton. Owner Jane Brown is herself a knitter and quilter whose wizardry at crocheting is particularly advanced. In fact, this retired art teacher has written for *Crochet* magazine. Many of her own quilting designs are on display at Craftique, where lines of reproduction fabrics from the 1930s and '40s, the Civil War and even the 1700s are very popular. Contemporary quilt fabrics include batiks, Americana and flannels in sports, garden and floral themes. Craftique also carries needlepoint and cross stitch supplies. More specific in its focus, Never Enough Knitting is a full-service yarn shop packed with more than 35 brands of yarn in such materials as wool, alpaca and camel. The owner sells her own original patterns under the JMB Designs label and those of her daughter, called Jean Austin Designs. Both stores offer classes and plenty of assistance for your projects. Find crafts supplies along with ideas to inspire your creativity at Craftique and Never Enough Knitting.

119/121 N Main Street, Wheaton IL (630) 221-1007 or (630) 752-9192
www.craftique-neverenoughknitting.com

Chicago Metro—Arts & Crafts

The Fine Line Creative Arts Center

The Fine Line Creative Arts Center is a not-for-profit art school that offers classes in the fine arts and fine crafts. More than 35 dedicated, professional teachers, many with national reputations, teach 200 classes to about 1,100 students each year. Topics include weaving, fiber, glass, metal and jewelry, pottery, painting and paper arts. The center has two buildings on four rural acres of land. The barn houses a yarn and supplies shop and the textile classrooms. The Dempsey Gallery, in the barn, exhibits the work of Fine Line members. The newer Kavanagh building contains teaching studios and the Kavanagh Gallery, an open, light-filled space. The Kavanagh's six or seven yearly exhibits range from nationwide juried shows of paintings, pottery, textiles and sculpture to one and two-person shows, student and faculty exhibits and the annual Christmastime Show and Sale. Raku Day, a public pottery outreach program in the summer, and Uncommon Threads, a wearable art fashion show in the fall are sponsored by the Fine Line annually. The Fine Line dates to 1979, when it was founded by Denise Kavanagh. She was a member of the School Sisters of St. Francis, an international community of sisters who serve in education, and has a strong tradition in music and art. Denise had been a school principal earlier in life. After retiring, she pursued the dream of exploring her creative spirit. Denise passed away in 2002, but her joyful spirit continues to animate the center. Lynn Caldwell is the director today. Come visit the Fine Line Creative Arts Center, a passionate project run almost entirely by volunteers.

6N158 Crane Road, St. Charles IL
(630) 584-9443
www.fineline.org

Arts & Crafts—Chicago Metro

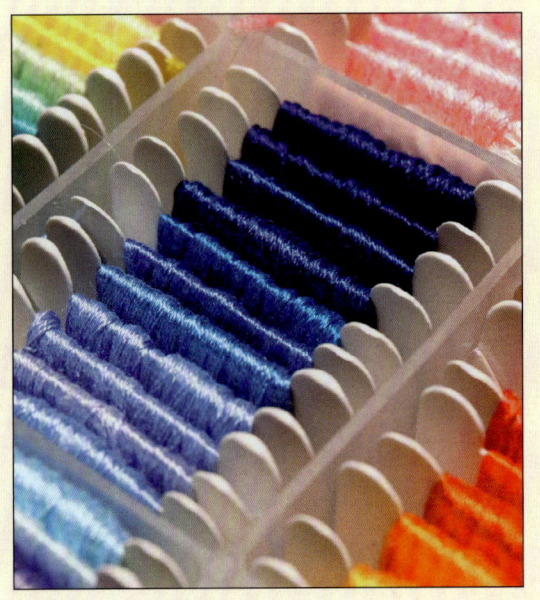

Designers Desk, the Complete Needlework Shop

Designers Desk, the Complete Needlework Shop began with a mere 330 square feet and has since expanded to nearly 4,000. One of the largest needlepoint shops in Chicagoland, it offers everything a needlework crafter could wish for. Supplies for punch needle, cross stitch, needlepoint and silk ribbon embroidery fill the shelves. You'll find complete lines of threads in every color and strength. Over 7,000 hand-painted needlepoint canvases provide you with an array of design options, from traditional to whimsical. Accessories galore, including scissors, laying tools, beading and needles, fulfill your artistic needs. Unfinished needlework projects such as purses, trays, boxes and foot stools are available for you to complete. Classes in needlepoint, punch needle, cross stitch and embroidery are offered and taught by professionals. Owner Pat Delp has been an avid needlework crafter since childhood. Closing her Bloomingdale store after twenty three years, she moved to the store to its current location in a restored 1861 home in 2007. If you share her passion for the art of needlepoint, don't miss Designers Desk, the Complete Needlework Shop.

216 James Street, Geneva IL   (630) 262-1234 or (800) 377-8087

Wool and Company

A kaleidoscope of yarn awaits you at Wool and Company. Owner Lesley Edmondson creates a paradise for passionate knitters and weavers. Explore the overflowing cases and corners filled with the finest supplies and thousands of sumptuous yarns. You may have trouble deciding between a pastel alpaca and a vibrant Peruvian wool. Luxurious qiviut yarn, made from the soft undercoat of musk oxen, is softer and lighter than cashmere. Shimmering silk and hand-painted yarns will make selecting your next skein a wonderful challenge. Browse through accessories, patterns and books galore to spark your creativity. The talented and dedicated staff offers classes for beginners to experts in a range of techniques, including Fair Isle knitting, cable knitting, felting, crocheting and lace. Whether you want to create a tote, sweater or hat, you'll find a class that fits your needs. Love for the community and the community-building nature of knitting permeates Wool and Company. Whether by hosting the annual Knit-Out during Swedish Days, sponsoring weekly knitting group sessions or offering school enrichment programs that help kids discover the joys of knitting, Wool and Company is out to spread the joy of the traditional handicraft. Find the yarn of your dreams at Wool and Company.

23 S Third Street, Geneva IL   (630) 232-2305
woolandcompany.com

Stained Glass Emporium

You will want a little time to spare when you shop at the Stained Glass Emporium (SGE) in Skokie, because this shop is alight with inspiring glass art, as well as the supplies to make your own pieces. Here, you will find hundreds of stained glass windows, lamps and gifts, plus an extensive inventory of glass, tools and books. Owners Jennifer and Tony Kuzminski recently purchased the business from Jan and Dave O'Malley, who owned the store for 26 years. The helpful staff prides itself on customer service and years of experience. The store also offers classes that provide the knowledge and inspiration that you need to design your own masterpieces. Interested in making a window or a glass mosaic? Does fused glass jewelry intrigue you? Need repairs? SGE replicates most colors and textures of antique glass. Skilled, in-house artisans repair copper foiled panels and lamps, as well as zinc and leaded windows. Additionally, SGE stocks clear and colored glass in large sizes that can be custom cut and installed in your kitchen cabinet doors or elsewhere in your home. Often you can bring in your cabinet doors and browse through the shop while the glass is cut and installed. Explore the colorful world of stained glass and prepare to get creative at Stained Glass Emporium.

4031 Oakton Street, Skokie IL   (847) 677-0811
www.stainedglasschicago.com

Chicago Metro—Arts & Crafts   13

Photo by JP Photography

Ayla's Originals

On a dreary winter day 12 years ago, Ayla wandered into an art store looking for an escape from the winter doldrums. She selected two art kits: one for pottery, one for beading. She chose to open the beading kit first and immediately fell in love. Ayla discovered an artistry through beading she had never known. She discovered that creating jewelry calmed her and gave her a way to express herself. In 1996, Ayla's favorite bead shop closed. "Hum," she thought. "How cool would it be to play with beads all day?" Two months later, the shop reopened as Ayla's Originals. Today, Ayla's is known as the best and most complete bead store in Evanston. Ayla carries an extensive selection of unique beads, including a large supply of African Trade beads, Swarovski Crystal, glass, pearls, gold, silver, gemstones and more. You'll find every type of chain and clasp, along with a fine array of finished jewelry and unique flourishes. Ayla sponsors bead shows and offers classes through her International Bead Bazaar. If you're a beader or a jewelry lover, you should find a way to visit Ayla's. If you can't get to Evanston right away, you can shop on her very informative and extensive website, which is bursting with products and information.

1511 Sherman Avenue, Evanston IL
(847) 328-4040
www.aylasoriginals.com

The Painted Penguin

The process of creating a ceramic work is a labor of love, and many people consider the best part of ceramics to be painting the pieces. The Painted Penguin offers families and friends the opportunity to get together and to tap into their artistic natures by painting the ceramics they choose, with no waiting time for firing. The business began with Michael and Robin Nasitir, a couple with two small daughters. The Painted Penguin was a way to spend creative time with their children and provide a place for other families to do the same. The daughters are now teenagers with a storehouse of memories from the family business, which has now expended to six locations in the Midwest. Participants work on their projects in a giant art studio with no pressure. The studio time is free and the experts on-site can be a second pair of eyes when needed. Budding artists take pride in their work and leave with a finished creation. Other featured activities include beading and archaeological digs. The Painted Penguin often hosts community events and holds field trips, parties, charity events and corporate events that build team morale. Franchise opportunities are available. Make a memory of your own at the Painted Penguin nearest to you.

2244 Fox Valley Center, Aurora IL
104 Stratford Square, Bloomingdale IL
(630) 820-0005
632 Hawthorn Center, Vernon Hills IL
(630) 894-0005
www.ThePaintedPenguin.net

14 Attractions & Recreation—Chicago Metro

Chicago Metro—Attractions & Recreation 15

Bristol Renaissance Faire

It's 1574, and Queen Elizabeth is visiting the port of Bristol. The festival prepared in her honor is much like the Bristol Renaissance Faire. On weekends and Labor Day throughout the summer, the faire, located at the Wisconsin-Illinois border just west of Interstate 94, promises many a *hail and well met* along with opportunities to laugh and make merry with costumed magicians, jugglers, street performers and musicians. Cheer as your favorite knight jousts; feast on fish and chips, Shepherd's Pie and a tankard of ale; visit shops filled with handicrafts and artwork like those you might have encountered during this spirited age of discovery and invention. Renaissance Entertainment Corporation has created an annual event Where Fantasy Rules and celebrates 20 years of rambunctious good times in 2007. Bristol Renaissance Faire is proof that people of all ages can find delight in a well-organized fantasy experience. The faire takes place on 30 wooded acres with open-air stages and more than 1,000 costumed performers. Activities abound for children, who are naturals at the fantasy game. Participating in the action begins when you don the clothing of a courtier or a lusty wench, just some of the costuming available for rent at the faire. Enjoy a juried art show and purchase food, furnishings, jewelry, glass, clothing and leatherwork from 180 independent merchants, offering goods from around the globe. The theme for each year's celebration varies, but the consistent gaiety assures *we shall see you anon* at the Bristol Renaissance Faire.

12550 120th Avenue, Kenosha WI
(847) 395-7773
www.renfair.com/bristol

Shadowbrook Farm

Shadowbrook Farm offers horse-lovers a triple crown of beautifully bred animals for sale, impeccable boarding facilities and educational opportunities for both horses and people. The farm has been a Libertyville landmark since it was built in the mid-1930s by the Rossiter family. It was sold to the Huthsings in the 1950s, who bred thoroughbreds at the facility. Tom Foran took over in the 1970s. In 1986, Tim and Moppy Towne purchased the farm and continued the tradition of breeding hunters and jumpers. Boarders and their animals are treated like family. The barn and stalls are heated for maximum comfort for both man and beast. Work your horse in the 189 by 81 square-foot arena or enjoy the outdoors in an arena measuring 100 by 200 square feet. Enjoy the half-mile track and the nearby trails. Located on 40 acres, Shadowbrook Farm offers plenty of natural beauty for you to observe as you ride. At Celebration Farm, located on the premises, the Townes' daughter, Amy Farmer, offers riding lessons for folks aged 5 and up. Riders can also learn how to bathe horses and even watch them being shod. Amy has shown on the A circuit for more than 20 years, so it's natural that the farm offers training for horses, preparing them for shows nationwide. Shadowbrook Farm offers a fun, safe environment for people and horses looking to excel in the ring—or just spend an afternoon riding the trails.

14341 Old School Road, Libertyville IL
(847) 367-1050 (Shadowbrook Farm)
(847) 553-8939 (Celebration Farm)
www.celebrationfarms.com

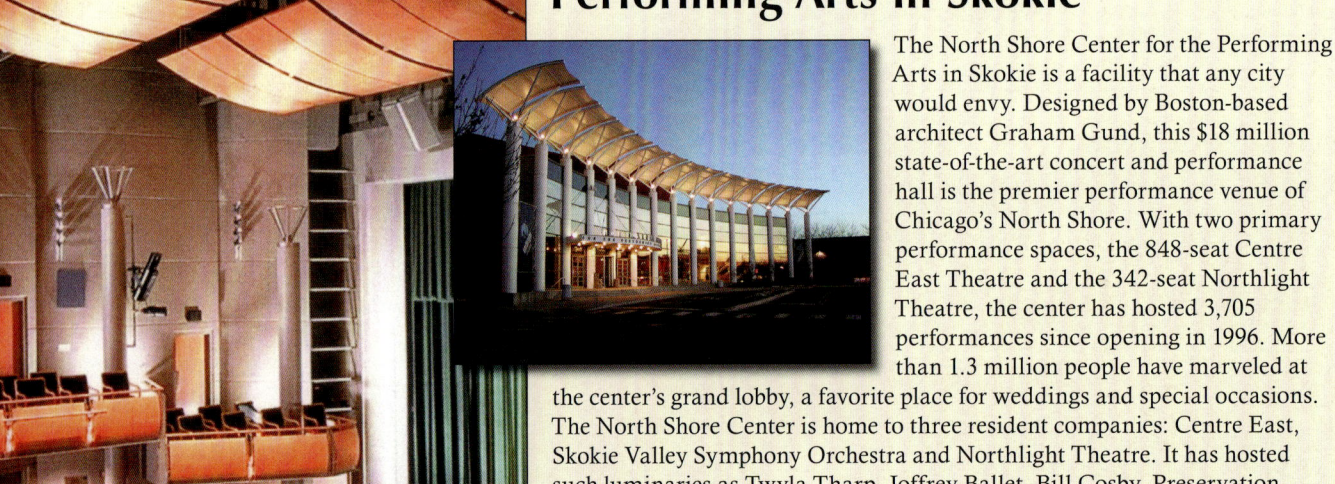

North Shore Center for the Performing Arts in Skokie

The North Shore Center for the Performing Arts in Skokie is a facility that any city would envy. Designed by Boston-based architect Graham Gund, this $18 million state-of-the-art concert and performance hall is the premier performance venue of Chicago's North Shore. With two primary performance spaces, the 848-seat Centre East Theatre and the 342-seat Northlight Theatre, the center has hosted 3,705 performances since opening in 1996. More than 1.3 million people have marveled at the center's grand lobby, a favorite place for weddings and special occasions. The North Shore Center is home to three resident companies: Centre East, Skokie Valley Symphony Orchestra and Northlight Theatre. It has hosted such luminaries as Twyla Tharp, Joffrey Ballet, Bill Cosby, Preservation Hall Jazz Band, Bill Maher and many others. The building houses a variety of family and community-based educational programming, and is used by numerous cultural, school and civic groups. Because of the North Shore's rich ethnic and cultural heritage, the center has hosted events in many languages, including Korean, Polish, Russian, Indian, Romanian and Thai, to name but a few. The North Shore Center for the Performing Arts in Skokie is a jewel of the Midwest. The next time you're heading to the Chicago area, check the center's website for upcoming events and plan to catch a performance.

9501 Skokie Boulevard, Skokie IL
(847) 673-6300
www.northshorecenter.org

Chicago Metro—Attractions & Recreation

Kane County Cougars

The Cubs may have their Bleacher Bums and White Sox fans may forever exalt their team for winning the 2005 World Championship, but the Kane County Cougars have the statistics to prove that their fans may be the best in the Chicago area. Average attendance per game has exceeded ballpark capacity for 16 straight seasons in Cougar Country. That's right, an average of 7,354 fans turn out every game to cheer on the Cougars, the Single A affiliate of the Oakland A's, when the seating capacity of the stadium is just 7,300. What is so special about a Cougars game? Well, if you truly love baseball, here is your chance to think like a major league scout, as you size up the talent on the field and predict which players are destined to make it to the Big Show. Cougars alumni in the major leagues include 2003 World Series MVP Josh Beckett, 2003 N.L. Rookie of the Year Dontrelle Willis and 2005 A.L. Rookie of the Year Houston Street. In all, about 80 former Cougars have worn the uniforms of major league teams. Even if you don't know the Infield Fly Rule from a Ground Rule Double, you will have a blast at the ballpark. A Cougars game offers outstanding and affordable family entertainment with nightly souvenir giveaways as well as on-field antics and contests between innings. For food, the offerings are strictly Americana and simply delicious. How about a boneless barbeque pork chop sandwich with roasted corn on the cob? Head to the ballpark and join the fans roaring for their beloved Kane County Cougars.

34 Wood Cherry Lane, Geneva IL   (630) 232-8811
www.kccougars.com

Attractions & Recreation—Chicago Metro

Long Grove Confectionery

Since 1975, the Long Grove Confectionery has been making delicious chocolates, first in the original store located in Historic Long Grove and then in a larger production facility in Buffalo Grove, which also offers a year-round Chocolate Factory Tour. The Long Grove store still maintains its history in a turn-of-the-century replicated schoolhouse accentuated with an antique stained glass ceiling dome, along with other pieces of stained glass from the owner's private collection. The Confectionery is noted for creating specialty molded chocolate items, beautifully packaged boxed items and special event custom items. You can watch the ever-popular chocolate-dipped fresh strawberries being made at the Long Grove store through a leaded glass window. Visitors from near and far make sure their visit to Historic Long Grove always includes a stop at the Long Grove Confectionery.

220 Robert Parker Coffin Road, Long Grove IL
(Long Grove store) (847) 634-0080

333 Lexington Drive, Buffalo Grove IL
(Chocolate Factory Tour, Factory Outlet Store and Corporate Office)
(847) 459-3100 or (888) 459-3100

www.longgrove.com

Long Grove Apple Haus

Reminiscent of a cider mill, the Long Grove Apple Haus has everything you can imagine—as long as it's made with apples. The bakery on premises sends wonderful smells through historic Long Grove, enticing you to come in and taste. Everything from the famous Uncle Johnny's Brown Bag Apple Pies, apple cider donuts, locally-made apple cider, jams, jellies, salsa and ice cream will be found in Apple Haus Square.

230 Robert Parker Coffin Road, Long Grove IL
(847) 634-0730

Chicago Metro—Attractions & Recreation

Pine Cone Christmas Shop

Christmas all year-round, what could be more fun than that? Stepping into the Pine Cone Christmas Shop is like stepping into yesteryear at Christmas time. Ornaments from all over the world fill every nook and cranny, along with beautiful accessories for Christmas decorating. Steinbach Nutcrackers and Department 56 are showcased along with a wall of exclusively designed Cobane Studio ornaments.

**210 Robert Parker Coffin Road,
Long Grove IL   847-634-0890**

Farmside Country Store & Winery

At the Crossroads of Historic Long Grove stands one of the oldest landmark buildings, the Farmside Country Store & Winery. As you walk up the steps you enter into what it was like in the mid-1880s. Expect to find tin ceilings, wooden planked floors, shelves filled with food delicacies and a marble counter where you can chat with the sales clerk. Specialty food items and a large selection of wines will make any shopper's dream come true at the Farmside Country Store & Winery.

**303 Old McHenry Rd, Long Grove IL
(847) 913-9002**

Attractions & Recreation—Chicago Metro

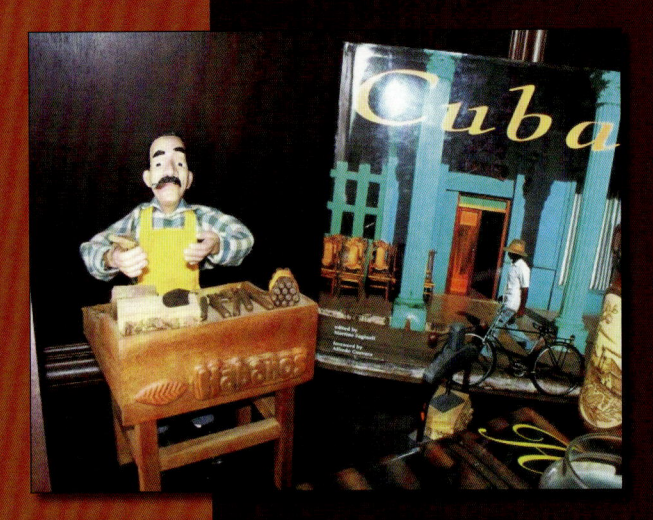

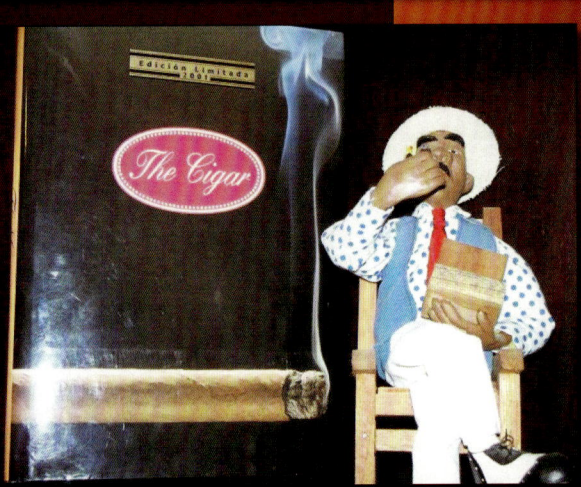

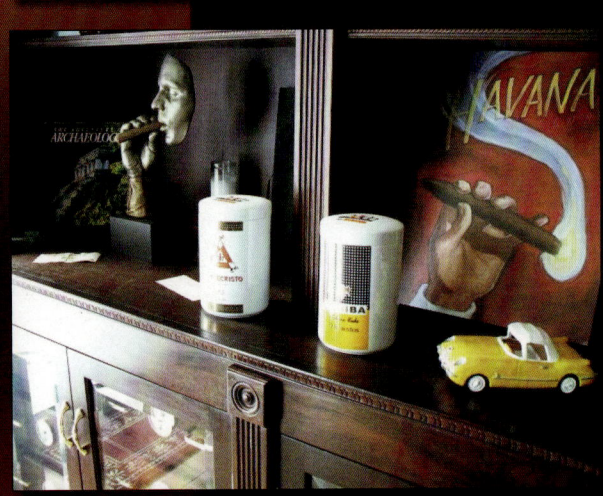

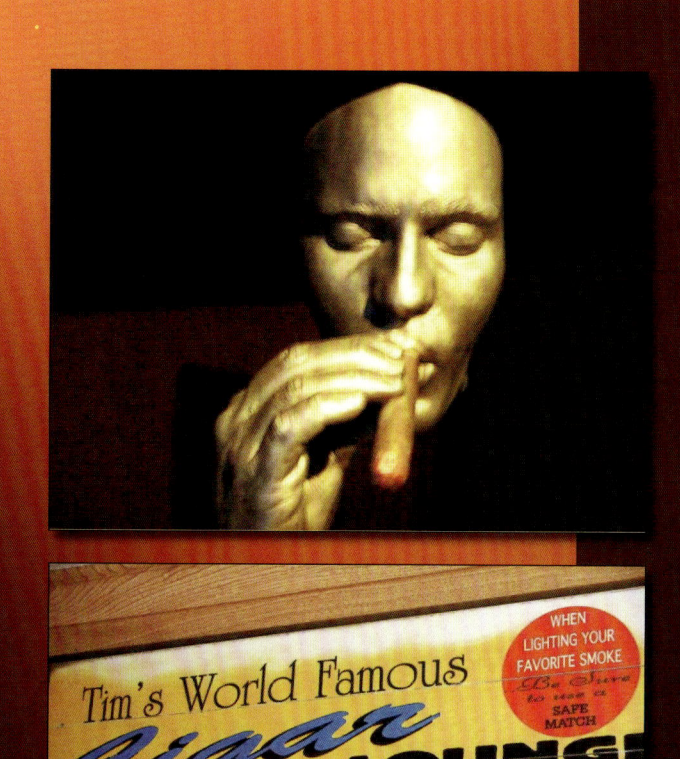

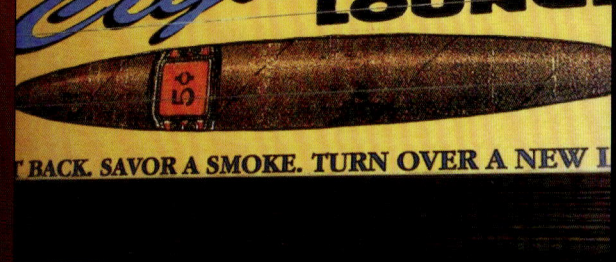

Little Havana Cigar Factory

When you pull up in front of the unassuming little building housing the Little Havana Cigar Factory in Elgin, you wonder if you're at the right place; there is nothing to mark it as the home of a shrine to the vintage cigar. The glass front has no lettering and window shades prevent you from peering inside—this treasure is as hidden as it gets. You simply must be in the know to find the best kept secret. Tim Hartke, owner and operator, greets you at the door (call ahead to let him know you're coming) with a warm smile and high-energy personality that puts you in mind of a favorite uncle—one passionate and knowledgeable about his favorite pastime. For Tim, the passion is channeled into his cigars. Over 30 years of his life have been spent in pursuit of creating the perfect cigar. "It's what gets me up and going in the morning," he readily admits. "I want to introduce people to real vintage cigars aged five to 20 years. There are many vintages put out by bigger tobacco companies that just haven't got all the aging they should have."

Tim ushers you into his smoking club, as he calls it, and hands you one of his hand-rolled vintage cigars with its carefully selected blend of tobaccos. "Try it," he says with a proud twinkle in his eye. "This one's on me. I want your opinion." You sit down in a comfortable easy chair and Tim instructs you in the proper way to cut and light your cigar. The vintage cigars Tim manufactures are smooth and rich in flavor; the smoke is thick and aromatic and far superior in flavor to many cigars of much higher cost. Tim offers his vintage cigars in a price range from $2 to $10, with a few rare cigars a little higher. "I want to educate my consumers," Tim says earnestly. "An educated cigar aficionado will demand a better quality cigar from the industry and force all the companies to raise the bar. Vintage cigars should be the standard rather than the exception."

As you gaze around the room and discover the ornate cigar boxes, decorative humidors, hand-carved wooden statues, artwork and memorabilia from Cuba, where tobacco and cigars originated, you realize, in this place, the cigar is not a momentary pleasure, but an art form to be cherished. Tim also carries all the cigar accessories, from cutters and lighters to humidors. "I don't try to make money on accessories," Tim says in all seriousness. "I just cover my costs. I'm not interested in that stuff beyond making sure my customers have what is needed to store and enjoy a well-maintained vintage cigar. For me, it's all about the cigar." When the time comes to take your leave, Tim shakes your hand, thanks you for dropping in and extends an invitation to come back again. Savoring another puff of vintage cigar smoke, you nod and agree that, yes, you will be back.

554 N Weston Street, Elgin IL
Office: (847) 742-1694
Mobile: (847) 338-5492

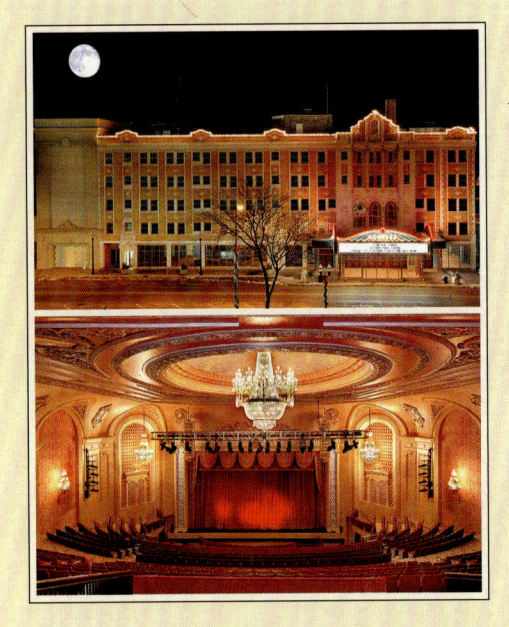

Genesee Theatre

A 23 million dollar restoration project brought this grand theater back to life after 20 years of sitting idle. Today, the 2457-seat Genesee Theatre retains its original colors, patterns and detailed wallpaper. With hundreds of yards of lush tapestries, abundance of marble and $350,000 Baccarat crystal chandelier in the Grand Lobby, this theatre has a rich soul that radiates from every corner. The 115,000 square-foot theatre draws performers from all over the nation. In fact, the grand re-opening of the Genesee Theatre featured two sold-out shows of world-class comedian Bill Cosby. Since then, performers such as Jerry Seinfeld, Ringo Starr and Martina McBride have graced the stage. The Genesee Theatre is not limited to comedy performances and live music. Musicals such as *Chicago*, *Rent* and *Cats* have been enhancing the culture of downtown Waukegan and its surrounding communities for years. Most importantly, the revitalization of the Genesee Theatre has brought back a sense of community to this culturally rich and diverse city. For a truly wonderful cultural experience, come to the Genesee Theatre and discover why this elegant landmark is really quite special.

203 N Genesee Street, Waukegan IL (847) 263-6300
www.geneseetheatre.com

Prairie Landing Golf Club

Prairie Landing Golf Club, designed by Robert Trent Jones Jr., has consistently ranked among the top public courses in Illinois. In 2007, the readers of *Chicagoland Golf Magazine* again rated Prairie Landing a five-star golf experience. The prairie links style, par 72 golf course plays as long as 6,950 yards and has a slope rating of 136. The meticulously groomed course features large undulating greens, rolling bentgrass fairways, massive sweeps of native grasses and strategically placed bunkers and grass mounds. Prairie Landing is also home to the Chicago area's finest practice center, which includes a driving range, two regulation par-four practice holes, nine-hole chipping area and two practice putting greens. The McChesney Clubhouse at Prairie Landing is a beautifully restored historic West Chicago farmhouse. It is home to The Grill Room restaurant, scenic banquet facility's, locker rooms, and an award-winning pro shop staffed by PGA golf professionals. The high tech golf club is also equipped with free Wi-Fi Internet access, high-definition televisions, XM satellite radio, an ATM machine and a full color GPS on every golf cart. In 2002 Prairie Landing received the honorable distinction as a Certified Audubon Cooperative Sanctuary.

2325 Longest Drive, West Chicago IL (630) 208-7600
www.prairielanding.com

Arrowhead Golf Club

A centerpiece for the community since 1929, Arrowhead Golf Club is grounded in local history. Its cornerstone is a 1850s stone farmhouse that once served as a residence on the property. The course is surrounded by acres of mature forest preserve. In 1982, the Wheaton Park District purchased the property in order to preserve the open spaces and provide a major recreational area for the community. The course has been constantly updated since that time, with the addition of hundreds of trees over the past 23 years. Today it includes three challenging nine-hole courses that can be combined various ways to create an 18-hole challenge. You can also enjoy a driving range, putting green and chipping green or sign up for private or group lessons at the club. After your round, stop by the American Grill and sample lunches and dinners for the freshest fish, steak, chops and salads and seasonal produce. Plan your corporate outing, wedding or banquet at the club with the assistance of a staff devoted to detail and to making every special occasion just right. Arrowhead Golf Club garnered a 4 ½ star rating from Chicagoland Golf in 2005. Visit to experience a community treasure that is sure to please golfers for generations to come.

26 W 151 Butterfield Road, Wheaton IL (630) 653-5800
www.arrowheadgolfclub.org

Chicago Metro—Bakeries, Treats, Coffee & Tea

Casteel Coffee

Open the door to Casteel Coffee and caress your senses with the aroma of fresh roasted coffee, a cozy atmosphere and shelves of engaging specialty gift items. You have found Casteel Coffee, a coffee nirvana just north of Chicago in Evanston. Casteel is a small-batch specialty coffee roaster. Co-owner and roastmaster Lee Casteel brings out the subtle characteristics of each variety of coffee, yielding rich, flavorful and always fresh coffee for enjoyment at the store or at home. Like fine wine, the handcrafted specialty coffees can be pungent, piquant, subtle or sweet. From the first sip you'll know you have encountered something far superior to bulk-roasted beans from the grocery store. For those of us who must have decaffeinated coffee, Casteel Coffee features CO_2-processed decaf. CO_2 processing retains more of the bean flavor and does not use chemicals that are harmful to the environment. Both the store and the website feature an array of coffee and tea gifts, such as the Tea Lovers' Basket, a collection of Harney & Sons loose tea, Ghiradelli chocolate bars and tea accessories surrounded by a birdhouse and a picket fence. For coffee to start your day, share with friends or serve for the finest occasions, visit Casteel Coffee.

2924 Central Street, Evanston IL
(847) 424-9999 or (877) 560-8335
www.casteelcoffee.com

Graham's Fine Chocolates and Ice Cream

Making chocolate and ice cream is a creative pursuit for husband and wife team Robert and Beckie Untiedt, who opened Graham's Fine Chocolates and Ice Cream in Geneva in 1987. You can watch through a large window as the chocolate is made in the 1868 Greek Revival house. Everyone loves the skalies, a Swedish-style turtle. The caramel apples use Granny Smiths from Washington State. The family excels at English toffee, truffles, peanut butter diamonds and chocolate-covered strawberries. Graham's also makes custom chocolates for weddings and special functions. Down the street is Graham's 318, a lounge for the enjoyment of coffee, chocolate fondue and gelato. You can sip frozen hot chocolate on the outdoor patio or try one of 50 gelato flavors, such as Double Dark Bitter Chip and Honey Lavender. Success has led to a second Graham's in Wheaton and inclusion in a chocolate exhibit that's touring the United States. In 2007, *Lucky* magazine featured the shop, which has been called the Best Chocolate Shop by *West Suburban Living*. Robert's first career was as a music teacher, but as schools started to close, he began working at a friend's candy company. He trained at several candy shops before opening his own store with Beckie, a fellow musician. Beckie's twin sister Bonnie Pechous is production manager, and daughters Jayni and Maddi contribute as well. Taste the artistry at Graham's Fine Chocolates and Ice Cream.

302 S 3rd Street, Geneva IL
(630) 232-6655

Pick a Cup Coffee Club

Pick a Cup Coffee Club is more than a place to simply get a cup of coffee. Pick a Cup is a place to congregate, talk, write, read or just pass the time. The Evanston café was opened in 2003 by Carol and Steven Kent with an emphasis on quality and the belief that coffeehouses should serve as community gathering spots, where people can share cultures and philosophies. Pick a Cup features live entertainment most weekends, an open drum circle on Fridays and the occasional documentary film during the week. The café decorates its walls with artwork for sale by local artists. Pick a Cup's menu reflects its diversity and attention to quality. The café features homemade muffins, soups, panini sandwiches, salads and its famous scones. Fruits and vegetables come from local growers and breakfast is served anytime. Coffee, roasted by local artisans, is served in a ceramic or china cup of your choice. There are literally hundreds of cups to choose from. Put delicious food and stimulating coffee together with conversation at Pick a Cup Coffee Club.

1813 Dempster Avenue, Evanston IL
(847) 332-2834
www.pickacup.com

Chicago Metro—Bakeries, Treats, Coffee & Tea   25

Deerfield Bakery

Baking is in the Schmitt family's blood, which accounts for more than a century of success and three popular locations, in Deerfield, Buffalo Grove and Schaumburg. Fresh, high quality ingredients and a commitment to flavor and freshness are at the heart of the gorgeous goodies found here. If you are planning a wedding, you'll find more than 100 wedding cake designs at Deerfield, including such fantasies as the April in Paris design, with tall pillars and pink icing roses, and the Cupid's Love Song, decked out with pretty bells. You can also design your own cake with the assistance of Deerfield Bakery's friendly, knowledgeable staff. In fact, there isn't much in the way of themed cakes that this bakery hasn't explored, from Fourth of July models featuring Uncle Sam and firecracker themes to fantasy cakes shaped like dragons and castles. Deerfield Bakery also offers cookies, in textures ranging from soft to crisp and crunchy. Patrons can order in person, by telephone or from the bakery's website. Those looking for a quick bite to eat along with some coffee and dessert will enjoy the bakery's café. What's a piece of cake for you is a way of life for the Schmitts, who invite you to celebrate every occasion with a visit to Deerfield Bakery.

813 N Waukegan Road, Deerfield IL (847) 945-0068
201 N Buffalo Grove Road, Buffalo Grove IL (847) 520-0068
25 S Roselle Road, Schaumburg IL (847) 534-0068
www.deerfieldbakery.com

Kernel Fabyan's Gourmet Popcorn Shoppe

Dann and Cathy Villwock take popcorn seriously. At Kernel Fabyan's Gourmet Popcorn Shoppe, named for a generous community philanthropist, they devote themselves to providing the highest-quality popcorn available. Popcorn enthusiasts will revel in the selection of flavors. The finest ingredients go into the recipes, and so when you bite into the popular caramel corn or the irresistible white cheddar popcorn, you'll understand why connoisseurs prefer Kernel Fabyan's. Purchase single, double or triple flavors in distinctive black and gold tins, or order a gift tin for special occasions. Kernel Fabyan's ships anywhere in the United States. Gourmet popcorn makes a fun alternative to candy as a gift with nostalgic overtones of country fairs and handmade fun foods. If you thought old-fashioned popcorn was a thing of the past, you'll delight in discovering a popcorn shop where your tasty crunch craving can be satisfied. Expand your popcorn repertoire at Kernel Fabyan's Gourmet Popcorn Shoppe.

511 S Third Street, Geneva IL   (630) 232-7151
kernelfabyans.com

Conscious Cup Coffee Roastery & Café

Through the giant picture window of Conscious Cup you see a big, cherry-red coffee roaster slow-roasting some of the finest, freshest coffees to be found. By purchasing green coffee and roasting it in-house, CC controls the freshness and quality of the drinks it serves. The result, in just its second year of business, was the 2007 Fox Valley Readers' Choice Award for best coffee. Try the sweet and spicy Mexican El Triunfo or the Ethiopian Harrar with its deft balance between bold richness and berry acidity. With the artisan roaster, even dark-roasted Sumatran and Papua New Guinea coffees come out rich and smooth, without bitterness. The Conscious Cup Cafe is a free Wi-Fi hot spot and offers pastries, cakes and freshly baked scones to go with the exceptional drinks. Conscious Cup rotates its brew schedule among its carefully roasted world coffees through the week. Conscious Cup buys only socially and environmentally sustainable coffees. By using Fair Trade and organic standards, owners Roseanna and Jack Shipley, along with their sons, Jason, Michael and Jeremy aim to help coffee farmers and workers get a fair share of the fruits of their labor. Stop in to Conscious Cup Coffee Roastery & Café today and take a sip of rich integrity.

625D Cog Circle, Crystal Lake IL   (815) 356-0115
www.consciouscup.com

Jarosch Bakery

At Jarosch Bakery, high quality bakery goods made from scratch have been a family affair since 1959. The bakery was established by the father and son team of George and Herbert Jarosch, with their wives Kathe and Betty. Ken and Kathy Jarosch, the third generation, operate the bakery today with the help of more than 50 employees. Every day, bakers and cake decorators create delicious cakes, pastries, strudels, tortes and cookies. The éclairs are popular all year long. Jarosch Bakery beautifully decorates cakes for all occasions. The shop has become a tradition for many families—customers have asked the bakery to re-create for their kids that special cake they remember from their own childhood. Jarosch Bakery has an extensive album of wedding cake possibilities to inspire you. Staff members work directly with the bride and groom to create the perfect cake for the perfect day. The bakery can decorate cakes or cookies with a corporate logo for special company events. The bakery has won multiple Reader's Choice awards and was featured on Channel 2's Best Of series. Whether you need a cake for a special event or just want a delectable treat to celebrate the day, be sure to visit Jarosch Bakery.

35 Arlington Heights Road, Elk Grove Village IL   (847) 437-1234
www.jaroschbakery.com

Chicago Metro—Bakeries, Treats, Coffee & Tea

Three Tarts Bakery and Café

Three Tarts Bakery and Café features a vast assortment of temptations. This Northfield business combines made-from-scratch sweets and pastries with appealing luncheon fare. When Kate Coyne, Ann Heinz, and another partner bought the bakery nine years ago, Three Tarts was just a temporary nickname for their business, but customers liked the name so much that they kept it. French doors, rattan café chairs and mellow wood shelves stocked with enticing goodies give the quaint shop a cozy charm and invite customers to linger. When Three Tarts says it's Simply a Butter Bakery and the employees wear T-shirts announcing the fact, you can rest assured the bakery is making a claim it can back. Three Tarts employs traditional baking methods and such ingredients as butter. In addition to muffins, scones and Danish pastry, you'll find more than 35 kinds of cookies plus cakes creatively decorated to celebrate just about any occasion. Three Tarts can turn icing into garden flowers so realistic you'll wonder if they are edible. Custom cake orders are always welcome, and brides can work with a wedding consultant to select just the right wedding cake. Many shop specialties are so popular they're sold by the bag, including malted chocolate chip cookies and Sesame Crisp crackers. Lunch is served inside or out and includes sandwiches on freshly baked bread along with salads and soups. Give in to temptation with a visit to Three Tarts Bakery and Café.

301 S Happ Road, Northfield IL
(847) 446-5444
www.threetartsbakery.com

Marked for Dessert

Cake specialist and sugar artist Mark Seaman creates cakes so beautiful that you would almost rather display them as art than eat them—that is, if they weren't so delicious. Such is the dilemma that a Marked for Dessert cake presents. Mark turns out his high quality cakes in low volumes. Clients meet with him at his Chicago cake boutique to come up with a one-of-a-kind design that reflects the personality of the person for whom the cake is intended. The Food Network featured Mark making his award-winning Butterfly Garden, a cake designed according to a Versace china pattern, for the Oklahoma Sugar Art Show. Marked for Dessert has provided cakes for events at many elite Chicagoland venues, including the Chicago Cultural Center, the Peninsula Hotel and the Adler Planetarium. When the Lincoln Park Zoo held the grand opening of its Regenstein Center for African Apes, Mark contributed an artistic cake in the shape of an ape to the occasion. At Mark's second location in Libertyville, you'll find all the fixings of a neighborhood bakery, including a variety of pies, tarts and muffins in addition to cakes. Consider Marked for Dessert when you want a cake that will taste as good as it looks.

1812 W Greenleaf Avenue, Chicago IL
(773) 761-3800
518 N Milwaukee Avenue,
Libertyville IL (847) 367-9898
www.markedfordessert.com

Infini-Tea

Infini-Tea, in beautiful downtown Antioch, with its quaint hometown atmosphere and antique and craft shops, is the perfect place to find a quite moment and enjoy some tempting delights. This tea room is as serious about tea as it is about real clotted cream. High tea is served all day long in two styles: the Royal Treatment Tea with four courses and the Tea Lite. Scones are made by master baker Kenelm Winslow Scheske, whose ancestors Kenelm and Edward Winslow came over on the Mayflower. Proprietor Lorrie Ferguson used to travel on business and always appreciated comfortable and accommodating places with good food. She retired early to create that kind of haven for others. Lorrie's daughter Leah Haling completes the management team. Infini-Tea is all about the guests and their comfort. The space is decorated with antiques, vintage hats, prints and tea pots. You can order any of a vast collection of specialty and herbal teas, as well as a variety of flavored coffees, cappuccinos and espressos. Visit the website for days and hours. You'll dine at an intimate linen-covered table. The dishes are not just served; they are created with an eye for beauty. Daily quiches are one of the most popular lunch options. Dinner offerings include beef Wellington, shepherds pie and duck Wellington with cranberry chutney. Scrumptious, fresh-baked goods are available, along with featured desserts. The restaurant sponsors tea-tasting nights, jazz, folk and other musical entertainment. Visit Infini-Tea and find a sweet retreat.

902 Main Street, Antioch IL
(847) 395-3520
www.infini-tea.net

Bakeries, Treats, Coffee & Tea—Chicago Metro

Coffee Drop Shop

It's not the 70 varieties of fresh roasted coffee or the 75 varieties of teas that keep people coming back to Coffee Drop Shop, but that doesn't hurt. Loyal customers return to this brew house for the Ma and Pa ambience, exceptional knowledge and personal service from the owners of this shop for the past 27 years. Regulars are called by name from owners Jerry and Judy Jendro. Whether you're into the rich coffees from Columbia and Africa, estate coffees from India, Indonesia and Costa Rica, or high-end coffees from Kona and Jamaica, you can drink it fresh-brewed or take home a bag. Flavors range from traditional vanilla, hazelnut and almond to unusual carrot cake, L'Orange and chocolate raspberry. Tea drinkers won't go away empty handed. White, red and herbals are among the 20 green teas and over 40 varieties of black in regular and decaf. Teas can be found in bulk and tea bags. Take home one of 200 teapots stocked for that special memory. Coffee Drop special orders, wholesales and mail orders daily. Stop in the next time you're in the neighborhood and say hello, and become one of its new regular customers.

12 N 3rd Street, St. Charles IL (630) 584-7989 or (888) 584-7989
www.3rdstreetshops.com/directory.htm

Morkes Chocolates

Rhonda Morkes was just seven years old when her dad and brother let her help make chocolate at Morkes Chocolates. By now, she has owned the 30-year-old Palatine store for 18 years. She opened a new location in Algonquin in 2007. Rhonda's family has been involved in hand-dipped, molded and enrobed chocolates since the 1920s when Rhonda's grandfather, William Morkes, Sr., left his sales position with Nabisco to open his own shop in Chicago. French creams were one of his specialties and continue to be a big seller for Rhonda, along with caramel apples, which sell by the hundreds of thousands during the fall season. Mid-September through Easter is the busiest time of year for the shop, which ships chocolate year-round throughout the country. Morkes Chocolates has freshly made candy canes, brittles and sponge candy. It offers a new chocolate silk line and an award-winning crunchy English toffee covered with chocolate. The shop provides candy for school fundraisers and offers chocolate-making parties customized for your group. Many of its molded candies feature unusual shapes, such as high heels. For a real candy indulgence, visit Morkes Chocolates.

1890 N Rand Road, Palatine IL
2755 W Algonquin Road, Algonquin IL
(847) 359-3454
www.morkeschocolates.com

Serene Teaz

The wonderful world of tea reveals its secrets to all who visit Serene Teaz. This specialty store features a full selection of loose tea, plus accessories and gifts. Step up to the tasting bar and sample teas before you buy. Choose from traditional and flavored varieties of black, oolong, green, yellow, white, rooibos (red) and herbal teas. Each cup is prepared as you like it, hot or cold. Magic Moon, a combination of green and black tea flavored with strawberry, delights the senses. For a real treat, order a cup of artisan tea, consisting of dried blossoms hand-sewn in green tea leaves that bloom when steeped in hot water. Owners Sarine and Robert Crotteau give workshops on tea preparation and tasting. Class times and dates are listed in the stores or on the website. Tea pots, tea kettles, cups and saucers fill the shelves. Fine porcelain lines include Royal Patrician and Franz. Tea collectibles and unusual jewelry make elegant gifts. The shop also creates pre-made and custom gift baskets for all occasions. Stop by Serene Teaz and discover the joys of tea.

118A N Hale Street, Wheaton IL (630) 784-TEAS (8327)
108 W Park Avenue, Elmhurst IL (630) 833-TEAZ (8329)
www.SereneTeaz.com

Photo by Louis Joy Photography

Chicago Metro—Bakeries, Treats, Coffee & Tea   31

Something Sweet and Gourmet

Chocoholics are always welcome at Something Sweet and Gourmet. This charming sweet shop is the brainchild of a fudge-making enthusiast. Michele Michel grew up in a family of entrepreneurs, so it's no wonder she turned her love for fudge and other treats into a business of her own. Michele used to work in an upstate New York fudge shop, and it was there that she began to dream of opening her own shop someday. Her fudge-making skills were soon so sought after that she sold her knowledge at local fairs and shows. Michele opened Something Sweet and Gourmet in 1998, and since then has continuously expanded her line of yummy fudges, barks, sugar-free candies and more. One of the shops signature treats is the Bearfoot, the tastiest turtle ever, made with four different kinds of nuts and three choices of chocolate. The shop has more than 20 kinds of fudge made fresh daily. The wonderful smells coming from the candy kitchen bring in new customers every day. Something Sweet and Gourmet is open seven days a week, so stop in today and find your own favorite treat.

891 Main Street, Antioch IL
(847) 838-9350
www.4somethingsweet.com

Tate's Ice Cream

Since the 1960s, cold, delicious ice cream has been a tradition at the parlor at 109 East Front Street. Starting out as Dipper Dan's, the shop underwent several name changes before becoming Tate's Ice Cream in the 1990s. Current owner Ann Wank bought the store in 2002. You'll find 50 different flavors here, which is only one reason why the Chicago Tribune name Tate's one of the Top 5 ice cream parlors of the region. Tate's is renowned for inventive homemade flavors such as fresh blueberry, cinnamon and coconut. Try the Tribune award-winning Coconut Dream sundae. Malts and shakes are hand-mixed at Tate's—malts with a vintage 1940 Hamilton Beach malt mixer. Those looking for lower-calorie alternatives will enjoy the shop's well-known sherbet, made from an old family recipe. Tate's is every bit the old-fashioned ice cream parlor, complete with pink and lime green décor and black and white checkerboard floors. Come chill out with a scoop of Tate's Ice Cream.

109 E Front Street, Wheaton IL   (630) 668-4434

Sweet Nostalgia

A walk down the aisles of Sweet Nostalgia is a walk down memory lane for those who savored candy treats in the 1950s and 1960s. Previously named Candy, Candy, Candy, the shop on West State Street became Sweet Nostalgia in 2002 after Tony and Cindy Godek teamed up to create a store that not only sells great candy, but great memories. The two did their research, located old-fashioned candy suppliers and stocked the store chock-full of Zots, Abba-Zabas and Necco Wafers. Voted the best old-fashioned candy store by *Chicago Magazine*, Sweet Nostalgia features more than 150 vintage brands. Licorice Pipes, Sky Bars, Walnettos, Slo-Pokes, Fizzies and Razzles line the shelves. Horlicks Malted Milk tablets continue to be a best seller. Bosco chocolate syrup brings smiles to those who remember the thick, rich milk flavoring. A line of Remember When greeting cards and videos of vintage television shows and musical groups carry viewers back. More recent popular candies have also found their way into the nostalgia-packed store. Jelly beans and handmade chocolates mix in among the sweets of days gone by. Bring your sweet tooth to Sweet Nostalgia and remember just how delicious life used to be.

318 W State Street, Geneva IL   (630) 208-9664
www.sweetnostalgia.com

Central Continental Bakery

When you see the extensive display cases filled with today's fresh baked goods, you will have some idea of the popularity Central Continental Bakery enjoys. The Mt. Prospect bakery, which opened in 1979, features the baking prowess of brothers Roger and Robert Czerniak, who continue to use many of their grandfather Teofil's recipes. Teofil came to the United States from Poland, opening his first Chicago bakery in 1922 and teaching the trade to his son Ted. You will find tortes, sweet rolls, butter cookies and assorted muffins, including ones filled with apple and cherry slices. On Fat Tuesday, sales of Paczki, a beloved Polish donut, soar into the thousands. More than 20 varieties of breads and rolls bring patrons in regularly. Custom novelty cakes are a Continental specialty, as are individually designed wedding cakes. The staff will work closely with you on cake design and flavor. They can also create a European sweet table to delight a party of guests. The pastry possibilities for the sweet table, like the choices in the bakery cases, are phenomenal. The bakery staff is made up of the brother's children together with Mariann Most, the bakery's first employee. Come to Central Continental Bakery, where your only dilemma will be which delicacy to choose.

101 S Main Street, Mt. Prospect IL   (847) 870-9500
www.centralcontinentalbakery.com

Chicago Metro—Bakeries, Treats, Coffee & Tea 33

Didier Farms

Folks in Prairie View can mark the seasons by what's going on at Didier Farms. The doors to the greenhouse swing open in April, the farm stand springs to life in July and the pumpkin patch begins welcoming visitors in late September. For decades, the Didier family has been planting and pampering its favorite annuals inside the greenhouse, including a bounty of petunias, begonias and geraniums. You will also find a vast selection of hanging baskets and wreaths, plus potted plants and vegetables galore. The Didiers grow the delicious sweet corn and just about everything else that they sell at the farm stand. Squeeze the tomatoes, sniff the peppers and fill up a bag. Produce doesn't get any fresher. You can pick your own pumpkin during Pumpkinfest, which starts the last weekend in September and runs through October. A spooky cabin, corn maze and hayrides make this event a family favorite. The farm has been in the Didier family since 1912. Mary Susan Didier turned the operation of the business over to her sons in 1994. These are people who take pride in preserving the rural lifestyle while supporting their families on the farm where they grew up. Join them in celebrating spring, summer and fall at Didier Farms.

16678 W Aptakisic Road, Prairie View IL (847) 634-3291
www.didierfarms.com

Gibby's Wine Den

Jan and Randy Gibson left the corporate world to create a store filled with their passion for wine. Gibby's Wine Den offers tastings, education and winemaker's events to please both the novice and expert wine aficionados. While constantly adapting to current trends in the industry, the Gibsons remain knowledgeable about the 500 wines available in their store. Well-appointed and contemporary, the store features a high black ceiling, modern lighting, wood floors and warm-colored walls. Inviting antique furniture welcomes you to sit, soak in the atmosphere and enjoy the good life. Often, live music ignites the air with a feeling of elegance and romance. Top sellers include B.R.Cohn Cabernet Sauvignon and Leaping Lizard Pinot Noir, but you choose the wine and snacks that most please your palate. Events include sangria night, ladies night out, gallery receptions and guest speakers. Gibby's Wine Club members receive a 10% discount on purchases, complimentary wine tastings and a quarterly newsletter. A full line of wine accessories and gourmet foods are on display in the gift area. Staff members can help you design a customized gift basket or select one ready-made. For an enjoyable jaunt through the vineyards, stop by Gibby's Wine Den.

1772 South Randall Road, #220, Geneva IL (630) 208-6424

Knightsbridge Wine Shoppe

Experience the thrill of discovering a great wine at Knightsbridge Wine Shoppe. Wherever great wine is being made, someone from the staff of Knightsbridge Wine Shoppe has been there to taste it, and to bring the best of the best back to the store. CEOs, socialites and even a Nobel Prize laureate or two trust the wine experts at Knightsbridge to select and offer the finest French and California wines, as well as extraordinary vintages from other regions of the world. The outstanding selection of port every winter gives Chicago-area epicures reason to look forward to the frigid season. Owner Kevin Mohalley estimates that he and his team have logged about 500,000 miles over the years, pursuing greatness. They've visited about 4,500 wine cellars, and gleaned insight from about 1,000 trade publications. "As a result, we frequently discover the superstars of the vintage before wine magazines rate them," notes Kevin, who adds that the success of Knightsbridge "stems from our passion and deep-abiding respect for the genesis of each artistically crafted wine." Honors for Knightsbridge include recognition from *Chicago Magazine* as the Best Wine Shop and acclaim from *MarketWatch* as "a feast of the senses, and one of the prettiest wine and spirits shops in the U.S."

842 Sunset Ridge Road, Northbrook IL (847) 498-9300
www.knightsbridgewine.com

Chicago Metro—Farms, Markets & Delis 35

Lynfred Winery

Lynfred Winery is the love child of two self-proclaimed crazy people who took an innocent wine hobby and turned it into an award-winning passion. Lynn and Fred Koehler, pioneers of the Illinois wine industry, began their project more than 30 years ago when they took a historic 1912 home originally constructed by the Hattendorf family and returned it to its former glory. Shortly afterwards, they opened a winery that's the oldest and largest continuously operating winery in the state. Lynfred Winery has won an extensive array of awards and accolades, including a Gold at the Lone Star International and a double gold at Reno. The winery boasts an impressive array of red and white vintages. Among the reds are an organic Cabernet Sauvignon, a barrel reserve Merlot and a delightful Chambourcin. The whites include dry and off-dry varieties, such as Fume Blanc, Chardonel and the signature Lynfred Legacy, an American Chardonnay of distinction. The winery also produces divine fruit, sweet and holiday wines, such as Cranberry-Rose, Apricot and Montmorency Cherry. Lynfred Winery sponsors several wine clubs and has a welcoming tasting room where you can sample wines and then choose great wines for your cellar. The winery's chefs put on special dinners, offer cooking classes and fill the gift shop with wonderful baked goods. Lynfred Winery even offers bed-and-breakfast accommodations in four luxurious suites. Enjoy a tour of the winery, sip the fruits of the Koehler's labor and discover new favorites at DuPage County's own Lynfred Winery.

15 South Roselle Road, Roselle IL
(630) 529-WINE (9463) or (888) 298-WINE
www.lynfredwinery.com

Farms, Markets & Delis—Chicago Metro

Le Petit Marche

Le petit marche is French for the little market. Le Petit Marche may be cozy, but this wine and cheese shop and artisan-style bakery and café offers a big selection and an even bigger taste. Owner Dawn Gerth hand-picks more than 50 varieties of cheese from small cheese makers and matches them with exquisite selections of wines from all over the world. Guests are welcome to sample the goods and invited to stay and enjoy the local art adorning the walls in the café or check out the gift baskets. Satisfy your sweet tooth with gourmet pastries such as the triple-layered opera torte, or a rich, flourless chocolate cake. The French macaroons are filled with lavender buttercream and will make even the most seasoned sweets lover swoon. Be sure to taste Dawn's baguettes, named by loyal customers as the best this side of Paris. Le Petit Marche also offers a variety of lunch items, including homemade soups, fresh salads and sandwiches. The shop is open until the opening curtain at Raue Center for the Arts, the theater across the street, and Dawn can be seen wetting whistles of playgoers and devoted regulars alike. Stop in for a bite at Le Petit Marche and enjoy a creamy latte or steaming cup of tea with your French-inspired meal.

19 N Williams Street, Crystal Lake IL (815) 477-3296

Nuts About Nuts

Julia and Ayhan Alsirt met by chance while living in neighboring townhouses, a meeting that led to a marriage and the 2005 opening of Nuts About Nuts in the Berry House. The store introduces Geneva to some of the world's best-tasting nuts, often purchased directly from orchards. The shop also sells nut butters and oils, dried fruits, chocolates, coffee, tea, sauces and dips. You can buy bulk nuts in various flavors and combinations, such as cinnamon roasted almonds or Ayhan's own creation, a combination of roasted and salted pistachio kernels and cranberries. Ayhan grew up in Turkey, where he picked nuts directly from his family's trees. He adds to his passion for nuts an educational background in plant breeding, which has allowed him to research his product thoroughly and make purchases with an eye for freshness, flavor and health benefits. Julia teaches home economics and loves to cook. Her passion has led to a collection of recipes she shares with customers. Julia and Ayhan treat their customers to generous samples. They enjoy sharing knowledge about the health benefits of nuts and create ready-made and custom gift boxes. Find out why the Alsirts love nuts when you visit Nuts About Nuts.

227 S 3rd Street, Unit 107, Geneva IL (630) 232-NUTS (6887)
www.nutsaboutnutsonline.com

Parkview Gourmet

You'll find plenty of food samples at Parkview Gourmet, a specialty food and wine market with a European feel. Charley Colette and Patricia Sweeney opened the Libertyville store in 2003 after leaving their corporate jobs. Their shop carries more than 40 artisanal cheeses, 170 wines from boutique wineries and a selection of original gourmet creations, including cakes, breads and pies made fresh daily. You can put some extra spark into your next dinner party with one of the more than 15 cheese spreads made at the store and some ready-to-bake hors d'oeuvres. Charley and Patricia know their customers by name and take time to answer questions. They can help you successfully pair food with wine and arrange a gourmet cheese platter for a special event. You can try the premium extra-virgin olive oils and aged balsamic vinegars, stored in stainless steel tanks, before they are bottled for you. Free wine tastings are a regular Saturday activity, and the store offers wine dinners and demonstrations. Gift choices include custom-made gift baskets featuring food items from around the world as well as ceramic serving pieces and tabletop décor. Before you entertain, visit Parkview Gourmet, where specialty food and wine are passionate concerns.

524 N Milwaukee Avenue, Libertyville IL (847) 549-0663
www.parkviewgourmet.com

Chicago Metro—Farms, Markets & Delis

The Olive Mill

Learning about olive oil got easier with the opening of the Olive Mill. Debbie and Ed O'Connell opened the Geneva shop in 2005 after a trip to California's wine country that inspired their investigation into olive oil, a food that defines many Mediterranean dishes. Debbie and Ed store the oils in stainless steel tanks that the Italians call *fusti*. You get to taste the oils and choose what you would like bottled for you. The O'Connells introduce their customers to the flavors, cooking properties and health benefits of cold-pressed, unfiltered extra virgin olive oils. They carry 20 olive oils from artisan operations throughout the world. They also carry macadamia nut and walnut oils, plus 10 balsamic vinegars. Customers who know what they like can shop online. Olive oils range from classic Greek, Californian and Spanish selections to exotic concoctions infused with blood orange, basil, garlic, lemon or porcini mushroom. You can buy an 18-year-old balsamic vinegar from Modena, Italy or try vinegars flavored with such fruits as fig, pomegranate or strawberry. You will find stores in Galena and Saugatuck as well as Geneva. Call to arrange a group tasting party. The store also offers recipes and an array of olive products. Olive oil contains healthy fats that promote strong bones, lower blood cholesterol and calm the stomach. Like olive oil, balsamic vinegar's antioxidant properties fight infection, cancer and inflammation. Come to the Olive Mill, where Healthy Eating Tastes Good.

315 James Street, Geneva IL (630) 262-0210 or (866) 548-3844
www.olivemillgeneva.com

The Spice House

The Spice House was founded in 1957 by Ruth and Bill Penzey in Milwaukee. Their daughter Patty grew up working in the shop as a way to earn her allowance. Patty and her husband, Tom, took over the business in 1992, carrying on her family's tradition. Patty and Tom opened the second Spice House in Evanston in 1997, giving the business their personal stamp. The store has become an icon in Evanston, with coverage from all of the region's media outlets and earning recognition throughout the nation by culinary institutes, publications and organizations. The Spice House was named Evanston's Small Business of the Year in 2000. In 2001 Tom and Patty opened a store in Chicago, adding to the legacy started a half century ago. The Spice House is a chef's dream store, carrying herbs and spices from all over the world. All spices are prepared by hand in small batches, and are prepared weekly to ensure freshness and quality. Both Tom and Patty are in demand as lecturers and speakers and have won numerous awards. We cannot begin to give justice to the list of items carried by The Spice House, or to the number of honors bestowed upon these second-generation spice merchants. We suggest you visit their extensive and informative website, which includes information, history and recipes, as well as a complete listing of the gift baskets and spices they carry. The Spice House is a model American business, the kind of establishment that makes a city proud. The next time you are in Evanston, make it a point to visit this unique and successful treasure.

1941 Central Avenue, Evanston IL (847) 328-3711
1512 N Wells, Chicago IL (312) 274-0378
www.thespicehouse.com

Bearj Antonio Salon & Spa

When customers at Bearj Antonio Salon & Spa say "Fabulous," they could be referring to their latest haircut or to the product line, Fabulous, that owner Bearj Antonio created to condition hair. "We believe that when you look your best, you feel your best," says Bearj, who is the driving force behind the Buffalo Grove salon and spa. The magnetic personality of this Armenian native attracts loyal customers and a talented professional team that includes his nephew and business partner Eddie Antonio. You'll know you've found a treasure when you walk away from the salon with natural-looking corrective color and cuts that honor your features and hair type. The spa offers a choice of body wraps and nail services, including private lessons in makeup application. You'll also find facials that control acne, defy aging and deep-clean pores, including one just for men. Bearj started out in the corporate world, but needed a more creative profession. He attributes his drive and inventive personality to growing up in a war-torn country and to his mother, who taught him to believe that if he was passionate about success, the world would come to his door. He took out a second mortgage on his home to start his business and launch his product line. He also relied on advice from such mentors as Michael Thomas and John Sahaj, a fellow countryman and hair designer who became well known in New York for his dry cuts. Put artistry to work for you at Bearj Antonio Salon & Spa.

730 Buffalo Grove Road, Buffalo Grove IL
(847) 520-7719
www.bearjantoniosalonandspa.com

Fashion & Beauty—Chicago Metro

Perlman Fine Jewelry

Perlman Fine Jewelry began its rich history in 1960, when Milton Perlman established the family business in downtown Elgin, Illinois. He was educated at the famous Elgin National Watch Company's Watchmakers College, where he acquired his watch repair skills and jewelry arts talents. His jewelry business prospered and Perlman, along with his two sons, have been dedicated to serving the greater Fox Valley area with their store locations throughout the years in Elgin, St. Charles, West Dundee and Geneva. His son, Corey Perlman, owns the store at Geneva Commons. The ambience of the spacious 5,000-square-foot store is inviting and elegant. Nowhere else in the vicinity can you find such an exciting array of products from the world's most renowned jewelry designers, watch makers and artisans. Brands, including Rolex, Mikimoto and Fabergé, are all symbols of excellence and are all represented at Perlman's. And if you are searching for that one truly breathtaking diamond, the one that will win her heart, then look no further. Perlman Fine Jewelry specializes in offering the most beautiful patented cut diamonds available anywhere. What's more, Perlman's hosts a professional in-house service team like no other in the area, providing custom jewelry designs, expert jewelry and watch repairs, pearl stringing, engraving and jewelry appraisals from its GIA Graduate Gemologists. You can visit Perlman's website too, for round-the-clock shopping enjoyment. Come to Perlman Fine Jewelry today and discover an Illinois Treasure.

Geneva Commons, Geneva IL (630) 262-9090
www.perlmanfinejewelry.com

Chicago Metro—Fashion & Beauty

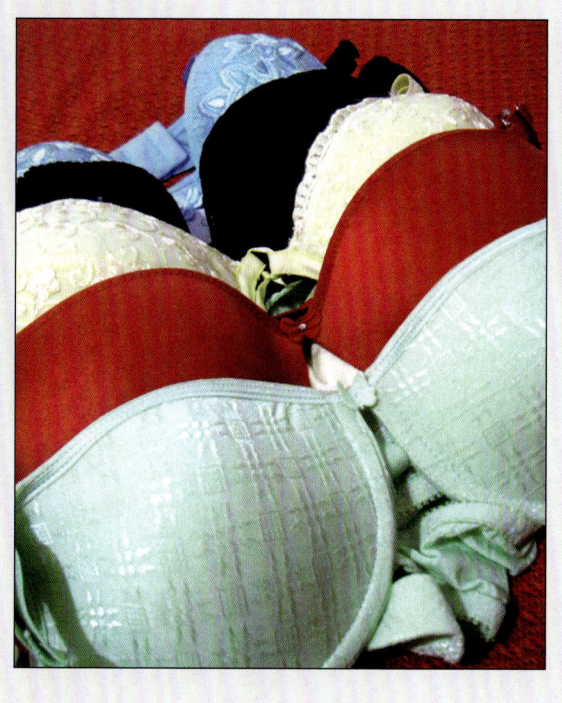

Betty Schwartz's Intimate Boutique

There is no need to feel intimidated by intimate apparel at Betty Schwartz's Intimate Boutique. The family business has grown since its origins as corsetieres, and the second and third generations proudly continue the tradition of offering top-notch personal service and selection in order to help you feel comfortable and confident. Once you step into the elegant interior, you'll receive personal and professional attention to help you find the perfect foundations or swimwear. The experienced staff identifies your correct size and shape so you won't end up with lingerie that isn't right for your figure. Comfortable lingerie isn't just about delicate lace or sleek design. It's about the fit, and the friendly, attentive staff won't give up until they find the perfect shape, size and style that fit your needs. You'll quickly realize why *Today's Chicago Woman* voted Betty Schwartz's Intimate Boutique Chicago's number-one lingerie store. The large inventory, including enticing selections from Wacoal, Calvin Klein, Chantelle, Cosabella, Hanky Panky and Le Mystere, lets you explore items to suit your mood, personality and taste. If you feel practical or provocative, sensual or serious, visit Betty Schwartz's Intimate Boutique for sleek and stylish items to flatter every contour and curve.

1833 Second Street, Highland Park IL (847) 432-0220
1152 Lake Cook Road, Buffalo Grove IL (847) 459-5846
720 D W Waukegan Road, Deerfield IL (847) 374-9833
www.bettyschwartzs.com

Wilmette Jewelers

Wilmette Jewelers is a family-owned and operated store known throughout the North Shore for its fine jewelry, professional expertise and diverse merchandise. Founded by Lester Inbinder in 1954, it is currently managed by Gayle Inbinder, a gemologist who grew up in the business. Assessing a gemstones quality and authenticity can be confusing, so Gayle and her knowledgeable staff are available to answer questions and have implemented a newsletter with pertinent advice and information. Wilmette Jewelers has evolved into an international business and carries such specialty lines as Waterford and Orrefors crystal, Mont Blanc, Longines, Tissot and Swiss Army timepieces. Always aware of current trends and advances in technology, its latest acquisition are the Hearts on Fire diamonds, one of the world's most perfectly cut diamonds. Custom-designed jewelry is a specialty of the store, and if an item is not stocked the staff will order or create it for the customer. In addition to the full-time gemologist on staff, there is also an in-house goldsmith, watch and jewelry repair services and engraving. Wilmette Jewelers provides exceptional quality and personalized service delighting generations past, present and future.

1149 Wilmette Avenue, Wilmette IL
(847) 251-1061
www.wilmettejewelers.com

Yaya's Unique Clothing & Accessories

"If you don't find shopping relaxing, you need to shop at Yaya's." That's how Yaya's Unique Clothing & Accessories owner Sherree Rothstein sums up the difference between her casual women's clothing boutique and the hustle and bustle of the big stores. Before Sherree and her husband opened Yaya's in 2002, they had worked in the clothing business for many years, owning a store in Crystal Lake. Yaya's, named after Sherree's sisterhood of friends, offers everyday clothing for women in a relaxing environment. You'll find lots of great-fitting jeans, as well as plenty of fun, casual and elegant tops from designers such as Skinny Minnie and G Wheels. Sherree takes care to stay on top of the latest fashion trends. Yaya's also offers a full line of accessories to complement any wardrobe. Whether it's a beautiful belt from Brave Leather or the latest Hobo International handbag, you'll find it here, plus hats, scarves, jewelry and other extras. The store offers a variety of special events throughout the year, including birthday events and trunk shows with massages, music, treats and specialty drinks. For fine fashion in a fun atmosphere, do your shopping at Yaya's Unique Clothing & Accessories.

608 N Milwaukee Avenue, Libertyville IL
(847) 367-1740
www.shopyayas.com

Chicago Metro—Fashion & Beauty

Peter Daniel
Apparel for Men and Women

Peter Daniel Apparel for Men and Women is a trendy, upscale clothing store that offers its customers a unique selection, superb service and great quality that you won't find anywhere else. Co-owners and sisters Becky and Beth Johanson and their staff truly enjoy working with customers and helping them find the perfect outfit for every occasion. Peter Daniel has been turning first-time visitors into loyal customers for more than 34 years. Beth's father, Peter Hammond, and his good friend, Daniel Thomsen, founded Peter Daniel in 1973 as a gentlemen's shop. Since then, it has expanded into an exquisite store offering casual, sport and dress clothing for men and women as well as accessories, purses and jewelry. Beth and her sisters Becky and Bridget are proud to carry on the tradition and work in all aspects of the business. Whether selecting the new seasons' collections or assisting a customer, they can be seen daily in the store. Quality lines from Debra de Roo, J'envie and Louben line the walls, arranged in appealing displays. The men's department has evolved to include a selection of upscale European collections, exclusive in the area, along with such favorites as Tommy Bahama, Cutter & Buck, Allen-Edmonds and The North Face. The women's department continues to flourish as new designers and collections are introduced each season. Beth is proud of the ever-changing selection, where customers always find something new and fashionable to add to their wardrobes. Stop in to see what Peter Daniel has to offer. Your closet will thank you.

200 Applebee Street, Ice House Mall, Barrington IL (847) 382-6676
www.peter-daniel.com

1973 Opening of the original Peter Daniel Men's Apparel in Countryside Mall, Palatine. Left to right are partners Peter and Evelyn Hammond and Dottie and Dan Thomsen.

Adrienne Clarisse Intimate Boutique

Femininity is the focus at Adrienne Clarisse Intimate Boutique, a Libertyville shop devoted to fine lingerie. Adrienne McGill opened the shop in 2005 and drew the attention of the trade magazine, *The Best of Intima*. Its Best Shop Awards 2006 recognized the store as a top five finalist in the personal touch category, among 350 lingerie stores in the country. The shop was also named MainStreet Libertyville's Business of the Year in 2006. Customers keep coming back to Adrienne Clarisse thanks to extraordinary personal care. You can expect not only an expert fitting, but education on how an undergarment should fit and the steps to take to keep it beautiful and functional. Adrienne's love of lingerie and deep interest in exploring femininity led her to leave a corporate career to open her shop. You'll find basic foundation pieces, including bras, panties and shapewear, as well as couture for the boudoir. You are sure to feel pretty and confident in styles by Chantelle, Le Mystère and Prima Donna as well as Cosabella, Hanky Panky and Simone Perelle. Adrienne wants her customers to enjoy every minute of their shopping experience and starts with beautiful surroundings and sensitive guidance. She has a fine tuned sense of intimate style and offers sexy, unconventional items along with the essentials. For an intimate expression of your private side, visit Adrienne Clarisse Intimate Boutique.

531 N Milwaukee Avenue, Libertyville IL
(847) 573-8905
www.adrienneclarisse.com

Photo by Studio West Photography, Ltd.

Shop 38, For the Love of Shoes

If you love shoes, step on in to Shop 38, For the Love of Shoes, an attractive, upscale boutique in downtown Geneva. Here, owner Elisa Pantano has made it her business to offer the best shoes available for every budget. Whether you're looking for a pair of $10 shoes to knock around the house in or a pair of $300 high-fashion heels, you'll find them at Shop 38. The shop's wares are displayed on attractive tables, giving you an accessible, 360-degree view. You'll find old standby brands, such as Cole Haan and Kenneth Cole, and more elusive brands, such as Michael Kors and Havaianas. One of the biggest attractions to the store is the brand Carlos by Carlos Santana. "His shoes always have a fashion-forward design, are well-made and are usually under $100," Elisa says. Elisa, who inherited her shoe fetish from her mother, grew up commuting to the bigger cities to satisfy her tastes. When she decided to bring shoe fashion to Geneva, she recruited her mother, Alice, as a buyer. Elisa believes a great pair of shoes is a waste without the right accessories to match, so you'll find classy handbags, jewelry and belts at the shop to complement your shoes. You can even take advantage of personal shopping services to help you find the exact pair of shoes or accessory you're looking for. Indulge your passion for foot fashion at Shop 38, For the Love of Shoes.

228 S Third Street, Lower Level, Geneva, IL
(630) 262-1849
www.shop38shoes.com

Chicago Metro—Fashion & Beauty   45

Blue Violet Body Works

Reach a new level of relaxation at Blue Violet Body Works. With a highly trained and devoted staff, Blue Violet is much more than a massage business. It is a health-centered facility, specifically geared at healing and prevention of a variety of ailments through heartfelt massage, aromatherapy and holistic medicine. Owner Barb Baran not only wants to improve the health of her patrons with alternative healing, but strives to educate them about its life-altering benefits. Insomnia, arthritis and headaches are among the many common ailments that are virtually eliminated after receiving routine massages from Blue Violet. Types of massage include Swedish, shiatsu and specialized massages, such as sports therapy, deep compression and reflexology, to target specific areas in the body. Also available is the ancient art of Reiki, which involves energy channeling and the laying on of hands. Exclusively at Blue Violet are the pregnancy and postpartum massages, designed especially for mothers and mothers-to-be. Looking to treat a friend or special someone? Gift certificates are available for a wide array of facials, massages and herbal body treatments. If you're interested in learning the art of massage yourself, Barb also offers classes in Reiki and reflexology. Indulge in whole body and soul health when you visit Blue Violet Body Works in Elgin.

2000 Larkin Avenue, Suite 301 & the Lighthouse, Elgin IL
(847) 697-5522
www.bluevioletbodyworks.com

Photos by Paul Swanson

Fashion & Beauty—Chicago Metro

Young Tootsies

With over a hundred years of collective experience, Young Tootsies owners Doug Pekarek and Frank Haslwanter make up a knowledgeable shoe-fitting team specializing in children. Young Tootsies offers the personalized service that only these local shop owners can provide. Doug and Frank think of each child as one of their own grandchildren. Relax and browse the women's line of shoes while these patient professionals find the exact size and fit for kids. With quality brands for boys and girls ages 2 to 12, you're sure to find anything from comfortable and functional to the hottest new trends for babies and tweeners. Young Tootsies carries popular brands that include Stride Rite, as well as special brands such as Umi. The colorful dress and casual shoes from Umi have a trendy European flair. Young Tootsies is one of the only stores where you can find specialty dress shoes for your little ones. Your little ring-bearer or flower girl will stride down the aisle with style and poise in their custom-fit and matched shoes. To really shine at a school play or parade, girls might enjoy some of Young Tootsies' sequined shoes, which come in various bright colors. Young boys will be intrigued by the fun shoes that leave dinosaur footprints in the ground. For one of the easiest shopping days you've ever had with the kids, stop into Young Tootsies. Let Doug and Frank do all the footwork for you.

200 Applebee Street, Barrington IL
(847) 277-1381

The Dreamwear Shoppe

It took a heart attack at age 37 and a strong reaction to 9/11 to shake up Nancy Burkhart's thinking about the need for comfort in our lives. Nancy used to work as a corporate vice president, but these days she goes to work in pajamas, along with her employees at the Dreamwear Shoppe. When Nancy ended up in the hospital, she was wearing her husband Kevin's old T-shirt, her standard pajamas at that time. She mentioned to Kevin that she looked and felt terrible. The next day, he brought her poodle-themed pj's and a pink chenille robe, items that started the healing process. Nancy opened the Dreamwear Shoppe in Long Grove in 2002 and in Geneva in 2004 to help others find comfort in their homes and recover from stress. The shop offers nurturing clothes and accessories for sleeping and lounging. You'll find a section for infants and children, another for grandmothers and one for men and women. The clothing is soft and friendly, featuring locally made lines as well as name brands such as Life is Good, Bunnies by the Bay and Sara's Prints. Pillowcases with lavender sewn in, linen sprays, aromatherapy and heat therapy products promise sweet dreams. Brides and attendants are not overlooked. Thongs and T-shirts make fun bridal party gifts, while brides delight in the flip flops that leave the imprint "Just Married" in the sand. The checkout counter is an antique bed, and all gifts, whether purchased at the store or online, include free gift wrapping. Lighten your spirits with a visit to the Dreamwear Shoppe.

407 S 3rd Street, Geneva IL (630) 232-2725
www.funandrelaxation.com

Deb-betts

One day Debi Cohen was forced to face the fact that her women's clothing business was too good to keep in the basement. The popularity of her product prompted her to move her home-based operation into a store front, thus bringing Deb-betts to life in 1983. From the start, this has been a place to find stylish lines not readily available elsewhere. Women of all ages and sizes count on Deb-betts for the latest from Bianca, Marc Ariel and Womyn, as well as Joie, Jenne Maag and Billy Blues. Debi practically grew up in a Chicago clothing store, Handmoor, that her parents owned for more than 40 years. She learned the business from them, but her sense of style is all her own. It did not find full expression until it was liberated from the basement and could be put to use not only in selecting stock, but in creating atmosphere in the store. Warm colors and backlit displays set a sophisticated tone, making Deb-betts a pleasant and attractive place to shop. Debi is joined in the business by her daughter, Robbyn Ratskoff. They know their customers well and keep in touch, informing them of great deals and special events, such as the popular trunk and fashion shows. Stay in style by shopping at Deb-betts.

100 Village Green Drive, Lincolnshire IL (847) 821-7400
www.shopallaboutme.com

All About Me

Robbyn Ratskoff was only 21 years old when she opened All About Me with her mother, Debi Cohen. Robbyn and Debi both grew up with retail backgrounds, so after graduating from college and working in the clothing business, it was a natural progression for Robbyn to join forces with her mother to open their own specialty store. They launched All About Me in 2002 to represent the cutting edge of fashion. Robbyn and Debi create a fun and trendy atmosphere at the store. The cement floors are painted with fun phrases and graffiti, and the displays incorporate vintage pieces. They make custom mix tapes to set the shopping mood and keep an English Bulldog named Gus as the store mascot and personal greeter. Fashionistas love the big selection of denim fashions and the creative new brands, such as Genetic, Rebel Yell, Kasil and Three Dots. As an example of a successful young entrepreneur, Robbyn serves as a role model to many up-and-coming young women. If you're wondering what's new in the fashion industry, stop by All About Me to see it first-hand.

300 Village Green Drive, Lincolnshire IL (847) 821-7400
www.shopallaboutme.com

Sole Searching

Perhaps no one understands the tastes of Lincolnshire women better than the mother/daughter team of Debi Cohen and Robbyn Ratskoff. Already the owners of two women's clothing stores in the Village Green Shopping Center, All about Me and Deb-betts, they added Sole Searching, a shoe store, in 2007. Style meets comfort in the shoes that they offer, which run the range from funky to sophisticated. The owners know of very few stores that carry Taryn by Taryn Rose, just one of the featured lines. They also stock such brands as Anyi Liu, Faryl Robin and Tsubo in their bright, fun and welcoming store known for its shabby-chic displays. The staff prides itself on being able to find the right shoes for any outfit. When you're in the fashion business, keeping up with what's in style in Manhattan and Milan is important, but having a sense of what trends could catch on in your town is even more crucial. Debi and Robbyn possess this instinct. By combining the resources of all three of their stores, you can create amazing outfits. Slip your feet into something neat at Sole Searching.

300 Village Green Drive, Lincolnshire IL (847) 415-2525
www.shopsolesearchingshoes.com

Chicago Metro—Fashion & Beauty

Eliza Jane

Do you have the stuff to be an Eliza Jane girl? According to owners Nicole Guvenoz and Megan Hernandez, their shop caters to, "the up-and-coming school girl, the all-that college girl, the look-at-me career girl, the hip mom and the cool grandma." All feel right at home shopping for jewelry, handbags and other accessories at Eliza Jane. Featured items include many seen on the *Today Show* and *Oprah*. The owners also like to carry Fair Trade lines made by women in Third World countries who are working to support their families. Just coming into Eliza Jane will make you feel good, but visiting the spa in the back will make you feel even better. Getting your nails done at this color-splashed pampering palace might include the addition of some Nail Bling in the form of Swarovski crystal jewels. The Ice Cream Pedi treats your feet to a scoop of bath ice cream, a matching flavored scrub with massage and a marshmallow masque to moisturize. Other services include facials, waxing and eyelashes. Eliza Jane also teaches debutantes table manners and other social graces at its etiquette university. The format is fun and entertaining as classes cover such topics as how to hold and control a knife, how to write a good thank you note and how to make a fine first impression in any social situation. "There is no other shop like Eliza Jane," say Nicole and Megan, who clearly enjoy spreading beauty, style and grace throughout St. Charles. Drop by and revel in being an Eliza Jane girl.

322 W Main Street, St. Charles IL
(630) 457-1821
www.elizajanegirl.com

Fashion & Beauty—Chicago Metro

Clarice's—Creating Beautiful Looks

Women in Wheaton turn to Clarice Loiacona for skin care. Clarice, who opened Clarice's—Creating Beautiful Looks in 1989, is an award-winning aesthetician with 25 years of experience. Her private label skincare line was developed by a UCLA teacher of cosmetic chemistry. Her theater background serves her well in applying makeup for special events. Her makeup lessons show women of all ages how to achieve classic good looks. Clarice customizes facials to address your skin's idiosyncrasies. The most popular facial is Clarice's Complete, a luxurious blend of cleansing, Shiatsu massage, skin-appropriate exfoliation and extraction. While the mask works, Clarice massages feet and hands. When Clarice spoke at a San Francisco trade show, she presented her Journey of Inner Peace facial, which adds relaxing imagery, chakra balancing and Reiki to her signature facial. Her customers like the Queen Pedicure so much that Clarice created a one-and-a-half-hour version called the Diva Pedicure. A visit to Clarice's is a pleasant interlude spent in a charming house. Customers often linger to catch up on local events over coffee and green tea extracts. Choose a package or plan a party at Clarice's—Creating Beautiful Looks.

326 S Main Street, Wheaton IL (630) 690-2266
www.creatingbeautifullooks.com

The Country Cobbler

Three generations of the Adams have made footwear their life's work at The Country Cobbler. Ace Adams founded the Glenview store in 1949, and his grandson Jim continues as owner and president today. The store can keep you and your family in brand-name shoes from infancy through your senior years. Since customers need many pairs of shoes over a lifetime, The Country Cobbler's loyalty program can add up to big savings as customers earn credits on future purchases. You can expect some old-fashioned measuring and fitting from the experts at both Country Cobbler locations—Glenview and Wilmette. The Country Cobbler also stocks handbags and accessories. Jim began working in the family business in the sixth grade, a circumstance that has led him to know both shoes and local community members well. The store is an active partner in the community through sponsorship of Little League Baseball and the Glenview and Wilmette chambers. Next time you need shoes, visit The Country Cobbler and let the Adams family keep your family comfortable and stylish.

1708 Glenview Road, Glenview IL
(847) 724-3131
1163 Wilmette Avenue, Wilmette IL
(847) 256-0165
www.thecountrycobbler.com

Chicago Metro—Fashion & Beauty   51

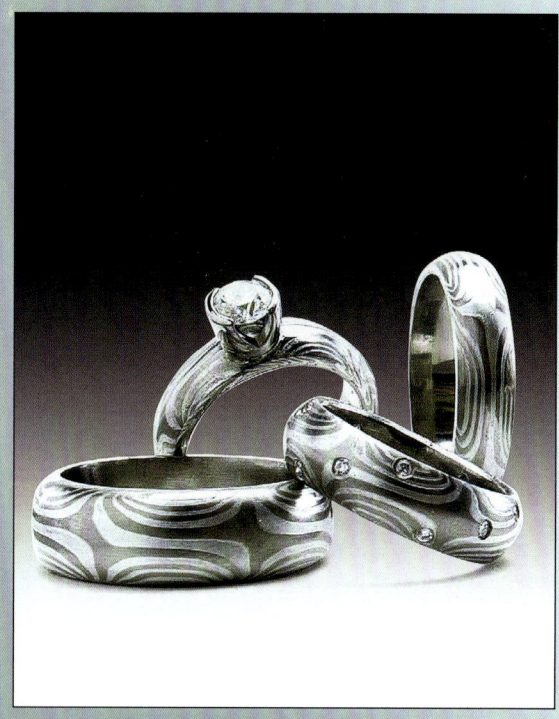

Peggie Robinson Designs

Peggie Robinson uses traditional Japanese *mokume-gane* to create stunning pins, pendants earrings, bracelets and rings at her jewelry studio, Peggie Robinson Designs. She began creating jewelry from home in the early 1970s. Early in 2001, she learned the ancient Japanese art form of mokume-gane. In the fall of 2001, she showed her first collection of pendants and earrings using mokume-gane, a mixed-metal laminate with distinctive, layered patterns. Developed in the 17th century by master sword smiths, mokume-gane was first used in the hilts and pommels of the katana swords wielded by samurai warriors. The name translates as wood grain metal, a term that aptly describes the lovely patterns in the laminated metal. Later, mokume-gane was fashioned into high-quality jewelry. In 2002, Peggie added mokume-gane wedding and engagement rings for both men and women to her collection. Peggie now creates mokume-gane using 14/18K gold and platinum silver. Layer upon layer of colored metals are painstakingly fused together and manipulated to make unique mokume-gane patterns that are incorporated into wearable art jewelry. Customers can choose from mokume-gane or other original jewelry designs, or have a piece created especially for them. Jewelry from the studio of Peggie Robinson Designs will be treasured into the next generation. To make an appointment with Peggie to see the collection or to create a special piece, please phone the studio for an appointment.

1601 Payne Street, Suite 1, Evanston IL
(847) 475-2121
www.peggierobinsondesigns.com

Lori's Designer Shoes

Lori's Designer Shoes, affectionately known as the sole of Chicago, hit the northwest suburbs in 2005 with a store in Lincolnshire that makes shoe fanatics shout with joy. The selection of 200 styles of shoes can rightly be called huge, yet the shopping experience is fun and casual, not overwhelming. Owners Kelly McCormick and Beth Sussman do a great job of maintaining a comfortable, boutique atmosphere, despite the exciting prospect of so many higher-end, hard-to-find shoes together under one roof. Whether you're looking for casual or dressy, you'll discover plenty of choices. Poetic License, Frye and Me Too are just a few of the appealing lines. The moderate prices only serve to feed the adrenaline rush. Founder Lori Andre is a self-declared shoe addict whose addiction has transferred to thousands of women since she opened Lori's Designer Shoes in 1983. Her loyal customers wish her well when she sets off on one her biannual buying trips to Europe, and then mark the days until she returns. They know that she'll be bringing home the newest, trendiest and most cutting-edge styles that she can find. Indulge your passion for shoes at the Lincolnshire branch of Lori's Designer Shoes, located in the City Park Shopping Center.

275 Parkway Drive, Suite 613, Lincolnshire IL
(847) 947-4851

Persin & Persin Jewelers

Susan and Julian Persin scout jewelry trade shows throughout the world to assemble the distinctive collection at Persin & Persin Jewelers. Susan's trips to Ireland have resulted in the largest selection of Irish jewelry in the region. If you have something special in mind, Julian can create a customized design to meet your tastes and budget. He begins with a sketch, then makes a wax model so you'll know just what to expect. He's been a jeweler for 53 years and learned the trade from his late father. He offers repairs, antique restorations and appraisal services. Customers have been coming to this Antioch location for jewelry since 1902; Susan and Julian bought the business in 1984. You will find superior diamonds, wedding sets and popular platinum, gold and palladium jewelry. The shop owners can help you select jewelry to celebrate special occasions, as well as Waterford crystal and fine Irish china by Beleek. The store's collection of Lladro porcelain figurines rivals any in Lake County, making it easy to find that missing collectible or limited-edition piece. For personal attention and jewelry that stands apart, visit Persin & Persin Jewelers.

913 Main Street, Antioch IL
(847) 395-8855

Teddie Kossof Salon, Spa & Wellness Center

Comparing the Teddie Kossof Salon, Spa & Wellness Center to your average salon and spa combo would be like comparing your neighborhood park to Disneyland. Kossof, long known as a hairdresser to the stars, began his prestigious career in 1975 and has since coiffed the tresses of such famed personalities as Lauren Bacall, Mary Tyler Moore and Poet Laureate Maya Angelou. His beauty emporium is the largest of its kind in the nation and features a staff of more than 70 professionals in the salon alone. At Teddie Kossof Salon, Spa & Wellness Center, services range from cosmetic dentistry and surgery to catching a healthful and delicious meal with friends at the in-house Richard's Café. After a massage and some aromatherapy, you can stop by Rita's Design Studio where Rita, an expert seamstress and designer, can create a masterpiece for your next gala function. In the salon you can relax and enjoy a full range of traditional services, secure in the knowledge that Kossof's expert and pampering staff will give you a perfect cut, color or curl and ensure that your nails are in tip-top shape. The spa offers facials, massages and makeovers, while the wellness center offers tanning, body contouring, hair removal and other discreet services designed to improve your well-being. Give yourself the grown-up vacation you deserve with a day at Teddie Kossof Salon, Spa & Wellness Center.

281 Waukegan Road, Northfield IL (847) 446-9526
www.teddiekossof.com

Chicago Metro—*Flowers & Events*

Floral Gardens

Floral Gardens of Highland Park is a full-service florist that provides flowers, plants and trees for weddings, graduations and showers, and for social and corporate events. Until 1988, Floral Gardens was known as Bahr's Floral Gardens, and under one name or another it has been a leading Highland Park business for more than 80 years. Today, Floral Gardens is managed by two sisters, Rosann Santi and Renee Santi-Ruedig, who were born and raised in Highland Park. The sisters studied at a school of floral design and have more than 30 years of floral experience. Renee also worked as an interior designer early in her career. Providing complete floral design services for any occasion, the sisters and their staff are proud of their personal touch and artistic flair. If you have a vision, Floral Gardens can turn it into reality. Consider flowers for fall and winter festivals as well as for spring and summer—Floral Gardens can create arrangements to help brighten Rosh Hashanah, Thanksgiving or Christmas. Come to Floral Gardens, where innovative ideas and personalized service will leave you with a lasting impression.

2109 Green Bay Road, Highland Park IL
(847) 432-3420 or (888) 432-3420
www.floralgardensofhighlandpark.com

Barrington Flower Shop

Floral designer Glen Egeland and his wife Mary Cay own one of the most creative and eclectic flower shops in Barrington. Barrington Flower shop offers high design floral arrangements, simple but sensational bouquets and gifts. Glen's flair for edgy floral creations is a testament to his lifetime in the industry. His mother and uncle both owned flower shops, and Glen prides himself on having continued the family tradition for over 40 years. Barrington Flower Shop believes in color. One of Glen's best-selling arrangements combines sunny lilies, blushing roses and magenta snapdragons with a vibrant green fern. If you're looking for something contemporary and original, check out his arrangement of orange roses embedded in river rocks. Glen is happy to provide on-site consultations to assist you with custom arrangements and themed designs for your wedding or event. In addition to some of the best floral arrangements in the area, Barrington Flower Shop is home to antique furniture, vintage accessories and silk flowers. Let Glen's taste and imagination makeover your home or event with products from Barrington Flower Shop.

201 S Cook Street, Barrington IL
(847) 382-4090
www.barringtonflowershop.com

Chicago Metro—Flowers & Events

Joseph's Floral & Gift Showroom

For more than five decades, Joseph's Floral & Gift Showroom has provided beautiful flowers and décor for events throughout Lake County. Christy Dugo-Rudie and her brother, Daniel Dugo, maintain the traditions of service and quality established by their parents, Joseph and Joan Dugo. Entering Joseph's is like walking into a wonderland of colors and scents, with a variety of themed areas set up throughout the store. Each season brings a variety of new and colorful plants and home décor items to the shop, and the entire store is updated several times a year. You'll find the freshest, most fragrant flowers from Holland, along with expert designers who will help you realize your floral vision for any event. Most of the friendly staff has been at Joseph's for more than 10 years. Specializing in weddings, bar mitzvahs and other social occasions, Joseph's can create a vision of beauty for your special event, with everything from beautiful flower arrangements to lighting, centerpieces, napkins and other necessities. In addition to flowers, Joseph's offers an array of pretty plants, as well as baskets and home décor items ideal for gifts. The store also stocks a variety of greeting cards and beautiful art objects. Let the staff at Joseph's Floral & Gift Showroom put a bloom of joy on your next special event.

1022 N Milwaukee Avenue, Libertyville IL
(847) 362-2224 or (888) 447-4882
www.josephsflorist.com

Flowers & Events—Chicago Metro

Antioch Floral

Since 1995, owners Dave and Joanne Hoeh have provided a full line of fresh flowers to Antioch and all of Lake County. Everything from roses to tropicals are cut fresh daily to assure that customers get the freshest, longest lasting arrangements possible. You can welcome the seasons with bouquets of lush colors or honor a special day with beautiful long-stem roses. Choose from thoughtfully done sympathy arrangements that convey your deepest thoughts. Antioch Floral has a wonderful selection of corporate gifts to brighten workplaces and show appreciation. Dave and Joanne are known throughout the area for their creative designs and are sought after for their wedding and party arrangements. Wedding consultations ensure that the flowers for your special day are exactly as you dreamed. Every customer is treated with care and receives the attention to detail and assurance of quality that they deserve. Whether you are expressing condolences or celebrating a birth, birthday or anniversary, Antioch Floral is sure to give you service you can count on.

959 Main Street, Antioch IL (847) 838-0300 or (800) 300-0522
www.antiochfloral.com

Fresh Flower Market

A European-style open market, Fresh Flower Market has delighted Barrington shoppers since 1987. The perfume of fresh flowers greets you the moment you enter. Buckets of flowers are artfully arranged amidst bird baths and antiques. The Market's gifted design staff specializes in European garden designs, including French country, Tuscan, Dutch and English styles. In addition to its arrangements, the shop offers topiaries and seasonal plants such as orchids and hydrangeas. Have your order placed in a gift vase, urn or other special container. Additional home decor items are found artistically displayed throughout the store. Fresh Flower Market's superior flowers are the result of painstaking selection from around the world. The shop has its own buyer at the Dutch auction in Aalsmeer as well as long-standing connections with growers in South America, the West Coast and the Midwest. The Market receives its flowers within 24 hours of harvest and expertly cuts and conditions them to guarantee quality and longevity. Owner Elizabeth Bremner has lived around flowers all her life—her mother and grandmother were gardeners. Come to Fresh Flower Market for fragrant blooms to brighten your rooms and lighten your heart.

122 W Main Street, Barrington IL (847) 381-7800 or (888) 381-7800
www.barringtonfreshflowermarket.com

The Grove Banquets

Planning, organizing and hosting special occasions can make even the most stalwart person cringe. The folks at the Grove relieve the stress of dealing with all kinds of events by offering a premier banquet hall and a full range of planning services. The Grove specializes in wedding receptions, proms and business meetings, but you can also book your graduation party, reunion, bar or bat mitzvah or any other occasion. The Main Room offers a spacious setting for your gathering, with chandeliers providing elegant lighting. The smaller Club Room offers a quaint setting for a business meeting, dinner party or shower. The Bride's Room is a perfect place for bridal parties to apply finishing touches to makeup or attire before greeting guests. Select delectable menus served family, buffet or individual service styles. Owners Adom and Hanna Hryniewicki specialize in Eastern European and Polish cuisine and are passionate about offering a choice of pierogis, chicken paprikash, schnitzel and sauerkraut and sausage in addition to the more traditional banquet fare of baked chicken, beef roulade, Greek chicken or Swiss steak. A wide range of side dishes, salads and desserts are also available. With efficient attention to every colorful detail, the Grove Banquets will make your next event a spectacular success.

301 N Weiland Road, Buffalo Grove IL (847) 229-1000
www.thegrovebanquets.com

Chicago Metro—Flowers & Events 57

Libertyville Florist

Beautiful, fragrant flowers and service with a smile are a family tradition at Libertyville Florist. The store opened in 1985 and is owned and operated by Jan and Kristen Lindell, a mother and daughter team. It was a natural fit, because Jan and Kristen are both very creative and believe in personal service. Freshness and beauty are the order of the day at Libertyville Florist. The store stocks fresh, high-quality flowers from all over the world. In addition to fresh flowers, the shop has many different varieties of green and blooming plants. You'll find arrangements for everything from weddings to corporate events. No matter what you're looking for, the expert staff can design something to your exact specifications. If you're looking for longer-lasting beauty, check out the silk and everlasting arrangements. Libertyville Florist accepts orders 24 hours a day by phone or on its website. In addition to beautiful flowers, the shop stocks a variety of attractive gift items, including themed baby or other special occasion gift baskets, and gift baskets featuring gourmet food and fruit. The shop carries a full line of Door County coffees and offers samples while you shop. Find a greeting card that says just what you mean from among the many on display. Let Libertyville Florist make your special occasion bloom with color and beauty.

1348 S Milwaukee Avenue, Libertyville IL
(847) 816-6900 or (800) 656-5488
www.libertyvilleflorist.com

Mille Fiori!

Mille Fiori! is a blossom-filled emporium of all things floral with an Old World touch of distinction that puts it well above the par. Mille Fiori stocks a full inventory of regal flowers with which to create stunning bouquets and arrangements for weddings, corporate events and special occasions of all kinds. The shop further offers a selection of topiaries, as well as dried flower arrangements and wreaths, expertly hand made on the premises. In Italian, *Mille Fiori* means one thousand flowers, a term that most aptly describes what visitors will find as they walk through the door. In addition to offering a glorious sampling of nature's bounty, Mille Fiori also offers a wide array of floral scented body oils, soaps and personal care items, as well as a line of candles. The shop is a terrific place to find elegant gifts, whimsical water fountains and creative décor for the home and garden, along with antique pottery vases and unusual pots. Partners Tracy Rosenquist and Charles Mullenix took over this 11-year-old European-style floral boutique in 2005. Give the gift of flowers, to yourself or a loved one, with Mille Fiori's creative floral designs.

**1943 Central Street, Evanston IL
(847) 570-0300
www.millefioriflorist.com**

Twinkle Teas
& Twinkle Tots Boutique

With Twinkle Teas & Twinkle Tots Boutique, Hillary Wertz brings the magic of childhood and tea parties together under one roof. Since 2002, Twinkle Teas parties have sparkled so little princesses can shine. Made-to-order party menus include treats such as peanut butter and jelly sandwiches, gaily decorated cupcakes and pink lemonade. Parties are hostess-guided so little guests and their moms can relax and enjoy the puppet shows, crafts, manicures and makeovers. Bridal and baby showers and special ladies tea parties are also available. Teas, coffee and sodas are served along with homemade scones and assorted pastries and treats. Twinkle Tots Children's Boutique features specialty designs that are not easily found elsewhere. Girls' clothing from newborn to 12 years old includes dresses and outfits by Catimini, Kate Mack and Biscotti. Boys' clothing runs from newborn to age five. The boutique also stocks dress-up costumes for girls and boys. With fantasy wall murals and magical nooks and crannies you'll delight in spending time at Twinkle Teas & Twinkle Tots Boutique.

**212 W Front Street, Wheaton IL
(630) 588-9898
www.twinkleteas.com
www.twinkletotsboutique.com**

Chicago Metro—Flowers & Events   59

Riverside Receptions & Conference Center

Celebrating a wedding in historic surroundings next to the Fox River is a dream come true for many brides and grooms. The family-owned business has been satisfying such dreams since opening Riverside Receptions and Conference Center in 2000. The Geneva facility, built by William Howell as a foundry for sad-iron manufacturing in the 19th century, features its own chef and areas suitable for outdoor or indoor weddings and other events attracting up to 275 people. The lower floor gets its distinctive and intimate atmosphere from natural brick and stone, three fireplaces and a pub-style bar, while an upper level delights guests with enchanting views. The staff thinks of every extra to enhance the candlelit dining room. Two bridal suites offer an elegant place for the bride to prepare for her wedding. The attentive and experienced staff orchestrate each event to assure a smooth and enjoyable affair, whether you plan a business meeting, a corporate holiday party or something more intimate, such as a shower or anniversary party. The superior food and excellent service, combined with a river location, won the facility a local Reader's Choice award for Best Banquet Facility. Being just steps away from the famous Herrington Inn and Geneva's shopping district is an added bonus. Plan your next event at Riverside Receptions & Conference Center.

35 N River Lane, Geneva IL
(630) 232-1330
www.riversidereceptions.com

Galleries & Fine Art—Chicago Metro

William E. Miller—*Young Boy With Riding Crop*, English 1896, Oil on canvas
Photo by Aaron Schneider

Maclund Gallery

A welcoming gallery with a small-town charm, Maclund Gallery shows and sells a variety of 19th and 20th century fine art, antique furniture and jewelry. Owners Ro McLaughlin and Barbara Lund pride themselves in the fact that they can offer many different types of art to appeal to a diverse audience. With a knack for finding rare antiques, Ro and Barbara maintain a loyal customer base, who are enthusiastic about quality originals. Whether you're looking for antique hand-painted porcelain dishes or 19th century paintings, the art at Maclund can't be found anywhere else. Among the jewelry collection are sparkling brooches and vintage Tiffany treasures. If you're looking for an antique rocking horse or aged end table to give your home that country flair, look no further. Maclund offers charm that just can't be recreated in modern designs. In the fine art, you'll find English portraits and dog and horse pieces, each reminiscent of a simple, elegant era. Dress your home in quiet history with pieces such as *Mother in Blue*, a graceful reminder of the pre-Raphaelite movement or the detailed painting *An English Valley*, where a gentle river flows through a serene village. Visit Maclund Gallery in Winnetka and journey back to a peaceful pastoral time in history.

1011 Tower Road, Winnetka IL
(847) 441-7890
www.maclund.com

Maple Avenue Gallery

Maple Avenue Gallery, in Evanston's Church Street Plaza, features original works by contemporary artists in a variety of mediums. Rotating exhibits include original prints, sculpture and paintings by both regional and international artists. The works of approximately 30 artists are on display at any one time. The 4,500-square-foot space, winner of a Design Evanston award, was created by Chicago-based architectural firm Nagle Hartray Danker Kagan McKay. It features a flowing, open layout with an undulating ribbon wall, a circular for highlighting sculptural pieces and a tastefully subdued color palette. Small alcoves allow display space for featured pieces, and a comfortable seating area invites one to contemplate the artwork. Recently featured artists include John Palmer, Sergei Kolevatykh, Lily Balasanova and Carol Sams. Although the gallery has a sophisticated, semi-urban feel, Manager Susan McMenamin says, "We're not intimidating, and we don't want to be." In addition to offering artwork for home or office, the Maple Avenue Gallery offers custom framing and provides art consultation services. Whether you're a serious art connoisseur or a casual collector, come to Maple Avenue Gallery for artwork that will enhance any living or working environment.

1745 Maple Avenue, Evanston IL
(847) 869-0680
www.mapleavenuegallery.com

Best Art Shop & Gallery

Would you like to discover the next Cezanne or Rothko? The Best Art Shop & Gallery may have him. For six years, Daina Pakalnis has provided a gallery for discriminating patrons of art. Her selection of fine art, jewelry, crafts, ceramics and sculpture comes from artists and artisans in Europe, the United States and Canada. The gallery promotes the highest quality of contemporary work by renowned artists. All items are selected for originality and quality. In most cases, the artwork is handmade and unique. Best Art Shop also specializes in fine art and crafts imported directly from Lithuania. Popular finds at the gallery are Venetian-styled glass goblets, elegant glass flowers and contemporary amber jewelry. The glass flower arrangements in the gallery's collection can stand a foot tall and include gladiolas, trumpet flowers, dahlias, tropical lilies, parrot tulips, freesias and much else. Here you will also find crafts from Harry Leaf and Soul Soup, bold and regal jewelry from a half-dozen leading designers and Mary Francis handbags. The Best Art Shop & Gallery is a destination for buyers of corporate gifts and couples who take advantage of the bridal registry program. The gallery website, which features images organized by artist and medium, is a useful tool for the gift shopper who needs ideas. Step into the Best Art Shop & Gallery and discover an artist today.

4 E Jefferson Avenue, Naperville IL
(630) 548-4003
www.bestartshop.com
www.basgallery.com

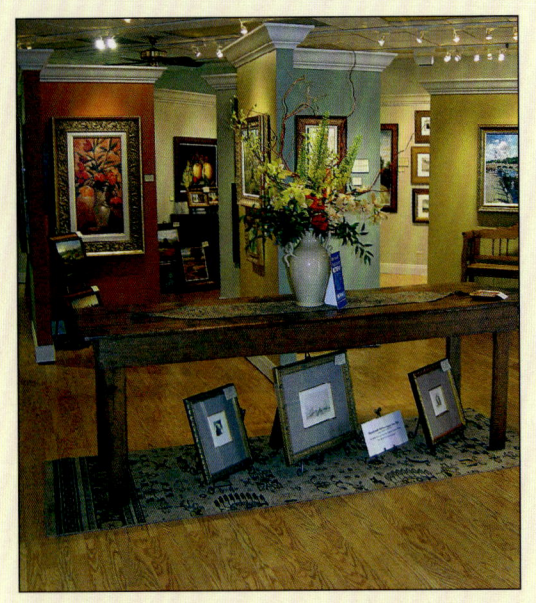

Art Post Gallery

Customers say that the Art Post Gallery is the best kept secret in Chicago. View the largest inventory of original artwork on Chicago's north shore at the Art Post Gallery, where an impressive roster of renowned national and international artists display their latest works. In 1980, owner Christina Bates purchased the established gallery, which opened in 1972, and proceeded to gain a large and loyal following of clients who appreciate her excellent service. Art Post Gallery exhibits a wide range of original artwork but is best known for Impressionist oil paintings, watercolors, etchings, vintage art and antique maps. The newly remodeled and masterfully designed gallery additionally offers conservation framing, which is designed to protect artwork and preserve its original condition. The framing is all done in-house by professional staff members who have innovative ideas for showing off fine art. They are also able to make custom mirrors of any size and offer a wide range of art restoration services. Art Post Gallery is centrally located in Carillon Square and is an ideal resource for art lovers of all kinds, from connoisseurs to the novice collectors. Expand your collection, restore an old piece or frame a masterpiece at the Art Post Gallery.

1452 Waukegan Road, Glenview IL (847) 657-9492
www.artpostgallery.com

The Art Store & Gallery

Turn your mementos, personal art projects and special collectibles into treasures that will last a lifetime with customized framing from the Art Store & Gallery. Jerry Meinhardt opened this popular shop in 1973 and has since gained a large and faithful cadre of loyal clients who return again and again for his quality craftsmanship and hands-on, old-fashioned customer service. The Art Store & Gallery, which now has both a Glencoe and a Lake Forest location, was voted Best of the North Shore by *North Shore Magazine* and offers a full selection of framing and graphic art services that are geared toward ensuring that your custom framing reflects your project and your personal style. Jerry can frame nearly anything you can imagine, including sports memorabilia, diplomas, awards and photographs, as well as original oil paintings and watercolors. Frame your child's school medals, report cards and craft projects so that you can proudly display them or show off your wedding pictures in style with quality custom framing from Jerry Meinhardt at the Art Store & Gallery.

668 Vernon Avenue, Glencoe IL (847) 835-2770
825 Waukegan Road, Lake Forest IL (847) 295-2777

Colbert Custom Framing

Kevin and Sue Colbert know you come to Colbert Custom Framing with an emotional attachment to the item you want to preserve. The special attention they provide has brought in customers for the last 20 years that include the Ronald Reagan Museum, the Pentagon and the Smithsonian Institute. Over the years, Colbert Custom Framing has improved its technique and business has grown extraordinarily as a result. The shop's work ranges from capturing family memories such as a tattered family Bible or Grandpa's war medals to framing valuables such as original Picassos and NASA flight badges that have orbited the moon. Colbert Custom Framing is the largest custom framer in western Chicagoland. Also an industry leader in the use of digital technology, the shop can take an image from your camera card, flash drive or CD and print it with graphic effects that give the illusion of a watercolor or oil on canvas. The Colberts can advise you on the safest way to preserve your child's precious first drawing or family reunion portrait. *Décor* magazine has named Colbert Custom Framing among the nation's top 100 framers. In addition to its Naperville location, Colbert Custom Framing has shops in Aurora and Geneva. See the website for details. You are going to love it at Colbert Custom Framing.

8 W Gartner Road, Suite 132, Naperville IL (630) 717-1448
www.colbertcustomframing.com

Chicago Metro—Galleries & Fine Art

Kamp Galleries

In drawing rooms and executive suites around the world, you'll find paintings that draw the eye and exclamation of visitors. These are the works of the *petit maitres,* or little masters, who are artists of merit treasured by collectors everywhere. Kamp Galleries, in Chicago's Drake Hotel and in nearby Winnetka, captivates visitors with works by American regional painters from the mid-18th century to the mid-20th century. You'll also find Russian post-impressionists active since 1950 and 400 years of European master works. Owner Nick Vahlkamp began the gallery 30 years ago to showcase his appreciation for period art and artists. Artwork by artists represented appears in prestigious art museums throughout the world. The gallery also includes contemporary works in keeping with its period focus and holds numerous exhibitions throughout the year. Look for paintings picturing Paris and other European cities, plus landscapes, beach scenes, portraits and still lifes. The gallery presents the art in ways to enhance your enjoyment and frames each piece beautifully, often in gold gilt. For paintings done by celebrated artists in classic styles, visit Kamp Galleries.

563 Lincoln Avenue, Winnetka IL (847) 441-7999
140 E Walton Place, Chicago IL (312) 664-0090
www.kampgallery.com

Galleries & Fine Art—Chicago Metro

FolkWorks Gallery

FolkWorks Gallery is the brainchild of Cease Giddings, who wanted to introduce the world to the treasures of American folk art and antiques. Cease and her husband, Paul, settled down and opened the gallery after a nomadic life that included 28 overseas moves in almost as many years during Paul's military career. They chose Cease's childhood neighborhood in Evanston as the home for their gallery, which features a literal treasure trove of items ranging from Santas, angels, birdhouses, cats and witches to quilts, vintage jewelry, art pottery and garden antiques. Each piece is original, giving it a special and timeless quality. The range of artists and artistic styles offered here are impressive and eclectic. Cease and Paul stage a show every month to spotlight the more than 300 artists from 44 states who supply their unique merchandise, which ensures a rotation of pieces through the gallery. FolkWorks Gallery has been featured by numerous media outlets, including *Chicago Shops, Country Marketplace, Niche* and *Decorating Ideas*, for their unique approach and exciting shows. The next time you are looking for a fun and imaginative shopping trip, visit FolkWorks Gallery, a one-of-a-kind destination.

1310$^{1/2}$ Chicago Avenue, Evanston IL (847) 328-0083
www.folkworks.com

Neville-Sargent Gallery

The Neville-Sargent Gallery has changed its location and focus during more than 30 years of family ownership, but remains as devoted as ever to fine art. Jane Neville started the gallery in 1974 in Evanston. Today Jane and her husband, Don, a fine art appraiser, own the gallery, and it has been a part of the Libertyville scene since 1994. In recent years, the gallery has moved from contemporary art and crafts to antique prints and furniture. Botanical prints before 1900 are a specialty. You can also find prints of shells, animals and maps. Cigarette prints from old cigarette packs can be framed to make reasonably priced gifts. Other subject matter includes flowers, farm animals, trains, planes and bicycles. The gallery offers appraisal services on single pieces or entire estates. An in-gallery frame shop uses conservation materials to frame your artwork and memorabilia and places special emphasis on French and fabric-wrapped mats. Furniture and home accents change frequently and may include chests, cupboards and mirrors. Other services include painting restoration, glass repair and caning. For antique prints and a variety of specialized services, visit Neville-Sargent Gallery.

406 N Milwaukee Avenue, Libertyville IL (847) 680-1414
www.neville-sargent.com

Proud Fox Gallery

For years, interior designers and corporate buyers have come to Proud Fox Gallery to outfit homes and offices with extraordinary fine art and quality custom framing. Owners Patricia and Dean Farr have customers from all over the country and overseas who come for the diversity of artwork and their extensive experience conserving original oil paintings, original pastels and sports memorabilia. The finest custom framing entails securing the object in a chemically stable environment that minimizes deterioration resulting from environmental factors such as air, light and humidity. Proud Fox also has original etchings, watercolors and graphics. Artists from all over the globe exhibit landscapes, abstracts and three-dimensional works at the Proud Fox Gallery. You'll find vivid colors and cosmopolitan quality art. Patricia and Dean have commissioned pen and ink drawings of local scenes of quaint Geneva and sell them framed or unframed from the gallery. Certified conservation framers, Patricia and Dean offer in-home consultations to advise you on the placement, framing and lighting of your newly found masterpiece. Find your own treasure at Proud Fox Gallery and feel a bit foxy yourself.

213 W State Street, Geneva IL (630) 262-8797
www.proudfoxgallery.com

Chicago Metro—Home & Garden 65

Atrium Garden Center

August 2003 was a memorable month at Atrium Garden Center. That is when the business was featured on the cover of *American Nurseryman* magazine. Atrium's size is certainly one thing that makes it worthy of such recognition. Owner Tim James oversees a garden center and nursery operation that sprawls across 215 acres. At least 90 percent of stock sold at the garden center is grown by the center itself. This is in keeping with Tim's belief that the best way to control the quality of your product is to grow as much of it as possible. The center carries a vast selection of trees, shrubs and evergreens, in addition to annuals, perennials and hanging baskets. Since 1994, Tim has operated the business under the simple philosophy of offering the best possible product at the best possible price. To provide excellent customer service, employees undergo training to develop an eye for quality and to learn which plants thrive under certain conditions. This business will deliver anything they sell, even out of state. Being featured in a national magazine was a high honor, but it is hardly the only one Atrium Garden Center has received. *Lawn and Garden Retailer*, along with *Today's Garden Center* magazines have also recognized Atrium. The building that houses its retail operation has won its own award for architectural design. Drop by and see if it inspires you to declare Atrium Garden Center your favorite place for garden stock and supplies.

21481 N US Highway 12, Lake Zurich IL (847) 438-7100
www.atriumgardencenter.com

Chalet Nursery & Garden Shops

The dynamic innovations of three generations of Thalmanns make Chalet Nursery & Garden Shops a first choice for landscaping services and garden supplies on Chicago's North Shore. In 1917, Lawrence Joseph Thalmann launched a landscaping business, using a bicycle to get to his first jobs. In 1944, he purchased the property at Lake Avenue and Skokie Road that remains company headquarters. He gained a garden center and a company name when he transported a Swiss chalet-style building to his land. In the 1950s, folks crowded around L.J.'s prototype color television to watch the first color show record the growth of plants through time-lapse photography. He went on to sell the first Weber grill, firing enthusiasm for outdoor cooking with barbecue demos. Son Larry Jr. helped his dad try new ventures, while daughter Diane launched a pet department that continues to this day. In 2000, Larry Jr.'s son Larry Thalmann III took charge and, like the rest of his family, refused to be dull. He's made Chalet a green industry leader and winner of major awards from state, national and international trade groups, including Innovator of the Year from National Garden Retailers. You can enjoy free lectures, unusual gift selections and Chalet's own brands of everything from mulches to holiday lights at the shops. Certified nursery professionals help you with plant selection. For a yard that's a vital part of your surroundings, visit Chalet Nursery & Garden Shops.

3132 Lake Avenue, Wilmette IL
(847) 256-0561
www.chaletnursery.com

Chicago Metro—Home & Garden 67

Leider Greenhouses

What started as a small vegetable garden just north of Chicago has expanded to one of the largest floricultural companies in the Midwest. Leider Greenhouses is truly a leader in the flower and plant industry, providing over one-hundred years of experience to its loyal customers. Since opening, Leider Greenhouses has evolved from exclusively wholesaling vegetables and potted plants. Managed by the fourth generation, the Leider family now offers premium products at the retail garden center located at the fourteen-plus-acre greenhouse compound. A special treat is if you visit on a day a grower offers a behind-the-scenes tour, which garden lovers will really enjoy. Known mostly for selling color, Leider also appeals to independent growers and anyone who appreciates the fresh, vibrant hues of spring, summer and fall. Leider Greenhouses' primary goal is to produce and deliver the highest quality plants and meet the needs of its customers every day. A place to truly stop and smell the roses, Leider Greenhouses invites you to stop by for a relaxing and colorful experience.

855 E Aptakisic Road, Buffalo Grove IL   (847) 634-4060   *www.leider.us*

Anastazia—Treasures for the Home

You can change the whole look and feel of your home with the right accessories and accents, according to Tom Konopacki and Bob Wery. That was the inspiration for their store, Anastazia—Treasures for the Home. Tom held an esteemed position with the home décor department of the Spiegel catalog when he mentioned to Bob his longtime dream of owning his own store. At Anastazia, he would bring together only those items that represented his practiced eye for quality and his own personal taste. Bob, who shared Tom's dream, offered to be his business partner. Anastazia offers a wide variety of accessories and home accents, including wall décor, lamps, accent furniture, vases and frames. The display changes constantly, emphasizing current themes in home décor. The atmosphere is friendly, making it a place where shoppers linger and local residents frequently pop in to see the latest arrivals. Bob and Tom enjoy helping customers browse and pick out the perfect accents for their rooms. If you're looking for a gift, Anastazia offers the perfect gift for any special occasion. Each gift is wrapped in Anastazia's signature gift box topped with a hand-tied bow. Spend some time at Anastazia—Treasures for the Home, to experience what home décor can do.

447 S Third Street, Geneva IL (630) 208-8048
www.anastaziaonline.com

Gardens and Gatherings

If you happen upon this cozy cottage stocked with fresh and silk flowers, vintage furniture and home décor, you'll be glad you did. Gardens and Gatherings, located in a beautifully restored farm house built in 1896, is a rare find for shoppers, interior designers and floral customers. You'll enjoy the homey atmosphere as much as you'll enjoy the treasures you find. Ten rooms are adorned with décor items such as wall hangings, seasonal figurines and candles. Gardens and Gatherings has the entire Vera Bradley line, including luggage and trendy accessories. Owners James and Joan Folgers opened the shop in 2000 with credentials in horticulture and a passion for the home and garden industry. They provide an inspiring environment for elegant home items as well as custom floral creations. Planning a wedding? Get the personal attention you deserve in the bridal consultation room. Brides are encouraged to bring their wedding dreams to the shop. Joan and James are happy to design around colors and themes, and they can duplicate any picture. Stop in to Gardens and Gatherings today and browse through a historic home that's abundant with creative gifts and floral wonders.

4N901 Old LaFox Road, Wasco IL (630) 762-9092

Castle Gardens

At last count, the different varieties of perennials and ornamental grasses at Castle Gardens numbered about 1,700. Among the thousands of trees, shrubs and evergreens that fill the lots, customers typically find as many as 20 varieties of some plants, such as crabapples. Long gone are the days when this family-owned business operated out of three display garages on the corner of two busy roads. Its inventory spreads across 25 acres at two locations, with another 80 acres devoted to growing nursery stock. The garden center carries gardening tools, fertilizers and a fabulous selection of concrete statuary. Its full-service landscaping department offers services ranging from simple plant installation to brick patios and stone retaining walls. Many members of the staff have been working for owners Bob and Jackie Williams since they founded the business. Following the Golden Rule, treating customers as they would wish to be treated, has been a key to their success since 1983. Find flowers, trees and shrubs by the thousands at Castle Gardens.

31776 N Highway 12, Volo IL (815) 344-9000
5511 N Highway 12, Richmond IL (815) 678-7200
www.castlegardens.com

Chicago Metro—Home & Garden   69

Midnight Sun Antiques & Design

Annika Christensen travels to her Swedish homeland several times a year to hand-pick the furnishings in Midnight Sun Antiques & Design. Annika has been offering design services in the Chicago area for 15 years and opened her Libertyville shop in 2002. The store carries many 19th and 20th century Gustavian-style cupboards, chairs, tables and chests. Much of the furniture is painted and has an airiness and small scale that work well in contemporary surroundings. Annika carries some Gustavian reproductions, including Klismos chairs, the gingham-clad Gripsholm armchair, plus bedroom and dining room pieces made in a small Swedish workshop. You will find decorative Swedish transferware from the 1920s and 1930s, vintage chandeliers and sconces as well as 18th and 19th century Mora clocks. Other popular items include Biedermeier furniture and Rörstrand and Gustavsberg porcelain along with Swedish pillows and seat covers arranged in intriguing vignettes. Annika, who holds a degree in interior design from Chicago's Harrington School of Design, offers a full range of design services, including in-home consultations. She can handle one room or an entire house in any style the customer prefers. She has helped decorate show homes for charity and designed the distinctive white and platinum interior for the master sitting room in the 2007 Lake Forest Showhouse & Gardens. See what Swedish furnishings can offer your interior—or consult with Annika about the design that works best in your setting at Midnight Sun Antiques & Design.

110 W Lake Street, Libertyville IL
(847) 362-5240
www.midnightsunantiques.com

Northwoods at Home and Rain Collection

Whether you're in the market for rustic and woodsy or classic and contemporary, you'll find it all at this two-in-one home décor store. Anita Johnson owns Northwoods at Home, a collection of northwoods lodge furnishings, while her daughter, Karla Jordan, operates the adjoining showroom for the Rain Collection. If you like to bring the outdoors in, Northwoods at Home has just what you're looking for. Northwoods offers the finest handcrafted hickory furniture on the market, and compliments it with beautiful lighting. You'll find all-natural wood art pieces, rustic signs made from recycled barn wood and lamps made from twigs. Meanwhile, at the Rain Collection, you'll find lamps with wood and porcelain bases, and elegant home accessories of wrought iron, ceramics and other quality materials. You can dress your walls with modern art or classical architectural elements. Design professionals collaborate to bring together the newest and most innovative designs for the Rain Collection. Whether your tastes run rustic or elegant, you'll have a good time browsing Northwoods at Home and the Rain Collection.

507 S Third Street, Suite D, Geneva IL (630) 232-9464
www.northwoodsathome.com
www.raincollection.com

Honquest Fine Furnishings

When Richard Honquest started selling window treatments door to door, he had no idea his venture would grow into one of the best-known businesses in the Chicago area. Today, Richard and his wife, Rachel, own Honquest Fine Furnishings, a 65,000-square-foot showroom filled with items from all over the world. The showroom displays an impressive array of modern, traditional and ornate furnishings, from entire bedroom sets to decorative throw pillows and home décor. Pieces are arranged beautifully to spark your imagination and give you fresh ideas for remodeling. The expert Honquest staff members, many of them licensed interior designers, can help you decide how to arrange the furniture and décor in your home for the greatest effect. Richard and Rachel pride themselves on carrying only the finest furnishings by manufacturers that have long-established relationships with the store. Honquest Fine Furnishings offers everything from exquisite woods to smooth leathers and elegant fabrics, so you won't have to look anywhere else to create or recreate the home you want. If you're in the market for window treatments, the store still has them too. Stop in to Honquest Fine Furnishings today to make your dream home a reality.

1455 Barrington Road, Barrington IL (847) 382-1700
www.honquest.com

Motif—Accents for the Home

Located in the historic Proctor Building in Libertyville, Motif—Accents for the Home has all the décor items you need to turn your house into fantasy made real. After many years in the retail business, Allison Wonderlic realized her dream of opening her own shop when she purchased Motif from a friend. Now, Allison and her friendly staff, which includes her children Chase and Ryan, help customers to realize their dreams of beautiful homes that fit their personality and lifestyle. Motif stocks different furniture lines, giving customers a wide variety of options. Pieces can be special-ordered. A variety of lamps can light any room. Fragrant candles add light, warmth and color to your home. Motif also stocks soft, cozy linens and beautiful wall art. Many of the pieces are from local artists, reflecting Allison's love of Libertyville. Baskets and candelabras provide both function and beauty. The store also offers a variety of gifts, which it can dress up with special packaging and bows. Whatever your design motif, come to Motif to realize it in style.

526 N Milwaukee Avenue, Libertyville IL (847) 549-6898

Chicago Metro—Home & Garden 71

Van Kirk & Co.

"Well-designed treasures at good prices" is how Van Kirk & Co. owner JoAnn Horvath describes the selection of beautiful furniture and home décor items found in her store. JoAnn spent many years in the furniture business before opening the shop in 1991. An interior designer, she is full of ideas on how each piece can be best used in a home or office environment. Van Kirk & Co. carries furniture from around the nation and the world—lamps hand-forged in Vermont, Mexico and Italy; pre-Revolutionary War furniture from Massachusetts; beautiful pewter sculptures from Belgium. It's obvious that JoAnn has scoured the globe for the best pieces. Whether you're looking for upholstered furniture from Pearson or the elegant wood and metal of a Charleston Forge piece, you'll find it at Van Kirk. Home accents include shimmering art glass from New York and England. Fine china pieces from Portugal and Italy will add a fragile beauty to your table and cabinet. Looking for something beautiful to hang on your walls? Check Van Kirk's selection of paintings. Some antique prints date back to the 1600s. JoAnn and her staff can bring their interior design skills to work in your house and give your living space a complete makeover. Van Kirk & Co. can also provide expert floral designs for your home or special event, and it offers expert custom framing services and window treatments. Come to Van Kirk & Co. to find just the right treasure to make your home glow.

348 N Milwaukee Avenue, Libertyville IL (847) 680-9580 www.vankirkandco.com

Lakeside Interiors

You will always find a design expert to answer your questions at Lakeside Interiors, where owner Fern Allison and her staff realize they need to know you if they are going to help you create a stylish and comfortable environment. The Wilmette store, which opened in 2004, showcases many styles of furnishings in an inspirational setting, complete with environmentally friendly bamboo floors and an antique tin ceiling. You can buy rooms full of custom-built furniture and accessories or hire Lakeside to help you downsize to smaller quarters, rearrange your rooms or hang your artwork. Lakeside designers excel at preparing homes for resale. The store carries irresistible accessories that bring character to a home. A 2006 *Chicago Tribune* article featured Lakeside's spring debut of the Hudson Beach Glass Collection. Other choices include bronze sculpture, hand painted lamps and original oil paintings. You can order a mirror made to your dimensions or custom bedding, draperies and upholstery in designer fabrics. HGTV's *New Spaces* devoted programming to a parlor designed by Fern. Begin your home's transformation with a visit to Lakeside Interiors.

1111 Central Avenue, Wilmette IL (847) 512-5045
www.lakesideinteriors.com

The Painted Cupboard

Today's homes deserve tableware and accessories that are designed for cooking and serving with an elegant flair. You'll find just the right pieces at The Painted Cupboard. Kathleen Dobbler draws on her experience in the fine arts to create dazzling displays of tableware and decorative accessories. Her eye for quality allows her to offer the finest products, including pewter and porcelain collections from Arte Italica, imported from Italy. Set off your next dinner party with richly colored Madeira Harvest or Meridian stoneware from Casafina, imported from Portugal. Mix colors to create a distinctive dinner table. These pieces keep their beauty from freezer to oven to dishwasher. You'll also find a full line of serving pieces and serving accessories from Gracious Goods, a line that combines stoneware with intricate iron accents. Choose from a range of canisters, serving pieces and dinnerware. Gift items include burled maple and walnut jewelry boxes from Tyzo and eyecatching Mark Roberts Santa Fairies. These beautiful handmade dolls in seasonal clothing make charming additions to your table centerpiece, Christmas tree and wreath. Dress your kitchen and dining table with vessels and accents from The Painted Cupboard.

216 W State Street, Geneva IL (630) 232-9511
www.thepaintedcupboard.com

The Perfect Setting

The Perfect Setting brings beauty, style and function to your home entertaining and tabletop world. Both traditional and cutting-edge tableware fill the Geneva and Lake Forest shops. Your inner style will be inspired by pieces and ideas seldom seen, including full collections of MacKenzie-Childs, William Yeoward, Simon Pearce, Pickard, Juliska, Vietri, Gali, Michael Wainwright, Monica Willard, Spencer Peterman, Edward Wohl, Ricci, Match and much more. Each piece is handmade by a real person with no two exactly alike. Owners Sue and Chris Fichter search for high-quality artisans and designers wherever they may be found, usually in small studios and factories across Europe and North America. With an eye for quality, beauty and function, the Fichters monitor the latest trends from New York to Paris. If finding the perfect wedding, shower or hostess gift is on your list, the knowledgeable staff is there to help. Services include bridal registry, home entertaining and tabletop design. When you want to be spectacular, call on the experts at The Perfect Setting.

407 S Third Street, Geneva IL (630) 232-1040
624 N Western Avenue, Lake Forest IL (847) 234-9145
www.perfectsettingonline.com

Chicago Metro—Home & Garden

Red's Garden Center and Fireplace Logs

Family-owned and operated, Red's Garden Center has been a source for garden help and landscaping services since 1968. Customers marvel at Red's friendly spirit, attention to detail and high levels of service. With 14 greenhouses and acres of off-site growing area, Red's can stock plants of the highest quality. Red's retail center carries everything from soil amendments and tools to pots, statuary, fountains, garden gifts and home décor. Red Poehls started with a farm market selling fruits and vegetables and expanded a year later into nursery and firewood sales. The next step was to buy farmland in Lake Zurich and begin growing his own nursery stock, a way of guaranteeing quality at the best possible price. In 1994, Red's added a gift shop specializing in home and garden décor and began to offer complete landscape and design services. In 2002, Red's once again expanded its inventory to offer a huge selection of annuals and perennials, more than 40 varieties of roses and a new home-grown vegetable market. Red's also enlarged the gift shop to include even more outdoor furniture, statuary, candles, holiday decorations and garden doo-dads. Whether you know exactly what you're looking for or you need all the help you can get, Red's staff members will guide you to the answer. The Red's team, including Red, Cindy and Terri, invite you to come see what's growing at Red's Garden Center and Fireplace Logs.

3460 Dundee Road, Northbrook IL
(847) 272-1209
www.redsgardencenter.com

West End Florist & Garden Center

West End Florist & Garden Center excels at both parts of its business. As a florist, it offers high-style floral arrangements for any occasion, while specializing in dish gardens and blooming European baskets. As a garden center, it carries an outstanding selection of annuals, perennials and nursery stock, almost all of which—including 300 different perennials—are grown on-site. Seasonal items, including Christmas greens, wreaths, pumpkins, straw and cornstalks, are also available. The owners find themselves meeting the demands of more customers than their great-grandfather could have imagined when he founded the business nearly 100 years ago. Mathias Hoffman, an immigrant from Luxembourg, began growing vegetables and selling them to businesses in and around Chicago in 1908. Over time, he transitioned into selling cut flowers. Lilies, mums and roses were best-sellers then, just as they are today. During the 1940s and 1950s, the center began to incorporate bedding plants. West End Florist & Garden Center has enjoyed an amazing run as a family owned and operated business built on the kind of customer service that inspires local regulars. Drop by to shop for garden stock, pick up some flowers for Mom or decorate your home for Halloween or the holidays.

3800 Old Glenview Road, Evanston IL (800) 228-8755
www.westendflorist.com

Strawflower Shop & Rug Merchant

From flowers to furnishings, the Strawflower Shop & Rug Merchant has everything it takes to make your home beautiful, elegant and comfortable. Owners Mike and Susan Haas began the store nearly three decades ago, offering their one-of-a-kind floral arrangements. The arrangements, still a staple of the Strawflower Shop, mix dried and silk flowers to create lasting centerpieces, swags and flourishes. Today, the shop is a home furnishings emporium, known as a premier source for decorative lamps and mirrors and hand-knotted Oriental rugs. You'll also find durable, attractive traditional and French country furniture for every room in your home from such exclusive names as Sherrell, Theodore Alexander and Taylor King. The fine art department carries not only framed prints and canvas transfers, but also a variety of framed oil paintings. Most recently, the Strawflower Shop sent buyers to the highly touted New York Gift Show to bring back beautiful and affordable jewelry collections of sterling silver, turquoise and beadwork. Ask about home consulting services to put the Strawflower Shop's design talents and resources at your disposal. Make your house bloom with beautiful accents from the Strawflower Shop & Rug Merchant.

210 N State Street, Geneva IL (630) 232-7141
www.strawflowershop.com

Belongings

Fine home furnishings and accessories abound at Belongings. Tables of polished wood, upholstered furniture and unique table lamps, chandeliers and rugs are just some of the eclectic treasures found in the shop. Exceptional values await you, from select vintage and contemporary jewelry and collectible antiques to a variety of framed artwork and seasonal items, including holiday décor and garden furniture. Belongings loves change, and loves the unique. The finely crafted silver serving pieces and decorative glassware may be just the touch to enliven a table setting for an elegant event or a special dinner with your family. All merchandise is consigned or donated to benefit Wellness Place, a not-for-profit community cancer resource center. A group of dedicated volunteers contribute time and talent to maintain the shop. Wellness Place, privately funded through generous donations, provides its services at no cost to participants. Shop at Belongings to beautify your home, and at the same time, to help enhance the lives of those living with cancer.

205 S Cook Street, Barrington IL (847) 304-0504
www.shopbelongings.com
www.wellnessplace.org

Chicago Metro—Home & Garden

Rustique

Located in historic downtown Antioch, Rustique is a home décor store with a twist. Owners Jim and Nicole Hayes invite their customers to enjoy complementary coffee while they peruse the shop's antiques and one-of-a-kind merchandise. Antique furniture, iron pieces and local art are among the variety of items at Rustique. There is something for every customer, and you'll rarely see the same item twice. Jim and Nicole travel to markets throughout the United States and Europe, bringing worldwide treasures to their local customers. Besides gifts and home décor, the shop also provides interior design services and hosts private events. Jim and Nicole enjoy putting on wine tastings with live music. Starting with its first year of business, Rustique experienced wild success. In 2006, Rustique was honored with the National Retailer Excellence award for New Store Design. Join the customers who travel all the way from Chicago and Milwaukee to see the store. Rustique is worth the drive.

925 Toft Street, Antioch IL
(847) 838-2612
www.rustiquehome.com

Restaurants & Cafés—Chicago Metro

*© 2006 James M. Abrahamson
All Rights Reserved*

The Firkin

Beer aficionados find endless entertainment among the 25 draught beers at the Firkin. Your bartender can discuss the subtle flavor differences among the local microbrews and the rare Belgian, German, English and Irish imports. The Firkin, named after a unit of measure and the name given to a quarter barrel of beer in England, does in fact offer two cask-conditioned ales, hand-pumped in the English style. The Firkin's atmosphere and menu choices invite lingering over the steak, hamburger or fish prepared on a wood-burning grill. You will find meal-sized salads, lobster tacos, rotisserie chicken and bread just pulled from the oven, all fitting accompaniments to the beers and delightful fortification for an evening spent conversing with friends or listening to live American Blues or Caribbean reggae. Owners Rick and Linda Jansen and co-owner Terry Langworthy opened the Firkin in 1998. Terry is a fourth-generation Libertyville business owner, and Rick's family goes back several generations in the restaurant business. Linda is an artist, responsible for the vintage atmosphere of the Firkin and its sister restaurant next door, the Tavern. Linda's efforts have resulted in an interior that has the look of an old neighborhood Chicago bar, with vintage wallpapers and a 40-foot long bar made of antique salvage. The décor and the menu change frequently. Those who prefer spirits or wine will be well pleased with the Firkin's selections, which include international wine choices and 120 varieties of vodka. For drink, food and music in original surroundings, visit the Firkin for lunch or dinner seven days a week.

515 N Milwaukee Avenue, Libertyville IL (847) 367-6168
www.firkinoflibertyville.com

Chicago Metro—Restaurants & Cafés

The Tavern

The Tavern offers a plush combination of dramatic atmosphere, fine wine and some of the world's richest steaks and most desirable seafood. You can choose an eight-ounce USDA choice filet served with truffle butter and a slice from a chilled bloc de foie gras, or try the organic beef from Uruguay. This steakhouse has been searching out the best available foods since opening in 1983. It offers rare USDA prime beef and Texas-raised Wagyu, the breed used for Kobe beef, known for rich marbling and a higher percentage of omega-3 and omega-6 fats. You can start your repast with Shetland Island smoked salmon and move on to diver-caught Maine sea scallops or Narragansett calamari, flown directly in to O'Hare Airport. In season, the menu includes live Maryland soft shell crabs, wild mushrooms and locally grown vegetables. Open for dinner only, the establishment is the brainchild of Rick and Linda Jansen and their partners, the Langworthys and the Seilers, who have received many honors, including the 2006 and 2007 Award of Excellence from *Wine Spectator*, the 2006 Award of Unique Distinction from *Wine Enthusiast* and the 2005 Golden Spoon Award from *Chicago Free Press*. Two private dining rooms can seat up to 60 people. *North Shore Magazine* gave the Tavern its 2006 award for Best Décor, describing Linda's interior with its Brunswick bar and architectural salvage as a cross between a pasha's palace and a Montmartre bistro. Vintage wallpapers and hand stenciling add American charm. For rare foods and subtle flavor combinations, visit the Tavern.

519 N Milwaukee Avenue, Libertyville IL
(847) 367-5755
www.libertyvilletavern.com

Wolfgang Puck Grand Café

Do you need a dinner spot that satisfies a myriad of tastes? The menu at the Wolfgang Puck Grand Café includes meals for the refined palate of adults and the fun loving tastes of children. This Evanston establishment is just right for a casual lunch or dinner, a business meeting or a place to take the family. The expansive patio is a favorite during the summer months. The café also offers a private dining room for large group banquets. The staff is happy to prepare anything on the menu to-go. Many dishes here are inspired by Wolfgang Puck classics. You will find numerous freshly made soups, sandwiches and salads along with fish dishes and the signature Wolfgang Puck pizza, all prepared with fresh, gourmet ingredients. The restaurant features an excellent and affordable wine list with a strong showing of American wines. Wolfgang Puck's cooking techniques fuse ingredients that are often unexpected and always delightful. If you find yourself inspired to try a recipe at home, your server may be able to locate the recipe in the restaurant's file. Wolfgang travels to his restaurants and is happy to sign autographs, if he's there when you visit. You can ask your server to arrange for him to stop by your table. For a dining experience that embraces every generation, make a reservation at Wolfgang Puck Grand Café.

1701 Maple Avenue, Evanston IL
(847) 869-9653
www.wolfgangpuck.com

Gridley's Grille

An upscale yet casual atmosphere prevails at Gridley's Bar and Smokehouse Grille, where Black Angus steaks and various delights from the smokehouse out back top the menu. Indeed, apple hickory smoke infuses the pork, beef and fish that come to your table as barbecued ribs, salmon filet and Kobe beef burgers with bacon. Gridley's has been featured many times in Chicago-area publications, which have recognized Chef Danny Bilotta's inventive and healthful cooking. His apple onion soup was voted one of the top ten dishes in Chicago in one newspaper poll. Bilotta chose the Cedar Plank Roasted Wild Alaskan Salmon as his signature dish when the *Daily Herald* ran his profile. Served in a Thai broth, this pleasing entrée comes with a side of gingered spaghetti squash cake that is its equal for flavor and creativity. Everyone at Gridley's Grille, from the chef and owners to the wait staff, is committed to making the dining experience truly special. "A lot of customers are afraid to ask for something or to say anything," notes Bilotta. "That's why I do table visits. I would make anything for them." The bar at Gridley's Grille deserves the attention of any serious connoisseur of spirits—it has 123 different vodkas alone. The restaurant, located on land that once belonged to the 800-acre farm of John Gridley, embraces the Prairie Style of architecture prevalent throughout Illinois. Its interior combines old wood and iron with frescoed walls and modern glasswork for graceful results. Experience the excellent service and exemplary menu that make Gridley's Grille a Chicago-area favorite.

4868 Route 83, Long Grove IL (847) 478-3663
www.gridleysgrille.com

Danny's Tap Room

It always a pleasure to find an accessible place to gather with friends, where good brew flows freely and your favorite sports are always on the television. A friendly bartender, congenial customers, fair prices and great specials are what you will find at Danny's Tap Room. The bar belongs to Scott Tomczyk, whose parents originally opened it in 1972. Scott holds his employees, some of whom have been working at Danny's for more than 15 years, in high esteem. The bar is attractive and the atmosphere is exactly what you look for in a sports bar: enthusiastic, comfortable and sociable. Danny's offers eight beers on tap and 50 more by bottle. A number of wines are sold by the bottle or glass. When you visit, you will find yourself surrounded by like-minded friends, a glass of your favorite brew or wine in hand and a great view of the game in front of you. If this sounds to you like a good time, join the cheerful neighborhood turnout at Danny's Tap Room.

2218 N Western Avenue, Chicago IL   (773) 489-3622

Costello Sandwich & Sides

When still young, Chris Costello experimented with sandwich recipes and began serving his creations to family and friends. Everyone raved about the results. If anyone was destined to make his living from sandwiches, it was Chris. In 1998, Chris and his sister Lisa opened the first Costello Sandwich & Sides serving sandwiches and recipes from Grandma Costello. Their oven-baked sandwiches and homemade soups proved such a hit that they opened at a second location a few years later. In addition to the sandwiches such as the Costello and the popular turkey focaccia— crispy on the outside, melty on the inside— you'll find made-from-scratch sides, hearty chili, and tasty shakes and malts. Still only a buck, the coffee is the best deal in town. The secret is out, and every weekend, locals line up outside waiting for Chris to open. If it's worth getting up early on a Saturday morning, you know it's worth coming to Costello Sandwich & Sides.

2015 W Roscoe Street, Chicago IL   (773) 929-2323
4647 N Lincoln Avenue, Chicago IL   (773) 989-7788
www.costellosandwich.com

Around the Clock Restaurant & Bakery

With a lifetime of restaurant experience and the support of a close-knit family of restaurant professionals, owners Steve and Fano Theofanous have made Around the Clock Restaurant & Bakery the popular destination it is today. True to its name, Around the Clock serves any meal no matter what time of day or night. For breakfast, be sure to try the popular breakfast skillets, with spicy veggies, potatoes and eggs scrambled into a hearty meal. If you're in the mood for something sweet, try the Waffle Alaska, an ice cream and strawberry topped delight. Lunch and dinner menus consist of original recipes like Maria's Steak Fajita Pita and classic burgers. If you've got a real appetite, try one of Around the Clock's juicy premium broiled steaks. In addition, fish lovers can get their fill with the tasty dishes on the seafood menu. Looking for something light? Enjoy a Mediterranean salad, a zesty wrap or one of the many vegetarian or low-carb options. Make sure you try one of the Greek-inspired dishes, such as the gyro plate, filled with feta cheese, Greek olives, and fresh tomatoes. With a childhood in Greece, Steve and Fano bring an old-world flavor to these authentic dishes. In addition to providing some of the best cuisine around, the restaurant has an award-winning bakery with a pastry chef who can design and whip up virtually any cake, pie or delicacy you can imagine. For all your dining and sweet-tooth desires, Around the Clock Restaurant & Bakery welcomes you, no matter what time your craving hits.

5011 Northwest Highway, Crystal Lake IL   (815) 459-2100
www.aroundtheclockrestaurant.com

Chicago Metro—Restaurants & Cafés

Peapod Chinese Restaurant

Peapod Chinese Restaurant takes Cantonese and Mandarin cuisine to whole new heights with tantalizing dishes such as crispy shrimp with crabmeat sauce. The Peapod offers a generous choice of prepared-from-scratch Hong Kong-style delights. Owners Sam and Terri Szeto opened the popular restaurant in 2003 and have quickly earned rave reviews from the community for their incomparable service and fresh entrees. Sam, a retired engineer, has always been intrigued with the restaurant business. Combined with his genuine affection for people, this made opening his own place a natural choice. Peapod features enough individual entrees that you could come twice a day for weeks and enjoy something new each time. Popular appetizers include the shrimp dumplings and the crispy calamari, as well as the Peapod Tidbits for two, which offers a sampling of all the favorites. The menu features a variety of seafood, chicken and pork dishes, as well as traditional delights, such as Hunan fried rice, beef egg foo young and flavorful chop suey, chow mein and wor mein. The vegetarian egg rolls are excellent. Saturday nights feature live music. The Peapod offers both take-out and catering options. Enjoy the flavors of Cantonese and Mandarin cuisine in a welcoming, family setting at the Peapod Chinese Restaurant.

84 Biesterfield Road, Elk Grove Village IL
(847)-357-9999
www.peapodhome.com

Don Roth's Blackhawk

With a menu of elegant favorites old and new, and with décor steeped in the dining and dancing days of the World War II era, Don Roth's Blackhawk gives diners a taste of old-fashioned excellence. Now located in Wheeling, the Blackhawk began its life in Chicago during the 1920s. From 1926 on, the Blackhawk featured dance orchestras that were broadcast on WGN radio from the restaurant's bandstand. Among the famed jazzmen that cut their teeth at the Blackhawk were Glenn Miller and Benny Goodman. Other featured greats included Mel Torme and Perry Como. You'll find much memorabilia from that era at the restaurant. By the 1950s, the dine-and-dance craze had ended, in part due to television. The Blackhawk adapted by making food the show with its famed spinning salad bowl and beef cart. Don opened the Wheeling branch of the restaurant in 1969 in a converted suburban farmhouse. In 1984, the original Blackhawk in Chicago closed its doors, but its elegance and fun live on in Wheeling. The nostalgic music of that earlier era caresses your ears and the menu, with its mix of timeless entrées including steaks and seafood, will tickle your taste buds. Come to Don Roth's Blackhawk for a taste of the sweet sounds and flavors of a bygone era.

61 N Milwaukee Avenue,
Wheeling IL
(847) 537-5800
www.theblackhawk.com

Photo © jimi allen photography

Dockside Deli & Custard Shoppe

Friendly fun, a titanic meat-filled sandwich and a decadent cake await diners at the Dockside Deli & Custard Shoppe. Open for the past 10 years, this deli was recently purchased by Carolyn and Roy Kibbe and their son Jim, who added their own family-style charm to the restaurant. Large portions of freshly made food are the order of the day, served up with a smile by the friendly staff. The restaurant is renowned for its Titanic sub, which features ham, turkey and roast beef, along with two cheeses and three veggies. You'll find a wide range of sandwiches, Mexican-style wraps, soups and salads. If you're looking for a Chicago-style eating experience, try the Chicago Dog, piled high with peppers, onions, relish, cucumber and tomato. Better than Sex? That's the name of the moist, rich chocolate cake with caramel that's begging you to judge for yourself. Peanut butter balls and 12 different kinds of custard are also on hand. Dockside Deli offers delivery and carry-out, as well as a separate catering menu. Sail on in to Dockside Deli for a fun dining experience that'll leave you feeling full and satisfied.

1700 E 7th Street, Winthrop Harbor IL   (847) 746-7424

Lou Malnati's Pizzeria

If there is such a thing as Chicago pizza royalty, then the Malnati family of Lou Malnati's Pizzeria is it. Considered to be the oldest name in Chicago pizza, the Malnatis have been making the savory pies since the 1940s, when Lou began his pizza making career alongside his father Rudy in the city's first-ever pizzeria. Lou and his wife Jean branched out in 1971 and opened the first of several pizzerias in Lincolnwood. Sadly, Lou lost a battle with cancer in 1978; however, Jean and their sons, Marc and Rick, joined together to carry on Lou's pizza legacy. Today, more than 35 years later, Lou Malnati's Pizzeria, with 24 Chicago-area pizzerias, continues to serve handmade pies created from Lou's own special recipes, including the family's secret recipe for their flaky, buttery crust that has been passed down from generation to generation. Lou Malnati's Pizzeria specializes in traditional Chicago-style pizza, which is patted out by hand and carefully fit into a seasoned deep-dish pan before being layered with fresh slices of mozzarella and delicious toppings. The eateries additionally offer stuffed spinach bread, luscious desserts and a variety of other tasty options all made from fresh local ingredients. A phenomenal staff of family and friends, many of whom have been with the company for decades, ensures your satisfaction. Taste the pizza that gave Chicago its pizza tradition at Lou Malnati's Pizzeria.

3685 Woodhead Drive, Northbrook IL (Headquarters)   (847) 562-1814
www.loumalnatis.com

John Evans Restaurant & Lounge

John and Evan Archos opened the popular fine dining destination called John Evans Restaurant & Lounge 28 years ago in Crystal Lake. In 2001, the brothers decided to close that location. After four years and a great demand, John decided to re-open at a new location in Crystal Lake, which remains family owned and operated. The restaurant's cuisine is a mix of old country Greek and classic American dishes. The extensive menu features the house specialties of prime rib and Grecian chicken, as well as steaks, chops and seafood fare. When you stop in, be sure to try the signature flaming Saganaki, a Greek cheese appetizer, the signature house relish tray that includes a homemade cheese spread and liver pate, or one of the many other tantalizing appetizers it offers. Come in and enjoy the relaxing atmosphere of the restaurant and full lounge, complete with a bar menu and big screen television. With superb food and outstanding service, you'll feel right at home at John Evans.

394 W Virginia Street, Crystal Lake IL   (815) 455-0600

Chicago Metro—Restaurants & Cafés 83

Mickey Finn's Brewery

Connoisseurs of microbrews know that it's well worth the trip to Libertyville to visit Mickey Finn's Brewery. The brewery opened in 1993 as Lake County's first brewpub, but the bar itself goes back more than 100 years, disguising itself as a barber shop during Prohibition. Mickey Finn's crafts 25 distinct beers and serves them along with many comfort foods in a room featuring the original bar, wood floors and exposed brick walls. Brian Grano was a regular at the brewery, eventually leaving his corporate job to buy his favorite hangout in 2004. Among the beers on tap is the well-balanced 847 Suburban wheat ale, a good starting place for folks new to microbrews. A brown ale gets its bitterness from English hops, and several area golf clubs carry Mickey Finn's amber ale, known for its caramel sweetness. Summer brings out the popular hefeweisen, an unfiltered German wheat beer. Once you've tasted the food, you will be back for more. Top choices, which bring out families for lunch or supper every day, are the Mickey Burger, wings, pizza and the Reuben sandwich. You will find an outdoor beer garden and live music on weekends in the upstairs Amber Room. Private parties also use the room, which includes a state-of-the-art sound system, large screen television and separate bar. Crowds mount for the St. Patrick's Day bash and the Backlot Brew Fest on the first Saturday in August. Make a beer pilgrimage to Mickey Finn's Brewery.

412 N Milwaukee Avenue, Libertyville IL (847) 362-6688
www.mickeyfinnsbrewery.com

Nosh

Experience how much fun breakfast and lunch can be at Nosh. Owners Mike and Kim Dixon have converted a garage into an upscale eatery with a vibrant, colorful décor and a sophisticated yet satisfying menu. Dishes surpass the traditional breakfast fare. You will have a hard time choosing between the Il Tricolore Benedict, with oven-dried tomatoes, fresh mozzarella, poached eggs and basil hollandaise, and the Red-Eye Benedict, with coffee-crusted flat-iron steak, poached eggs and shitake mushroom hollandaise. Other temptations include Bananas Foster Pancakes and the house French toast, made with challah bread soaked in vanilla and orange zest and served with lemon crème anglaise sauce. Lunch offers specialty sandwiches and a fabulous mushroom and crabcake trio that includes a lemon caper crabcake with avocado aioli, orange bell pepper crabcake with garlic aioli and mushroom crabcake with sundried tomato aioli. Quench your thirst with freshly squeezed juices. Nosh also offers wine, beer and mixed drinks, including mimosas in raspberry and pear or mango and black current. Indulge yourself at Nosh.

211 James Street, Geneva IL
(630) 845-1570

Trattoria Pomigliano

The whole family will enjoy Trattoria Pomigliano, where the meals are authentically Southern Italian and dinner specials are "whatever mama feels like cooking," according to Patty Saladino. Mama is Patty's mother, Ann Panico, who started the restaurant with her daughter in 1995. The restaurant fulfills a dream held by Patty's dad and is named after his birthplace. Chances are a Panico family member will serve you, since many of Ann's relatives work at the trattoria, including her daughter-in-law, Deanna Panico, and Patty's husband, Nick. This happy Italian tradition of combining good food and family puts customers at ease while treating them to sit-down or carryout service. The restaurant serves the biggest meatballs in town and a memorable lasagna. The *zupa de pesce* is loaded with fish variety and served over pasta. Entrée choices feature pasta, fish, chicken, steak and veal. Grandma's tiramisu is a favorite dessert selection. There's a full bar with beer, wine and cocktails. This award-winning restaurant exudes Old World charm with its stucco walls and wood floors. Trattoria Pomigliano caters and can accommodate private parties. For cooking that only a Sicilian grandmother could dish out, come to Trattoria Pomigliano.

602 N Milwaukee Avenue, Libertyville IL
(847) 247-2208
www.trattoriapomigliano.com

Villa Verone

Pietro Verone's mother taught him to cook in their home in Naples, Italy, and he still uses many of her recipes at Villa Verone. After savoring the richly flavored traditional dishes, you'll soon see why this restaurant was voted one of the top three restaurants in the area.

Mature trees shade the brick courtyard, and cascading vines, lush hanging plants and a stone fountain allow you to imagine yourself in an Italian village. Inside, several small rooms offer perfect settings for romantic dining. The extensive menu of authentic Italian dishes includes Rotolo Mamma Carmela, a tri-colored pasta filled with ricotta, spinach and prosciutto and served in a light cream sauce, and Vitello alla Vincenzo Verone, tender slices of veal with portobello mushrooms and pearl onions in marsala wine. Another favorite is the Farfalla al Salmone, bowtie pasta with fresh salmon and asparagus served in a tomato cream sauce. After dinner, you can wander upstairs to the Upper Club with its martini bar and live music. Your quest for authentic Italian cuisine and a frolicking nightspot just upstairs can end at Villa Verone.

416 Hamilton Street, Geneva IL
(630) 232-2201

Wildwood

When Patrick Neary sought an executive chef for his new restaurant opened in April 2006, he found both a chef and partner in Christopher Corby. Chef Corby designed the extensive menu, which offers upscale American cuisine including oak-grilled steaks, fresh fish and seafood as well as poultry, pasta and vegetarian fare, and supervises the busy, open kitchen teaming with Wildwood staff and culinary interns. Patrick roams the dining room and lounge nightly to greet new and return guests, monitor quality and consistency, and gather guest feedback. You can have lunch or dinner at Wildwood seven days a week, including an a la carte brunch every Sunday and special brunch buffets offered for Easter, Mother's Day and Christmas holidays. Dinner entrées include both a salad and side dish and grilled meats are accompanied by signature onion rings and a grilled lemon. Popular dishes include Veal Oscar, Roast Prime Rib of Beef, Horseradish Crusted Grouper, and the Chicken Woodsman, a chicken breast filled with pistachios, shiitake mushrooms and fresh vegetables and served with a lingonberry sauce. Wildwood servers will help pair the extensive selection of wines and specialty beers with your dinner or lunch selection, and numerous half bottle and wine-by-the-glass offerings allow guests to expand their horizons. To fully enjoy a meal requires a restful environment, which Wildwood masters with warm woods, extensive stonework and lovely artwork in its main dining room. A large outdoor courtyard allows diners to enjoy Wildwood's fare in the open air while overlooking a delightful water garden. The Wildwood lounge features a long copper-topped bar, leather easy chairs and a baby grand piano where live jazz is heard several nights per week. Wildwood has developed a strong relationship with local merchants and charities whose framed pictures are featured on the walls of the Wildwood lounge. Make yourself at home at Wildwood.

477 S 3rd Street, Geneva IL (630) 377-8325 www.wildwoodsteak.com

Restaurants & Cafés—Chicago Metro

Stockholm's Vardshus

A local *vardshus*, or tavern, in Swedish, gathers contemporaries together who enjoy beer crafted with subtlety and a menu of food you won't find in any tavern. Michael Olesen, owner and brewer at Stockholm's Vardshus, is as discriminating about beer as any Viking. He has an approach to brewing that avoids the sharp flavors that many brewmasters strive for. For Michael, the ideal brew is cask-conditioned and unfiltered for full flavor and smooth taste. Stockholm's features seven home brews at all times. Michael's favorite is Mike's Blend, one-third brown ale blended with two-thirds pilsner. Many patrons come not for the beer, but for the food. Aged steaks, sushi-grade fish and a half dozen pasta dishes are all prepared from scratch. Seasonal specials supplement the hearty menu. A native of Geneva, Michael is proud of his friendly, old-style tavern. *Western Living* magazine gave Stockholm's a nod and named it one of the top three breweries in the Chicago suburbs. Set sail for Stockholm's Vardshus and enjoy a cask-conditioned brew.

**306 W State Street, Geneva IL
(630) 208-7070**

Wildberry Pancakes & Café

Fruit-filled buttermilk pancakes and breads are among the most famous offerings at Wildberry Pancakes & Café. Wildberry has earned high praise from Phil Vettel at the *Chicago Tribune* for such offerings as cranberry walnut and pumpkin cheesecake pancakes. The tiramisu pancakes combine cheeses with cinnamon and cocoa. It's a good thing breakfast is available all day, because you will want to return often to explore the broad choice in fruit-stuffed crêpes, French toast, Belgian waffles and egg dishes. Coffee drinks feature the Seattle's Best brand. Lunch is equally fulfilling with panini sandwiches and salads that feature the signature Cocoberry vinaigrette. Many baked goods are made on the premises, including strawberry-banana and cranberry breads, cheesecakes and pies. You can sit outside or enjoy a dining room that sports stained cement floors and a massive double fireplace with an intricate brick design. George Archos opened this Libertyville café with managing partner Kevin Betyo in 2004. George, who left a pre-med program at Loyola to go into the family restaurant business, also owns Seasons of Long Grove and Dunhills in McHenry. For breakfasts and lunches that demand attention seven days a week, visit Wildberry Pancakes & Café.

**1783 N Milwaukee Avenue, Libertyville IL
(847) 247-7777
www.wildberrycafe.com**

FoxFire

Geneva needed a good steakhouse and a location that would put customers at ease while they enjoyed aged prime beef, chops and fresh seafood. FoxFire came on the scene, earning a place on the *Daily Herald*'s list of Top Ten New Restaurants and capturing the Best in the West listing from *West Suburban Living* and Best Steaks award from the *Kane County Chronicle*. With three owners—Dick O'Gorman and father and son Curt and K.C. Gulbro—attending to customers and a kitchen manned by Executive Chef Kevin Gillespie, FoxFire convinced one diner after another that it was firmly in control of every aspect of fine dining. The restaurant occupies an early 1900s building that once served as a manufacturing facility for horse-drawn carriages. Diners appreciate the exposed brick walls, curved ceiling and outdoor patio umbrella-topped tables, where live music plays on summer evenings. Sit at the bar and enjoy a basket of freshly made chips seasoned with pepper and parmesan cheese, which is reason enough to visit. The owners are proud of their wine selection, including 100 wines by the bottle and 50 by the glass, and offer popular wine flights. The full bar features many fine bourbons and scotches. FoxFire ages meat up to 30 days and carries a variety of signature sauces." You can order prime rib in 12, 16 and 22-ounce servings. The ribs are extra-special, thanks to a house barbecue sauce made with Knob Creek Bourbon. You can savor beef tournados sautéed with a blackberry brandy demi-glaze or sashimi grade tuna pan seared with Cajun spices. Find out what Geneva means by "best" at FoxFire.

17 W State Street, Geneva IL
(630) 232-1369
www.foxfiregeneva.com

Plum Blossom

Hong Kong native Vince Mui brings together the best of Asian furnishings and gifts at Plum Blossom, his Geneva shop. Vince came to the United States at age 17 to complete his schooling. He never went home, but with family still living in Hong Kong, he never lost his connection to his homeland. At Plum Blossom, Vince is happy to share that connection with his lucky visitors. Take a journey into an exotic and fascinating culture. Browse authentic silk embroideries, wood carvings and oil paintings and admire hand-crafted furniture of carved teakwood, lacquered wood or rosewood with shell inlay. The ritual of tea is one of the most quintessential Asian experiences, and Plum Blossom makes it accessible in wondrous variety. You'll find more than 70 different varieties of loose teas at the shop, along with teapots and accessories. You can buy your favorite blend in bulk or even create your own custom blend. Martial arts buffs will delight in the popular collection of Samurai and tai chi swords at the store. If you're looking for a gift, you'll find decorative fish bowls, figurines and good luck tokens. You can also try on authentic Asian clothing, including dresses and jackets. The beautiful products of Asia await you at Plum Blossom.

477 S Third Street, Geneva IL
(630) 232-2290
www.shopplumblossom.com

How Impressive!

How Impressive! It's more than the name of this store—it's what you'll say when you see the impressive array of personalized gifts, cards and invitations. It's also what the person who receives your gift will say. In fact, the store's unique name comes from what owner Kristine Knutson's friends said to her when she began printing and personalizing napkins for friends. That led Kristine to open her first store in 2003, moving it to the current location in 2006. At this shop, you'll find a huge variety of colorful stationery and invitations that can be personalized to suit any occasion. Place cards and luggage tags can be made to order just for you. Looking to give someone a one-of-a-kind gift? Check out the personalized soaps, candles and guest towels. A personalized picture frame makes a picture-perfect gift for friends and loved ones. How Impressive! also carries playing cards, unusual drinking glasses and a variety of other elegant gifts. Two graphic designers can help you add just the right personal touch to your selection. You can now place an order from the shop's website as well. Come and find a gift that will have your friend or loved one saying "How Impressive!"

334 N Milwaukee Avenue, Libertyville IL
(847) 680-6458 or (877) 338-8697
www.howimpressive.com

Chicago Metro—Shopping & Gifts

Barrington Saddlery

Barrington Saddlery has been spoiling horses and horse owners since 1970. This full-service saddle, tack and equestrian resource store is one of the leading English saddlery, supply and repair shops in the nation. Offering the best in horse and rider apparel, English saddles and stable supplies, Barrington Saddlery makes it easy to find everything you need in one place. In addition, it stocks horse health supplies that include behavioral aids, grooming supplies, preventative care and supplements, so you and your horse can be confident at your next big competition. Whether you're looking for a new saddle or have a question about horse health, you can count on Barrington Saddlery and its knowledgeable staff to help you. Manager Kathy Cramer, a seasoned equestrian and breeder, brings a lifetime of expertise to the shop. With a Canadian National Champion title and her own line of riding apparel, Kathy is clearly in the right industry. She's happy to provide professional advice and assistance to veterans and newcomers to the sport. The saddle shop at Barrington offers repairs as well as custom merchandise. Barrington Saddlery's mission is to exceed every customer's expectations. While it leads the pack in pricing, variety and product quality, Barrington is completely committed to customer satisfaction. Barrington Saddlery invites you to come to where the professionals come for all your horse and tack essentials.

760 W Northwest Highway, Barrington IL (847) 381-6015 or (800) 560-8008
www.barringtonsaddlery.com

Crocodile Pie, A Children's Bookstore

Kim White will do whatever it takes to foster a love of reading in preschool children, including bringing in storytellers three times a week to tell intriguing tales while children perch on stuffed crocodiles. Kim opened Crocodile Pie, A Children's Bookstore in 1989 after researching a California store she admired. The store indulged her love of books while keeping her three young sons engaged in reading. The large Libertyville shop attracts families and educators from throughout the Chicago area with its stunning selection of books that take kids from the time they are born through their early teens. You will find hardcover and paperback books, books on CD, workbooks, cloth books and board books as well as accessories that help bring books to life, such as stuffed animals and puzzles. Kim puts on a summer crafts camp. She and her staff offer knowledgeable advice for anyone purchasing a gift, along with complimentary gift wrapping. Special orders are welcome. The store orders books for classrooms and arranges visits by authors and book characters. Browsing is a pleasure—the books are divided by subject and age group. Get your child started on books with a visit to Crocodile Pie, open seven days a week in Cambridge Plaza.

866 S Milwaukee Avenue, Libertyville IL (847) 362-8766 or (888) 680-READ (7323)
www.crocodilepie.com

Bears Gone Wild on Third

Creating a plush animal from Bears Gone Wild on Third is the kind of experience that results in a cherished toy and long-lasting memories. Sisters Kathy Anderson and Doey Sabella opened the shop in Geneva's Berry House in 2006. At the shop, they help each customer create their own custom stuffed animal. Bears are popular choices, but children also choose other animals from the forests and farms. After choosing the unstuffed animal, children send their toy through the stuffing process on a toy train called the Teddy Bear Express. Kathy and Doey close up the opening, filling each creation with sentimental items chosen by the child, such as hugs, kisses, angels or prerecorded voice boxes with songs or greetings. Children name their bears and receive birth certificates signed by the Bear Master. They can choose from many outfits and carry their new pals home in special boxes. Bears Gone Wild throws many birthday parties where each guest makes a bear. Former Disney artist R.J. Ogren painted murals for the shop that add charm and good cheer to the surroundings. One room holds puzzles, books, music boxes and other fun gifts for children of every age. Whether you are welcoming a new baby, offering get-well greetings or celebrating a birthday, stop by Bears Gone Wild on Third.

227 S 3rd Street, Geneva IL (630) 208-9885
www.bearsgonewildonthird.com

Fairy Tales

Who says youth doesn't last forever? Grown ups turn into little kids all over again when they step inside Fairy Tales. This shop of wonder and delight brings a smile to everyone's face with its adorable selection of stuffed animals, figurines and dolls. Snoopy hangs out at Fairy Tales, as do the characters from *The Wizard of Oz* and many Disney favorites. Start or add to your collection of Wee Forest Folk, those cute miniature mice at home, on vacation and enjoying the holidays. Collectible lines include Steiff Club Stuffed Animals, Boyd Bears and Mary George Bears. Jim and Rochelle Pokorn, who opened the store in 1993, arrive at work every day looking forward to the response of their customers. Their hard work and commitment to customer service has grown Fairy Tales into a successful international mail-order business. When Deb Canham came out with her latest creation, Quack the Dragon, Fairy Tales had it on the shelves right away. The owners hold special events for new collectibles, often featuring appearances by the artisans, who sign their items with airbrushes. Stay young at heart by taking a trip to Fairy Tales.

9 S Park Avenue, Lombard IL (630) 495-6909 or (800) 495-6973
www.fairy-tales-inc.com

Chicago Metro—*Shopping & Gifts*   91

The Crystal Cave

Light plays across the detailed lines of art and architecture in each piece at the Crystal Cave. Founder Josef Puehringer, owner Goran Paunovic and a team of master engravers bring passion and artistry to the exquisite crystal gifts found at this Wilmette business. Whether creating retail items for the store shelves or a special design for one of many corporate or sports clients, the craftsmen here employ meticulous detail to create items that will be treasured by their owners. The American Heritage collection features soaring eagles and colorful flags, as well as sun catchers, paperweights and ornaments. Plaques capture cityscapes, shorelines and sports activities. Classically engraved serving trays, stemware or clocks make lovely gifts for a special couple's wedding or anniversary. For the graduate you'll find glasses, mugs, jewelry boxes and paperweights engraved with the icons of individual professions. Sports trophies and corporate awards can be personalized for one or hundreds of recipients. Specialty engraving can extend to a mug or plaque to memorialize a hunting trip. The experts at the Crystal Cave pay close attention to your needs to assure the results are everything you imagined. Visit the shop to browse, to select an outstanding gift or to gather ideas for your company's next awards dinner. The Crystal Cave will surely capture your imagination.

1141 Central Avenue, Wilmette IL
(847) 251-1160
www.crystalcaveofchicago.com

The Canterbury Shoppe

Located on the Riverwalk in downtown Naperville, The Canterbury Shoppe has been brightening special events in the community for more than 10 years. Whether it's a once-a-year holiday or a once-in-a-lifetime event, the Canterbury Shoppe will help you celebrate in style with fine gifts, collectibles and décor. Find the perfect wedding gift among the classy selection of glassware, picture frames and decorative plates. Commemorate a baby or a First Communion with a one-of-a-kind precious keepsake. Unique ornaments, snow globes or gourmet food items make thoughtful remembrances for Christmas. The Canterbury Shoppe celebrates each of the four seasons with fresh arrays of gifts, decorations and gift-wrapping. There are also quality souvenirs of the Naperville/Chicago area. Customers come to the Canterbury Shoppe from near and far, but the great Canterbury Shoppe gift consultants particularly focus on local customers, who return repeatedly for the fine gift selection and customer service. Be sure to stop by the Canterbury Shoppe as the next holiday approaches.

175 W Jackson Avenue, Naperville IL   (630) 717-5005
www.canterburyshoppe.net

Charmed

Tracey Schulze has been an entrepreneur since grade school, making T-shirts and barrettes for her classmates. Today, she creates her Charmed line of children's clothing and accessories from her home studio and markets them through her website and through selected Wisconsin and Illinois retail stores. Tracey enjoys using bright, fun fabrics to create vintage reproductions. You will find Fancy Schmancy Burp Cloths and pretty changing pads that roll up in a diaper bag. Charmed blankets feature lively fleece prints with ribbon loops around the borders that make them visually and physically stimulating to a baby. Aprons by Charmed suit children with various interests and can be monogrammed with your child's name. You can purchase art supplies for the young artist or cake mix and cookie cutters the budding chef. Look for items for the small gardener such as a little shovel, rake and seeds. Tracey makes custom pieces on request. She markets cotton sweater and hat sets from Jack Rabbit Creations. For handmade gifts that combine modern prints and materials with old-fashioned charm, call Charmed or visit the website.

(847) 877-9803
www.charmedgifts.net

Country Naturals

Decorators and collectors alike love getting lost in Country Naturals. Sisters and owners Susan Hadley and Deb Hilton have filled the twelve-room 1850s Hannah House with an alluring array of treasures. The house was the childhood home of Charles Dawson "Daws" Butler, the voice of Yogi Bear, and the shop upholds its heritage by invoking a sense of nostalgia. Stroll across the original wood floors and immerse yourself in the textures and colors of country décor. Every room, closet and cranny overflows with primitives, candles and natural soaps. You will find a unique blend of floral, wreaths, pottery and tabletop accessories. Browse through the selection of handmade jewelry, hand-stitched pillows and home accents. The scent of fresh herbs in spring and summer and the color of gourds and pumpkins in fall accompany you as you browse. The displays change to reflect the season and offer holiday decorations. Visit the charming two-level shop around the corner for unique gifts and selfish necessities. You'll find something new that feels like something old at Country Naturals.

316 Campbell Street, Geneva IL   (630) 232-1172
www.shopcountrynaturals.com

Chicago Metro—Shopping & Gifts 93

Gurnee Antique Center

For an antiques dealer, being accepted at the Gurnee Antique Center is an honor. It means that your merchandise has met some exceptionally high standards. It says that you have agreed to create eye-pleasing displays for your wares and to provide honest services. For customers, the sport of antiques shopping doesn't get any better. One of Chicagoland's largest antique malls, the 24,000-square-foot center is home to 200 dealers of everything from fine porcelain and art glass to vintage jewelry, sports memorabilia and advertising. Art lovers have found Picassos, and fashion hounds have found furs like Mae West used to wear. The furniture selection is particularly strong, with a wide assortment of mahogany, oak and walnut pieces. All merchandise must be at least 50 years old, which automatically disqualifies new collectibles. Reproductions and crafts are strictly forbidden. If a leg of a table has been replaced or a chair repainted, the modification must be noted on the price tag. Customers appreciate this commitment to authenticity and aren't shy about expressing their gratitude to owners Luan and Jerry Watkins, who have received compliments every day since they opened the mall in 1998. If you love true antiques, head to Gurnee Antique Center.

5742 Northridge Drive, Gurnee IL
(847) 782-9094
www.gurneeantiquecenter.com

Cradles & All

At Cradles & All, Kristina Garcia can help you choose the right crib, bedding, artwork and lighting to create a dream nursery or big kid room to fit any budget and style. Whatever you prefer, Cradles & All will have traditional and modern furniture and accessories to match. Select from beautifully crafted hardwood lifestyle pieces that grow from crib to full size bed. Browse quality bedding by over 25 vendors or design your own with 1000s of custom fabric options. Accent your room with dazzling artwork from national and local aritisans, beautiful crystal chandeliers and a cozy upholstered rocking chair. You'll find the 3,500-square-foot boutique in the beautiful Dodson Place Plaza in historic downtown Geneva, 40 miles west of downtown Chicago. Cradles & All features the latest in car seats and strollers and Kettler toddler bikes. You'll also find playhouses, handmade wooden toys from Germany and clothing for children of all ages. It also offers a full line of natural and organic diapers and other environmentally friendly items. Kristina owns and operates the store and finds love and inspiration from her three sons, Michael, Matthew and John. Find beautiful furniture and accessories that your child can grow up with at Cradles & All.

407 S 3rd Street, Geneva IL (630) 232-9780
www.cradlesandall.com

Beyond the Garden Gate

Cathy Kraemer and Lyn Almone love to shop and they love being creative. Owning Beyond the Garden Gate, a gift store brimming with pretty and joyful things, satisfies both of these passions. Selecting merchandise for their shelves brings out the shopper in both of them, as they get to choose items that strike their fancy and will also delight their customers. Candles, jewelry and greeting cards are part of the amazing variety that Libertyville residents have come to expect. An infant gift room features clothing and toys from such brands as Little Giraffe, Bunnies by the Bay and Baby Gund. A cozy and private area in the back is filled with bath and body products, comfy slippers, night shirts and robes. Cathy puts her artistic talent to work painting glassware, which she sells at the store, while Lyn pours her creative energy into the charming displays that have earned Beyond the Garden Gate a Main Street Outstanding Display award, a top honor in the state. She has also won numerous window decorating contests. There is so much to see at Beyond the Garden Gate, and the look of the store adds to the fun. Bring your shopping list and spend some time enjoying it all.

505 N Milwaukee Avenue, Libertyville IL (847) 680-9585

Design Toscano

At Design Toscano, you can expect the unexpected. This garden and interior design gallery stocks pieces that you are unlikely to find anywhere else. Owners Michael and Marilyn Stopka show many wonderful works of garden art to help bring your imagination and creative spirit into the outdoors, creating pleasure throughout the seasons. You'll see reproductions of European antique statuary, medieval and mystically inspired pieces and grand fountains. The store has something to suit every taste, from classic and religiously themed pieces to animals and gargoyles. To add charm and character to the inside of your home, Design Toscano has handsome home accents and furniture, such as a 16th century Italian replica globe bar or the Lord Byron wooden side table that looks like a bookcase. Whether it's framed art or exotic décor, you will find it at this shop. If you are looking for a special gift, you'll find a delightful selection of jewelry, watches, pens and walking sticks. Choose from among intricately designed pieces that reflect historical design and contemporary flair for a style that is all your own. Visit Design Toscano online or at the store to add an exciting dimension to your home, or to find a gift that is certain to please.

17 E Campbell Street, Arlington Heights IL (800) 525-9659
www.designtoscano.com

Hannah's Home Accents

Here's a superstore you'll look forward to visiting—Hannah's Home Accents has such an extensive variety of home wares that it really deserves to be called a super store. Owned by Don and Jane Marski, Hannah's Home Accents is actually a conglomeration of 10 specialty shops under one roof. The 30,000-square-foot store carries a breadth of merchandise, from quilts and candles to scrapbooking materials and stamps. The store also carries an assortment of specialty goods from brands such as Vera Bradley and Life Is Good. Rest assured you'll find the perfect gift for any home at Hannah's. Owner Don Marski grew up in Antioch and began working at Hannah's, then named Ben Franklin, while still in high school. Don's two-week job at the store unexpectedly turned into a lifelong career. He and his wife, Jane, purchased the business in 1985 and changed the name to Hannah's in 1997. Don and Jane are dedicated to providing the best service around and always staying on the cutting edge of trends. Hannah's loyal customers travel from surrounding cities for gift-giving ideas and to be inspired by the store's special themes such as nautical, kitchen and cabin. The home décor vignettes are detailed and inspiring, the small touches never overlooked. The Marski family takes pride in its store, and for good reason. At Hannah's Home Accents you'll find quality goods and impeccable service, something you can't find everywhere.

455 Lake Street, Antioch IL
(888) 784-6638
www.hannahs.com

Faye's Attic

Half of the fun in collecting is the hunt for treasures. At Faye's Attic, you will benefit from Faye Rosenberg's lifelong passion for pursuing antiques and for rummaging in antique shops across the country in her quest for one-of-a-kind treasures. Vintage clothing items, one of the owner's long-adored collectibles, rub shoulders with vintage jewelry. Choose from brooches and bracelets, handbags and hats. In addition to the wide array of clothing and jewelry, Faye's Attic offers primitive furniture, Depression glass, vintage pottery and pewter. Select the right accent to set off your own collection or let Faye suggest a new use for an old favorite. Indulge your nostalgic urge by surveying the selection of antique toys and find a cherished reminder of yesterday's play time. French soaps, candles and other enticing new items round out the offerings, blending the old-fashioned with the contemporary. The owner's special bond with each piece ensures that each beloved item finds a good home, and patrons particularly enjoy the owner's enthusiasm for her collection. Visit Faye's Attic where treasured memories take shape and where a collector's dreams can come true.

4159 Dundee Road, Northbrook IL   (847) 509-3017

Gadjets Galore

Affordability and a fun shopping experience work together to draw customers who are looking for something original to Gadjets Galore. The shop offers souvenirs, sports memorabilia and gag gifts. It stocks jazz, blues and reggae CDs and Polish DVDs for home entertainment. Polish memorabilia and gifts, including a Polish flag umbrella, have found a regular niche among the diverse merchandise. The shop is a great source for goodie bag contents, motivational gifts and whimsical gifts for fun. Alex and Patty Zajac are the proud owners of this entertaining shop. Alex had a retail background. His goal in opening his own business was to offer something for everyone. From perfumes and sword sets to ethnic apparel, Gadjets Galore is the manifestation of his vision. Gadjet Galore is very much a part of the community and a host of many neighborhood events. Whether you are looking for a gift, a gag, or just an enjoyable time browsing through the incredible inventory, make a beeline for Gadjets Galore. Chances are very good that you will find something fun.

386 E Golf Road, Arlington Heights IL   (847) 364-6410
www.gadjetsgalore.com

The Gift Box

Drawing its selection from all over the world, the Gift Box offers gifts galore and much more. Owner Lennart Jonsson imports items from Sweden, Norway, Denmark, Finland and Germany. Two floors brimming with bright, attractive displays await you. Sweaters made from 100% wool capture the essence of Scandinavian design. Wooden clogs, pewter candlesticks, linens and paper goods provide a taste of Sweden. Orrefors glassware and antiques make elegant accents and gifts. You'll find a wide selection of books, candles and prints. Traditional seasonal ornaments and wreaths are available year-round. The charming shop has been an integral piece of Geneva history for 60 years. Original owner Edythe Anderson opened the shop in 1947, filling it with remnants of her parents' Swedish heritage. Jonsson arrived from Sweden in 1954 and worked alongside Anderson, eventually purchasing the store in the 1980s. He continues to expand its inventory with gifts and collectibles you won't find anywhere else in the U.S. The location is also home to Cole Travel Service, featuring trips to Scandinavia. He also has primative Swedish antiques. Visit the Gift Box to enjoy an exciting array of international delights.

310 West State Street, Geneva Il   (630) 232-4151
www.thegiftbox.com

Chicago Metro—Shopping & Gifts 97

Pickard China

When the U.S. Department of State needed a manufacturer for the official china used by U.S. embassies worldwide, it chose a fourth generation family-owned business with a 110-year history of American-made workmanship. Pickard China serves Air Force One, the Queen of England, fine hotels, leading universities and country clubs. The firm offers 50 active china patterns, plus custom dinnerware, executive gifts and awards. It makes lavish use of 24-karat burnished gold, platinum and pure cobalt. All production takes place in Antioch, where a factory outlet store offers terrific selection, discounts on sets and a display of Pickard antique china. Andrew Pickard Morgan runs Pickard China with the help of family members. His great grandfather Wilder Austin Pickard established the company in Edgerton, Wisconsin in 1893, later moving it to Chicago and finally, Antioch. He developed a specialty in hand-painted art pieces and dessert and tea sets that collectors prize today. Wilder and his son Austin together developed the company's signature warm white china with the lion trademark. It is rare for a small family business to produce such fine china, but it is also an advantage, since Pickard can maintain unstinting quality control, passing each piece through three full inspections. When quality counts, visit Pickard China, America's oldest china company.

782 Pickard Avenue, Antioch IL
(847) 395-3800
www.pickardchina.com

Shopping & Gifts—Chicago Metro

The Good Works Gallery

The Good Works Gallery is a one-of-a kind gift shop. The gallery features contemporary crafts, functional art and unusual jewelry, handcrafted by local artists. You'll find high quality along with friendly customer service, which makes the gallery a comfortable place to explore. Owners Brett and Michelle Beckerman are knowledgeable about arts and crafts in general as well as the items in their shop, so they are a great source of advice on what you might want to purchase. In addition to artwork, the Good Works Gallery carries such items as wines from the Lynred Winery, gift baskets and Michael Aram's internationally known metals. The gallery has operated at the same address for 13 years. Working with local merchants to discover talent, the Beckermans have made the gallery an integral part of the community. Stop by and check out the Good Works Gallery. You might just find something you can't find anywhere else.

485 N Main Street, Glen Ellyn IL   (630) 858-6654

Possibilities

Possibilities knows how to get the attention of you and your gift recipient with a mix of goods that appeals to every generation. In fact, this Evanston institution, first opened in 1978, has been featured on NBC Morning News and now appeals to second and third generation shoppers. Owner Kate Coil started working at Possibilities as a teenager. She designed jewelry for the store and loved the store so much that she purchased it from her former employer when it became available. There isn't an age group, taste or personality that this store hasn't considered. Fine glass collectible Christmas ornaments by Christopher Radko share shop space with delightfully tacky pink flamingo lamps. An assortment of hilarious Everyday Icon Devotional Candles promise powers and entertainment value. Light one up to invoke Our Lady of Abundant Chocolate or as Protection from Bad Hairdressers. The younger set will go wild over Curious George backpacks, alarm clocks and watches as well as all things Madeline. The King lives on at Possibilities in Elvis lunchboxes and totes, and you'll want to analyze the Sigmund Freud 50-minute hour watch and perhaps a snuggly pair of Freudian Slippers. Gift wrapping is free, and so is the helpful service from the friendly Possibilities staff. For gifts that range from the whimsical to the sublime, take a look at Possibilities.

1235 Chicago Avenue, Evanston IL   (847) 328-1235
www.possibilitiesshop.com

The Present Moment

With gifts and inspirational items to soothe the soul, The Present Moment offers ways to make anyone's moment, day or even their life a little more positive. Owner Sue Opeka opened the store in 2006, after having her own moment of clarity. Before that, she had worked in corporate finance. After quitting her job to care for her mother, she realized that it was time to follow her dream. That dream has been realized in The Present Moment. Sue likens a visit to this serene store as a mental vacation. Customers enjoy relaxing music and comfy chairs, as well as the inspirational quotes on the walls. Gifts include the trademarked Sue's Chocolate Moments treats, which combine delicious chocolate with life lessons. You'll also find jewelry, wall art, soaps and other items that provide both spiritual and corporal beauty. Those looking for words of enlightenment will delight in the many inspirational books, as well as the many workshops. Sue even offers a Pay It Forward program for girls, encouraging them to do good deeds and pay forward the deeds done to them. There's no time like the present to come enjoy the gifts, atmosphere and enlightenment you'll find in The Present Moment.

521 N Milwaukee Avenue, Libertyville IL   (847) 367-1581
www.thepresentmomentinc.com

Chicago Metro—Shopping & Gifts   99

Paddy's on the Square

When you pass under the shamrocks above the door at Paddy's on the Square, you step into a store where green abounds and the luck of the Irish brightens your day. Paddy's carries all things Irish, including clothing for men, women and children. This Long Grove store is the place to find T-shirts and hoodies proclaiming your love for the land of the leprechauns. Many of the collectibles in the store, along with a selection of pants, skirts and sweaters, come straight from Ireland. Paddy's carries books about Ireland that will evoke fond memories if you have been there or will provide information if you are planning a trip. Who are the hottest acts these days on the Irish folk and pop scenes? Owners Paddy and John Barry invite you to find out by perusing the largest collection of Irish music in the Midwest. Friendly Irish service is the custom at Paddy's, which has been making life a little greener in historic Long Grove since 1975. Paddy has been very involved in the planning and growth of this tourist area, where Irish goods are so popular that you'll find a second shop, known as the Irish Boutique, here, plus Irish Boutique locations in Crystal Lake and Schaumburg. Be sure to wear green in honor of the Emerald Isle at your next visit to Paddy's on the Square.

228 Robert Parker Coffin Road, Long Grove IL
(847) 634-0339
www.irishboutique.com

Jenny Sweeney Designs

The cards and stationery at Jenny Sweeney Designs offer a flirty feminine spirit, combined with one-of-a-kind wit and artwork. Before starting the company, Jenny Sweeney had worked in graphic design and advertising. It was only after a friend took note of the artwork on one of Jenny's homemade cards that Jenny began to have a vision of selling them. Starting small, Jenny first sold her cards to local merchants before hitting the big time at the National Stationery Show in New York City. Now, Jenny Sweeney products are sold in more than 1,500 stores around the world—in addition to Jenny's own retail boutique in Libertyville. You'll find cards for every occasion with messages both inspiring—"You are fabulous"—and whimsical—"I love you more than gum." You'll also find a full line of custom wedding and birth announcements, some of which have earned the praise of such celebrities as *Law & Order* star Mariska Hargitay and Nicole Richie. Jenny also can design gift bags, napkins and even temporary tattoos. Jenny's shop exudes a savvy chicks-rule vibe, with pink everywhere. On Thursdays, the store serves wine and the atmosphere grows even more casual. Each month, you'll find seminars on how to throw a party—the business even oversees parties occasionally. A great experience is in the cards when you come to Jenny Sweeney Designs for your next special occasion.

627 N 2nd Street, Libertyville IL
(847) 816-8387
www.jennysweeneydesigns.com

Greer

Beauty. Wit. Civility. These are the values celebrated in the beautifully designed stationery you'll find at Greer. If the number of accolades this store has achieved in both local and national publications is any hint, those values are alive, well and treasured. In Style magazine has featured the store twice, while Greer's works were among the Chicago Tribune's 25 Things We Love in Design. Chicago Magazine named the store the Best Boutique in the region. Owner Chandra Greer spent much of her life as an honors student who worked toward degrees in medicine and business. She spent seven years as an accountant before deciding to use her self-taught artistic talent to celebrate the value of civility in greeting cards. Chandra sold her designs to stores independently before deciding to open her own. At Greer, you'll find cards and stationery for every occasion in Chandra's fresh, modern, original designs. These cards are uplifting and fun, celebrating the best of human nature in clever and unique ways. You'll also find pens and gifts, including ceramic serving dishes and jugs with small words printed on them. The atmosphere here is fun and happy, with vibrant splashes of color everywhere you look. Celebrate beauty, wit and civility with fun, attractive stationery and cards from Greer.

1657 N Wells Street, Chicago IL
(312) 337-8000
www.greerchicago.com

Irish Connoisseur

If you love the cozy clothing, scrumptious foods and traditional wares of Ireland but can't make it to the Emerald Isle, then pop into Irish Connoisseur where owner Megan Quinlisk Van Treeck has been selling her classic Irish goods for more than 20 years. Irish Connoisseur stocks a bounty of gifts, including crystal by Waterford, Galway and Irish Heritage, as well as Belleek China and Lladro porcelain figurines. This is also an ideal place to find handmade Irish pottery and china dishes from Nicholas Mosse and Stephen Pearce. The shop further offers savory pork sausage and bacon, along with brown bread, authentic Irish Soda bread and such tasty tidbits as Jacobs Cookies in a tin, Christmas pudding and a selection of Butlers Irish chocolate. In addition to memorable foods and gifts, the Irish Connoisseur also stocks gorgeous sweaters, woolens, shawls and dress coats along with such conventionally designed jewelry as Irish Claddagh rings. Megan and her delightfully friendly and knowledgeable staff are always happy to help you select just the right gift and answer any questions you might have about the products they sell. Indulge yourself and your friends with exquisite goodies from the land of enchantment at the Irish Connoisseur, where Megan and staff greet their customers with *cead mile failt*, meaning 100,000 welcomes.

1232 Waukegan Road, Glenview IL
(847) 998-1988

Irish Claddagh Ring
Photo by Royal Claddagh

Chicago Metro—Shopping & Gifts 101

View from observation deck of Sears Tower. Navy Pier in distance.

102 Greater Illinois

4th of July 2007 Fireworks Show in Springfield Illinois
Photo by Dan

Peoria's riverfront
Photo courtesy of Cyrus Gifts & Home Accents

Greater Illinois

104 Accommodations & Resorts

114 Arts & Crafts

118 Attractions & Recreation

130 Bakeries, Treats, Coffee & Tea

135 Farms, Markets & Delis

140 Fashion & Beauty

144 Flowers & Events

145 Galleries & Fine Art

148 Home & Garden

152 Restaurants & Cafés

167 Shopping & Gifts

Lincoln Tomb at the Oak Ridge Cemetary, Springfield.
Photo by Sid Webb

River House Bed & Breakfast

Owner Patty Michalsen says she can feel her house smile from the happy guests who stay at the River House Bed & Breakfast in Rockford. The River House hosts romantic getaways, package retreats and leisure travel lodging in two guest houses situated on six acres along bank of the beautiful Rock River. Patty is a gourmet cook, serving delectable two to three plate breakfasts as she pampers couples who stay in one of the Getaway Lodge's three luxury suites. Getaway Suites are equipped with a fireplace, Jacuzzi, and cater to guest's romantic occasions with first class amenities. The comfortable Retreat Lodge guest house, in addition to its five guestrooms, features a large gathering room. It accommodates all travelers, whether coming for family, leisure or business interests, but what some like best are the regularly scheduled Murder Mystery weekends, the Crop 'n Stamp retreats for scrapbookers, and the Foodie Recipe Swap cooking getaways for amateur chefs. Guests should note that Patty is an ordained minister, qualified to conduct marriages, and has packages available for small weddings at either lodge. Just for fun, the multitalented Patty fiddles and sings with a local bluegrass band and on occasion, will present house concerts at the bed-and-breakfast. Whether you stay in the Getaway Lodge or in the Retreat House, the Rock River will be within sight and its soothing rhythms will be within ear's reach. "Yes, happy memories are made here—that's our specialty," says Patty. Stay at the River House Bed & Breakfast and leave refreshed and smiling.

11052 Ventura Boulevard, Rockford IL (815) 636-1884 www.riverhouse.ws

Greater Illinois—Accommodations & Resorts 105

Bundling Board Inn

You might catch yourself checking the calendar at the Bundling Board Inn to make sure that the year is not 1910. The Victorian era survives in everything from the Queen Anne architecture of the house to the antique furniture, vintage quilts and hand-embroidered pillows in the three guest rooms. Each room is named for a womens relative of the owners who exemplified the hospitality and spirit of their times. Hosts Merida and Russell Johns keep the rooms just as they would have looked when Mildred, Clara and Patricia lived in them, right down to the hats and shoes on top of the armoire. Wake to the aroma of home-baked breads and muffins that complement the hearty breakfast at the inn. The sumptuous morning feast may include a fresh fruit smoothie to go with the granola pancakes or the Baked Praline Apple French Toast. While battling a serious illness, Merida told the chaplain at the hospital that she had done everything she wanted in life except own a bed and breakfast. He challenged her to pursue her dream, which is exactly what she did when she recovered. The inn, located just three blocks from Woodstock's charming village square, has passed the rigorous quality standards of the Illinois Bed and Breakfast Association. All guest rooms are non-smoking and have a private bathroom. Experience the elegant grace of the Victorian era at the Bundling Board Inn.

220 E South Street, Woodstock IL   (815) 338-7054   www.bundlingboard.com

Victorian Veranda Bed & Breakfast

Loretta "Ret" McCoy enjoyed staying at cozy bed-and-breakfasts each time she traveled to visit her children in college and the Navy. When this home became available for purchase, she jumped at the opportunity. It really is the perfect fit for a lady who loves to cook, meet new people and even likes to clean. Ret opened the doors of the spacious Victorian Veranda Bed & Breakfast in 1993. With more than 6,000 square feet and several common areas, including a living room, dining room, reception area and kitchen, guests have plenty of space to make themselves at home. Each of the five guest rooms feature a distinct look all its own and a private bath. Stay in the colorful Tropical Room, complete with brass parrots and decorative flamingos, or the more serene French Provincial Room. The wraparound porch invites you to sit and relax while looking out over the four acres of grounds. In the morning, fill up on Ret's delicious home cooking. A full breakfast at the inn includes fresh fruit, an egg entrée, a side dish and pastries. If you plan to visit any of the numerous nearby attractions, such as Klehm Arboretum, Burpee Museum or Coronado Theater, be sure to check with your friendly innkeeper for any advice. Ret has lived in the area for over 50 years and is happy to make helpful recommendations. Enjoy the fine hospitality you will receive on your next visit to the Victorian Veranda Bed & Breakfast.

8430 W State Road, Winnebago IL   (815) 963-1337
www.bbonline.com/il/veranda

Goldmoor Inn

Imagine 25 acres of meadows, flower gardens and fountains on a bluff overlooking the Mississippi River. Add gourmet breakfasts, seven-course dinners and luxurious accommodations that can include whirlpool tubs, fireplaces and views. You are well on your way to describing the many charms of Goldmoor Inn. Guests at this Select Registry Galena inn enjoy the attentions and often the lasting friendship of owners and hosts Jim and Patricia Goldthorpe. Jim bought the mansion in 1981. The home was designed as a private residence by a Taliesin student of Frank Lloyd Wright's. Sparks flew between Jim and Pat from the moment Jim hired Pat to perform interior design work, which ended in Jim's marriage proposal nine days later. Since those early days, the couple has made many improvements to the property. Guests choose from individually decorated rooms, stand-alone cottages and log cabins. Each room offers the kind of extras you would expect from a fine hotel, including Egyptian cotton linens, heated towel bars, voice mail and mini-refrigerators stocked with complimentary beverages. A chef prepares meals to exacting standards. Seasonal tours of Pat's gardens are popular. You can order an in-room massage or a couple's treatment, where you'll indulge in hot stone massage, chocolate, champagne and a soaking tub with your partner. Jim performs about 50 weddings a year at the Goldmoor, which features a climate-controlled gazebo and an outdoor pavilion with seating for 125. Enjoy the good life at the sumptuous Goldmoor Inn.

9001 Sand Hill Road, Galena IL (815) 777-3925 or (800) 255-3925
www.goldmoor.com

Annie Wiggins Guest House

If you arrive at Annie Wiggins Guest House on the weekend, Wendy Heiken may greet you in Victorian garb. On Friday and Saturday nights, Wendy turns into Annie Wiggins for ghost tours of historic Galena. Wendy and her husband, Bill, moved to Galena following Bill's retirement and opened the 1846 Victorian charmer to guests in 1998. The house is an ideal backdrop for Wendy, or Annie, to share her passion for the Victorian era. The Greek Revival home with its stately ionic columns and marble fireplaces offers seven guest rooms with private baths, queen-size beds and period furnishings. You can choose a room with a veranda, a fireplace or a two-person tub. Your visit includes a full breakfast served in double dining rooms and featuring such specialties as stuffed French toast and pumpkin bread pudding with bourbon sauce. Guests enjoy two parlors, porches and gardens. For many, Wendy's knowledge of Victorian times is so captivating that they return to Miss Annie's Academy of the Victorian Arts, where you can spend a weekend immersed in Victorian living or learn to sew a corset or Victorian gown. Workshops include 19th century bonnet making and mastering the Viennese waltz. Change gears and centuries with a visit to Annie Wiggins Guest House.

1004 Park Avenue, Galena IL (815) 777-0336
www.anniewiggins.com

Carrie's Vintage Inn

Carrie's Vintage Inn is located in the heart of Galen, with specialty shops and restaurants just outside the door. The inn was built in 1845 and functioned as a general store until the 1970s. In 2001, Brent and Carrie Hongsermeier purchased the inn and treated it to major redecorating. Rooms feature such charming details as original stone walls and intricate raised tile walls and ceilings. Couples will find a romantic setting while families will enjoy space and privacy. The inn offers four cozy rooms with queen beds, fireplaces and two-person whirlpool tubs. The inn's three suites are set up like small two-bedroom apartments. You can choose a suite with a kitchen or porch. Guests enjoy a Continental breakfast and the opportunity to browse through vintage merchandise at Carrie's Vintage Retold, a quaint shop featuring quilts, antiques and reproductions. Immerse yourself in the historic character of downtown Galena with a stay at Carrie's Vintage Inn.

305 N Main Street, Galena IL (815) 777-9125 or (866) 777-9125
www.carriesvintageinn.com

Cloran Mansion Bed & Breakfast

The Cloran Mansion Bed and Breakfast was purchased in August, 2001 by Carmine and Cheryl Farruggia. It was Cheryl's dream for 20 years to own a B & B specifically in Galena. Although the Cloran Mansion was a popular B & B, it has gone through extensive changes and improvements since the duo purchased it. The Mansion has five guest rooms and an award-winning handicap-accessible cottage. All rooms have a private bath. Four of the rooms and the cottage have two-person whirlpools and fireplaces. The Mansion's unique rooms include Alice's Room. John's Room, Ann's Room, Sara's Suite (an elegant main floor suite), The Tower Suite (the most romantic and requested room in Galena), and Antonio's Cottage. The one-and-a-half acre, well-kept grounds offer guests a screened gazebo, pond with fish and two waterfalls, and a fire pit. All of the guest rooms have satellite television, VCRs, DVD and CD players. Complimentary movies, CDs, beverages and magazines are available in the library. A full, country-style breakfast is served daily, and for those who wish to be pampered on-site, a Massage Therapist and private dinner can be arranged. For a truly romantic getaway, plan your next Galena experience at the Cloran Mansion.

1237 Franklin Street, Galena IL (815) 777-0583 or (866) 234-0583
www.cloranmansion.com

Galena Log Cabin Getaway and Adventure Creek Alpaca Farm

In 2005, Frank and Ruth Netzel purchased land near Galena and thoroughly renovated 12 cabins to the delight of every guest who stays at Galena Log Cabin Getaway. Each cabin makes a cozy retreat for up to four people with a queen bed on the main floor and a double bed in the loft. You will central heat and air conditioning, a gas log fireplace, satellite television, refrigerator, microwave, fine bed linens and—behind a closed door —a double whirlpool bath. Larger parties appreciate cabins that are joined by a breezeway in the dogtrot style. Adventure Creek runs through the 45-acre property, creating a large wetland, which hosts many native plants, birds and wild animals. You can walk along over two miles of wooded, hilly trails. The star-lit night sky, free of light pollution, is a special treat, as are the alpacas at the Netzels' Adventure Creek Alpaca Farm. Frank and Ruth will introduce you to these gentle animals, who are fond of children. The fleece from their herd is sent to a local mill to be spun into skeins of yarn, for sale in the Gift Shoppe. Other alpaca items available in the Shoppe are teddy bears, sweaters, shawls, ponchos, scarves, hats, caps, socks and gloves. Guests enjoy an outdoor barbecue grill and two campfire rings. The property is available for group events, including weddings. Sample rural pleasures at Galena Log Cabin Getaway.

9401 W Hart John Road, Galena IL (815) 777-4200
www.galenacabins.com
www.adventurecreek.com

Farmers' Guest House

In 1867, a farmer coming into Galena to sell his goods might have stayed overnight at a hotel on Spring Street that also operated as a bakery and store. Today, visitors to this historic street enjoy the updated charms of Farmers' Guest House, Galena's only 19th century restored inn. The high ceilings and original wood of the Italianate structure remain, along with a style of luxury yesteryear's farmers could not imagine, thanks to a renovation by owners Jess and Kathie Farlow in 2001. Nine guest rooms offer many comforts. You can choose a suite with a fireplace and a two-person whirlpool tub that used to be a stable. Another choice is a separate deluxe cottage. The Farlows can help you plan your time in Galena. They have hosted scrapbooking weekends, family reunions and small weddings. An ordained minister, Jess has performed many of the weddings. Mornings begin with breakfast by Jess. The Orange Tarragon Croissant French Toast is popular, as is the house's signature Hobo Hash. Guests gather for wine and cheese in the evening. The living room is stocked with DVD movies and an extensive jazz collection. You can play board games, sit down at the piano or visit the Littlest Gift Shop. An outdoor hot tub serves guests year-round. Take pleasure in life's details at Farmers' Guest House.

334 Spring Street, Galena IL
(815) 777-3456 or (888) 459-1847
www.farmersguesthouse.com

Maple Crest Bed & Breakfast

Relax and feel the history of Petersburg while staying at the classic Maple Crest Bed & Breakfast. Innkeepers David and Sandy Lanier are your hosts. You will find their inn listed as the Gault House on the Historic Homes Tour of Petersburg. All towns in this area of Illinois feel some connection to Abraham Lincoln. Petersburg is no different. In 1836, Lincoln was the deputy surveyor in nearby New Salem and plotted the Petersburg map. It wasn't until 1865 that Elijah Gault built his beautifully understated two-story house. Bay windows and white-railed porches lend elegant touches. Today, two suites, the Gault and Fulton's Folly, and two rooms, the Vogt and the Oriental, await visitors seeking a peaceful getaway or a headquarters while touring such area attractions as the Lincoln Library and Museum in Springfield and the reconstructed 1830s New Salem village. David and Sandy make guests feel at home with a beverage and cheese upon their arrival. Sandy's recipes go into making the full breakfast in the morning. Be sure to enjoy a few quiet moments in the gazebo during your visit. Enhance your trip to Lincoln country with a stay at the Maple Crest Bed & Breakfast.

319 S 9th Street, Petersburg IL
(217) 632-0128 or (800) 653-8012
www.maplecrest.us

Greater Illinois—Accommodations & Resorts

The Henry Mischler House

The Henry Mischler House projects the stately charm of a proper Victorian, but guests feel at home in the friendly, family-run establishment. Manager Jane Murphy convinced her daughter, Rani Boas, and Dr. John Saint to purchase the house because she'd always wanted to run a bed-and-breakfast. The Mischler house, built in 1897, retains its period details, including intricate fretwork and original light fixtures, and guests can choose to enjoy its old-fashioned ambience while playing cards or games in the parlor. Accommodations include eight tastefully decorated guest rooms, all with private baths, as well as a three-bedroom guest house, which can be rented as a unit. Breakfast, served in the dining room on crystal and china, features such scrumptious offerings as quiche casserole and apple walnut cinnamon pancakes. The lovely private gardens contain several fountains, a gazebo and a beautiful arch and bench. Evenings often include dancing on the deck, and Jane offers wine on the patio on warm summer evenings. She also provides transportation to and from the train station and refreshes guests upon arrival with wine and cheese or tea and cookies. Located across the street from the Lincoln home site, guests can walk to all the Lincoln historical sites from the bed-and-breakfast. Come see why senators and authors, as well as many international visitors, choose the hospitality of the Henry Mischler House.

802 E Edwards, Springfield IL (217) 525-2660 or (800) 525-2660 www.mischlerhouse.com

The Oaks Bed & Breakfast

High on a hill overlooking Petersburg and the Sangamon River Valley, the Oaks Bed & Breakfast nestles on five acres among majestic oaks and captivating gardens. The Italianate Victorian, built in 1875 by Sen. Edward Laning, exudes warmth and romantic charm with its intricate architectural details and sense of history. Innkeepers Susan and Ken Rodger offer guests a choice of accommodations, all with private baths, and some featuring fireplaces, whirlpools and porches. The Oaks offers lunch to the public. Guests receive a gourmet breakfast, wine and cheese in the afternoon and opportunities to book romantic candlelight dinners. Susan, a graduate of Chicago's Kendall School of Culinary Arts, creates the Oaks' signature Brown's Bay Bananas, a half banana wrapped in puff pastry, deep-fried, then rolled in cinnamon sugar and served with vanilla ice cream and hot caramel sauce. The spacious facility features two dining rooms, a parlor and a library, making it an elegant location for celebrations. Consider one of the special packages, such as the relaxing Girlfriend Getaway, Wine Weekends or festive Wassail Dinners during December. Susan pens the scripts for Murder Mystery Weekends, where guests enjoy a two-night stay while hunting for clues to solve the crime in nearby Petersburg. For elegant accommodations in a park-like setting, make reservations at the Oaks Bed & Breakfast.

510 W Sheridan, Petersburg IL   (217) 632-5444 or (888) 724-6257
www.theoaksbandb.com

Queen Anne Guest House

Mike and Anita Reese often visited Galena to celebrate their wedding anniversary. They turned their visits into their livelihoods when they purchased the Ridd House, which is now the Queen Anne Guest House. This gracious 1891 Victorian is still considered one of the finest built homes in Galena. The house, which appears in America's Painted Ladies, retains the original woodwork and leaded glass. Its four guest rooms feature private baths, queen-size beds and Victorian décor. Guests also enjoy the use several downstairs parlors. Birds were quite common in Victorian homes and Nikki, their small parrot, greets guests at the Queen Anne. Previously, Anita was a registered nurse and continues to do so today. Mike owned an outdoor sports store and was a writer for Adventure Sports Outdoors. Today, Mike writes interactive mysteries and creates original recipes for a breakfast that Inn Traveler magazine calls the Best Breakfast in the Midwest. Guests enjoy such delicacies as flaming sherried eggs and gingered pears. You will find complimentary beverages outside your room morning and evenings and a delightful parlor party at five pm. The Reese's offer many innovative packages, so plan your escape to the Queen Anne Guest House today.

200 Park Avenue, Galena IL   (815) 777-3849
www.queenanneguesthouse.com

Route 66 Hotel & Conference Center

In this era of cookie-cutter hotels, Marc Evans knows that the Route 66 Hotel & Conference Center, where he works as the director of sales and marketing, is something special. For starters, this locally owned Springfield hotel houses a mini-museum of vehicles, signs and newspaper articles from the heyday of road travel on US 66. While that's reason for history buffs to rejoice, the hotel's banquet and convention center is good news for anyone planning an event. With more than 6,000 square feet, it will accommodate any function.

"We can host up to 500 guests or as few as five to 25," says Marc, who adds that what really sets his hotel apart from others is "customized attention and customized pricing." With the Abraham Lincoln Presidential Library and Museum making Springfield more popular than ever, the Route 66 Hotel & Conference Center is ready to serve overnight guests with 114 rooms, an outdoor pool and extensive room amenities. The Cozy Dog restaurant, home of the original hot dog on a stick, is just up the street, and the American cuisine at the hotel's own Filling Station Bar & Grill always pleases. The hotel was built in 1959 as the first Holiday Inn in Illinois along Route 66. Many changes and a major renovation later, it impresses as a place where completely modern lodging and event hosting blend gracefully with nostalgia. On your next trip to Springfield, try the Route 66 Hotel & Conference Center.

625 E St. Joseph Street, Springfield IL   (217) 529-6626, ext. 604
www.rt66hotel.com

Hotel Père Marquette

The Hotel Père Marquette has seen every kind of world-changing event from stock market crashes to world war, and has hosted countless entertainers and politicians, including five presidents. As the number-one preferred hotel of Caterpillar Inc., the Père has welcomed dignitaries and visitors from all corners of the world. Built in 1927 and listed on the National Register of Historic Places, the Hotel Père Marquette is still, after all these years, the heartbeat of the city and the place to go when the occasion requires the very best. An eager and award-winning convention and meeting service staff supports four elegant ballrooms and six conference rooms that can accommodate from 10 to 1,200 people. Guests can choose among 253 spacious rooms or 36 spectacular suites, six of them with Jacuzzis. During the most recent renovation in 2006, the owner's mantra was as much about preservation as renovation. Care was taken to preserve the secret liquor cabinet in the Presidential Suite, a throwback to Prohibition days. They also preserved two priceless 1926 murals by Philadelphia artist George Harding that depict Fr. Jacques Marquette and Louis Joliet's journey down the Illinois River to Peoria in 1673. The renovation enlarged the hotel's fine restaurant, Carnegie's 501. Carnegie's ambiance is now slightly more casual than before, but it continues to garner an excellent reputation for fine dining while offering a complimentary breakfast buffet to all guests. The stylish Rendezvous Lobby Bar has been revamped, as have the elegant ballrooms, lobby and conference rooms. The suites are spectacular, but all rooms have been redone and the Hotel is getting rave reviews on the new bedding. Hotel services include a fitness center, free deck parking, a concierge floor, complimentary airport shuttle, a business center and high speed and wireless Internet access. On your next visit to the Midwest, surround yourself in luxury at the grand Hotel Père Marquette. Stop and linger a while—this is as good as it gets.

501 Main Street, Peoria IL
(309) 637-6500 or (800) 774-7118
www.hotelperemarquette.com

Beaver Creek Pottery

If it's practical and can be made out of clay, Tom Guirl probably creates it. Tom is the owner and potter at Beaver Creek Pottery. He works out of his parent's former farm, where he has built a home in the silo, a potter's studio in the dairy barn and a gallery shop in the horse barn. The shop is open daily and features three sales each year and a holiday open house in November. Tom wants his customers to include pottery in everyday activities and shapes such functional pieces as mugs, bud vases, pitchers and casserole dishes. You might find a chip and dip bowl, or a cluster pot, invaluable for sauces, snacks or desk organization. Large bowls with spouts and handles are ideal for mixing batters. Tom puts pottery in the garden, too, with birdhouses and flowerpots. He mixes his own clay and employs muted organic colors, including cobalt blue, brick red, oatmeal and such green shades as loden, sage, moss and hunter. He studied geology in college, but it was a pottery class that really fired him up. For graduation, he asked for a potter's wheel and immediately got busy, first giving away his creations, then selling them from a shed on the property. Plan a rewarding country drive to Beaver Creek Pottery.

10000 Beaver Valley Road, Belvidere IL (815) 547-6723 or (877) 352-2029
www.beavercreekpottery.com

FiberWild!

Amy Loberg left career in Chicago for a simpler life in rural Galena, where she opened a yarn shop in 2004. FiberWild! is the best kind of yarn shop—extensive, inspiring and cared for by an ardent knitter who appreciates color, texture and design. Amy's family has been designing, handcrafting and writing how-to fiber arts books for many generations. Amy and her family have created a large selection of samples to show product possibilities for every skill level. The shop features thousands of skeins of quality yarns, project kits and patterns, plus buttons, hand-dyed ribbon, weaving looms, spinning wheels and an extensive selection of books—15,000 items in all. Discover wool and alpaca from local sources along with exotic cashmere, bamboo and organic cotton. Other choices include silk, mohair and baby camel. The shop also carries a large selection of finished items by local people, including sweaters, hats, purses, blankets and baby clothes. The clicking of knitting needles is a common sound as folks stop in to knit or to ask Amy for help. Amy publishes a newsletter filled with tips and teaches classes in knitting, crochet, weaving, spinning and tatting for hobbyists of every skill level. Plan some browsing time at FiberWild!

214 N Main Street, Galena IL (815) 777-3550
www.FiberWild.com

The Goose Barn

When you're in need of something extraordinary to stimulate your creative juices, empty the trunk of your car and head to The Goose Barn in Rockford. You are going to need the empty space. The Goose Barn is housed in a massive 150-year-old peg-and-post barn filled to the rafters with scrap-booking supplies, rubberstamp materials and a plethora of crafts materials. The Goose Barn is packed so full of art supplies it will require at least two trips to see it all, and probably more. There are literally thousands of rubber stamps here. If you don't see exactly what you're looking for, a custom stamp can be made for you. Owner Becky Wilson has any accessory you need for your art projects. Want to try your hand at polymer clay? She's got you covered. Do you need watercolor supplies? No problem. Becky stocks an enormous selection of papers, cardstock, stencils, ink pads and cleaners. You'll find embossing powders that run from the very fine to the ultra thick, along with heat guns. In fact, The Goose Barn is where Becky's husband, Gary, developed the Heat Gun Holster. A patented concept, the Heat Gun Holster is now sold internationally. See how The Goose Barn can inspire you. This is a shopping experience true scrappers will appreciate.

5311 Charles Street, Rockford IL (815) 397-9391
www.goosebarn.com

Greater Illinois—Arts & Crafts 115

The Fold

If you have a love for spinning, yarn, wool and weaving, you'll be welcomed with open arms into the Fold. The Fold had its beginnings when Toni Neil and her family began raising sheep on their farm. Toni decided she wanted to make use of the wool and learned to spin it on her great-grandmother's vintage spinning wheel. That led Toni to begin collecting spinning wheels and carding wool for friends. Eventually, Toni decided to take over a friend's store and then opened a store on the farm. Now, in addition to the wool and yarn spun by Toni, you'll find thousands of other skeins of every variety, ranging from the finest sheep wool to alpaca blends and super-soft vicuña from the Andes. The Fold stocks everything from basic yarns to elegant hand-painted varieties. Want to spin your own yarn? Check out the supply of vintage spinning wheels and spindles, just ready to go to work on the 30 varieties of unspun wool stocked at the Fold. The Fold offers bulk-buying discounts for those with many projects underway. You'll also find a variety of other tools, notions, patterns and accessories to help you create the perfect piece. Want to improve your skills? The Fold offers classes in spinning, knitting, felting and weaving, as well as natural and chemical fabric-dyeing. The Fold is where the sheep feel safest, and Toni has made the environment a welcoming one for fabric artists of all skill levels. For everything you need to have a wild and woolly time spinning and knitting, come into the Fold.

3316 Millstream Road, Marengo IL
(815) 568-5730
www.thefoldatmc.net

Katherine's Bead Boutique

Katherine Sheetz-Tatak is the proprietor of Katherine's Bead Boutique, a unique bead shop located on the historic Woodstock square. Katherine is also a jewelry designer and certified precious metal clay artisan. Selling her custom jewelry at her shop and teaching classes keeps Katherine's creative juices flowing. Her pieces are also inspirational to her jewelry making customers. In addition, her shop is supplied with beads from around the world. She specializes in semi-precious stones and freshwater pearls but also carries a nice supply of glass, wood, African, carved bone, Bali and Thai, silver beads and of course, Swarovski crystals. She carries everything you need to design your own work, including a nice selection of tools and stringing supplies. Classes are available from beginner to advanced levels and are taught on Tuesday evenings and Saturdays. Katherine also does precious metal clay (P.M.C.) workshops, teaching an interesting twist to silver work. You can find a class schedule on her website or stop in for a hard copy. Katherine's Bead Boutique is part of the thriving scene on the Woodstock Square. Consider it your one-stop shop to meet all of your beading needs.

120 N Benton Street, Woodstock IL
(815) 337-7540
www.Katherinesbeads.com

Greater Illinois—Arts & Crafts   117

Galena Beads "serving creativity"

Creativity is the theme at Galena Beads, ranked one of America's favorite bead shops by Interweave Press. Owners and bead divas Jan Ketza-Harris, Trish Italia and Jess Italia-Lincoln met at craft shows while selling their wearable art. Inspired by Jess' jewelry designs, Jan and Trish decided to take up beading. The three women moved to Galena and opened shop in 2004. Trish finds beading to be therapeutic. She says, "It's fun to see a tray of beads and have one spark something in you." The shop offers a wide array of beads for sale individually or by the strand, with specialty mixes and jewelry kits also available. The shop's main specialty is Vintaj Natural Brass jewelry findings, which originated in Galena. Jan, Trish and Jess are proud to be the first retailer of this special product line. Galena Beads has an extensive jewelry section, which showcases 15 area designers. The shop's displays include over 1,200 pairs of earrings, wire crocheted jewelry, Vintaj art jewelry, free-form wire wrapping and handmade lampwork bead designs, to name a few. Wishing to share its passion for beading and encourage others, Galena Beads hosts a series of hands-on workshops, such as Beads, Wine and Chocolate, the Mystery of Wire Crochet and Bead & Breakfast Couples (complete with coffee and breakfast treats). Galena Beads was also featured in *Midwest Living* and made the Fall 2006 cover of *Stringing* magazine. Inside, Jan describes how to create an asymmetrical necklace using semi-precious stones, dichroic glass, art glass, sterling and pewter. Galena Beads is a great place to spark your creativity. You can join a workshop, or simply let something catch your eye and see what happens.

109 N Main Street, Galena IL
(815) 777-4080
www.galenabeads.com

2 One 7 Skateshop

2 One 7 Skateshop gives kids quality products at fair prices and provides a safe place to hang out and skate. This popular skateboarder destination has been owned and operated by a skater since 1998. Founder Corey Howell started the company shortly after his marriage, using wedding gift money and income he earned by working at area restaurants. Originally he used donated space at the community's old asylum and later moved the business to a storefront on Macarthur Avenue, where he operated for five years. In 2003, Corey was able to open 2 One 7 at its current location and expand the shop to include a giant indoor skate park chock full of ramps, jumps and challenges. 2 One 7 Skateshop also hires skateboarders to work in the store in order to ensure that you're receiving help from someone who knows the sport and uses the products sold here. Corey stocks products from companies you know and trust, like Almost, Independent, Mystery and Phantom. You'll find decks, trucks and wheels, along with stellar accessories, like DVDs, stickers, wax and griptape. Wheelslide and kickturn your way to 2 One 7 Skateshop, where you'll find the gear and accessories you crave and a place to show off your coolest new tricks while supporting a small local business that truly cares about Springfield's skating community.

3415 S Chatham Road, Springfield IL   (217) 391-0037
www.2one7skateshop.com

Bloomington Indoor Golf Club

If you fantasize about playing a round of golf at the Kapalua Plantation or the famed Pebble Beach, but you just cannot get away to Hawaii or California, head on over to Bloomington Indoor Golf Club where the state-of-the-art full swing golf simulators give you the chance to play courses you have only dreamed about. Owner Greg Sheffield, a PGA professional, opened the club in 2001 after experiencing the thrill and realism of a golf simulator in another city. A choice of 50 courses ensures that everyone, from a beginning golfer to someone seeking a real challenge, gets a course that suits their needs. If you would like to improve your swing, the BIGC offers teaching academies that make full use of the simulator's advanced technology and the experience of a professional instructor. Keep your equipment in top condition with Bloomington's club repair, club building and fitting. Opportunities exist for joining a league and playing golf with your friends all year long, regardless of the weather. Call or check out the website for the weekly special, and score a great deal on a meal and a round of golf. You could travel around the world or let Bloomington Indoor Golf Club bring the world's courses to you.

11 Finance Drive, Suite 1, Bloomington IL   (309) 662-6439
www.golfbigc.com

Children's Discovery Museum

The Children's Discovery Museum is three stories of amazing hands-on fun. The surprising array of hands-on exhibits is enough to keep curious children and their playful grown-ups busy and happy for hours on end. Walk into the first floor of the Museum and you'll find Discover My World, the exhibit gallery that puts children in charge of the world around them. In it, you'll see scads of youngsters bustling around the Kids' Medical Center, Train Express, the Toddler Backyard, Sugar Creek Waterplay and much more. Venture to the Museum's second floor. Gain access to the two-story Luckey Climber, learn how to better treat the environment in Oh Rubbish, harvest corn and milk the cows in the world's largest children's museum agriculture exhibit, AgMazing, experiment with airflow in ImagineAir, then plop down to read a book in the Reading Garden. Visitors connect with their inner artist as they explore all the fun on the third floor of the Museum. The Art Studio is rich with tools and supplies used by artists. Visitors get down and funky in the multicolor Recollections Room and are enthralled with the gigantic Paint Wall with its tantalizing paint palettes and water bottles. There is plenty to explore, imagine, create and play with at the Children's Discovery Museum.

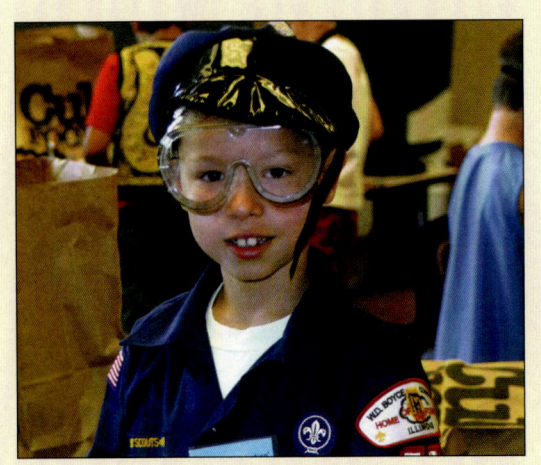

101 E Beaufort, Normal IL   (309) 433-3444
www.childrensdiscoverymuseum.net

Greater Illinois—Attractions & Recreation

Aldeen Golf Club

In 1934, the Rockford High School Yearbook contained this passage next to the photo of Norris Aldeen: "Norry says, 'Do it and do it well.' We know that whatever he attempts will be done that way." Truer words were never written. Norris Aldeen went on to become one of Rockford's most successful businessmen, a community benefactor and well-loved patron. Along the way he got hooked on golf. In 1987 Norris approached the city with an offer to donate land for a public golf course that is now one of the nation's best public golf clubs, the Norris Aldeen Golf Club. Designed by Dick Nugent, Aldeen is rated by *Golf Magazine* as one of the top 50 courses in America with greens fees under $50. *Golf Digest* gives the course four-and-a-half stars. Featuring bent grass greens, teas and fairways, a 26-acre practice facility, lots of trees, and water on 12 of the 18 holes, Aldeen Golf Club provides all the amenities of an upscale golf resort. The signature hole is the par-3 number 8, which features an island green. Club pro Duncan Geddes, who has been with the club from the start, owns the well stocked pro shop at Aldeen. Everything at this course is first rate, just the way Norris Aldeen did everything in his life. Aldeen Golf Club is a must-play course for true golf lovers.

1900 Reid Farm Road, Rockford IL
(815) 282-GOLF or (888) 4-ALDEEN
www.aldeengolfclub.com

Photos by Paul Hundley

Fever River Outfitters

Fever River Outfitters of Galena is an outfitter for all seasons. Located next to the Big Green Floodgates on South Main Street, Fever River Outfitters caters to the athlete and non-athlete alike. It rents out canoes, kayaks, bicycles, scooters and snowshoes. Canoe and kayak rental services include point-to-point trips with shuttle transportation services. Choose from a variety of paddling trips on the Galena River. In addition to daily rentals, Fever River Outfitters offers guided special events (see listings on website). One trip includes a paddle on the peaceful Mississippi Backwaters. Experienced guides share their knowledge of the birds and animal habitat on the popular Mississippi Backwater Tour. Mississippi Adventure Days are offered twice a year and include a seven mile paddle to Chestnut Mountain, followed by a chair lift to the top of the mountain, a hike in the woods, lunch and a 10 mile bicycle ride back to Galena. With advanced reservations, Fever River Outfitters will deliver rental scooters to your hotel or bed-and-breakfast. Also, stop by the store to shop for popular name-brand outdoor gear, as well as canoes and kayaks. Keep in mind, Fever River Outfitters always offers customers the option to test equipment on the water.

525 S Main Street, Galena IL   (815) 776-9424
www.feverriveroutfitters.com

Galena Trolley Tours & Depot Theatre

Once home to nine Civil War generals, Galena now boasts a historic downtown, beautifully renovated mansions, exquisite gardens and museums. Wondering where to start? Head for the Galena Trolley Tours & Depot Theatre and hop on one of Dee Levens' cherry red trolleys. The first option is a one-hour non-stop tour in which you'll pass by the Belvidere and Stillman mansions and cruise through downtown Galena. For the more adventurous, the two-hour tour includes a stop at the home of Ulysses S. Grant and a visit to the 3½-acre Limnar Gardens and its lush 35-foot waterfall, featured in *Country Gardens* magazine. The Depot has a courtyard and gift shop, and is also home to the Depot Theatre, which offers nightly showings of *Mark Twain and the Laughing River*, the acclaimed one-man musical play described by the Smithsonian Institute as nothing less than brilliant. Dee Levins started her business over 30 years ago with a 10-passenger van, then eventually hired a contractor to recreate the look and feel of an antique trolley. She now runs a fleet of four open-air trolleys and one executive mini-coach. Trolleys-are also available for private charters and weddings. Galena Trolley Tours & Depot Theatre is ready to jumpstart your Galena adventure. Just hop on board, sit back and relax for a truly historic ride.

314 S Main Street, Galena, IL   (815) 777-1248 or (877) 425-3621
www.galenatrolleys.com

Photo by Michael Burns

Henson Robinson Zoo

Open since 1970, the Springfield Park District's Henson Robinson Zoo offers visitors a glance at native and exotic animals in a park-like setting. The zoo is home to over 300 animals from Africa, Asia, Australia, and North and South America. Henson Robinson Zoo's animal collection encompasses approximately 90 species of native and exotic animals. While visiting the zoo, guests can observe animals in naturalistic environments and can even experience animals up close in the Australian Walk Thru. The zoo's contact yard offers visitors the opportunity to directly interact with animals. Sally Safari journal entries, which are posted at each animal exhibit, offer zoo visitors facts and information about each of the animals on exhibit. Once guests have toured the zoo they can relax in the zoo's pavilion and watch the children playing on the zoo's safari playground. Food and snacks are available in the zoo's concession stand. A visit to the zoo's gift shop to pick up a souvenir is an essential part of the trip. Henson Robinson Zoo is open year-round and is accredited by the Association of Zoos and Aquariums. The zoo participates in conservation efforts aimed at aiding endangered species.

1100 E Lake Drive, Springfield IL   (217) 753-6217
www.hensonrobinsonzoo.org

The Belvedere Mansion

It's a rare treat to tour a private mansion filled with priceless antiques. You can do just that from May to November at the Belvedere Mansion, one of the most famous homes in the Northwest Territory. This 1857 Italian Villa-style home was built by J. Russell Jones, steamboat owner, ambassador to Belgium and personal friend of Ulysses S. Grant. The 22-room Galena gem, with its carved marble fireplaces, sweeping staircase and views from the cupola, possesses an enchanting beauty and scale. Contents include lavish period furnishings and the present owner's collection of antiques and art. Your guide is sure to point out the green velvet drapes from MGM's *Gone With the Wind* and Liberace's boulle collection. From President Theodore Roosevelt's library comes a set of unusual Belter chairs with carvings of presidents' heads, which may have belonged to Confederate President Jefferson Davis. Visitors can also admire oil portraits and the dining room's signed Tiffany light fixture. Following the half-hour tour, you can take in the formal gardens at your own pace. See for yourself why the Belvedere Mansion is called the Crown Jewel of Galena.

1008 Park Avenue, Galena IL (815) 777-0747

Midwest Cimmaron Archery

If you haven't picked up a bow and arrow since summer camp, the Gussie family will show you how to start hitting targets again. Peter Gussie and his parents, Will and Norma, operate Midwest Cimmaron Archery. Will has been an avid archer for more than 40 years and has taught archery. Peter grew up immersed in his father's love for the sport and got his first bow when he was only four. It was only natural that the Gussies would find a way to make a living from their favorite activity. The grounds at Midwest Cimmaron Archery have it all—a 12-lane indoor range, a 30-station wooded 3-D course on 20 acres of land and an 80-yard distance range. Even the outdoor ranges are open year round, so there's no need to worry about losing your touch during the snowy winter months. Besides offering a variety of ways to practice, Midwest Cimmaron Archery sells everything needed for archery and will also service and repair your equipment. The Gussies want to help people become better hunters and archers, and they encourage the whole family to find out what fun archery can be. Tournaments, leagues and youth nights are commonplace at Midwest Cimmaron Archery. Whether you're looking to refine your skills or have never shot an arrow in your life, come down to Midwest Cimmaron Archery and let the Gussies show you what archery is all about.

9201 Main Street, Richmond IL (815) 678-7371
www.mcarchery.com

Photo by Iain Cuthbertson

Piper Glen Golf Club

Piper Glen Golf Club is one of the premier public golf courses in Illinois. Rated by *Golf Digest* as one of the top 200 courses in North America, and rated the 21st best public course under $50 by *Golf Magazine*, Piper Glen features a 6,985-yard championship layout consisting of immaculate bent grass tees, fairways, and greens. Strategically placed bunkers and water hazards, combined with the gently rolling countryside and wooded areas make for a challenging round of golf for players of all abilities. The course, designed by Lohmann Golf Designs, Inc., is one of the most challenging in the region. It incorporates a sophisticated, computerized irrigation system, which is one reason the course always seems to be in great shape. Piper Glen's 8,500-square-foot clubhouse boasts a number of amenities. The Golf Shop stocks a large assortment of quality merchandise, including logoed apparel and accessories, and the latest in golf technology. The Stewart Grill offers great food and beverages before, during or after your round. Piper Glen's banquet hall, The Palmer Room, provides guests with a comfortable atmosphere and tremendous views of the golf course. For a visit to one of America's best public golf courses, visit Piper Glen Golf Club.

7112 Piper Glen Drive, Springfield IL (217) 483-6537 or (877) 635-7326
www.piperglen.com

Rock Island Arsenal Museum

Rock Island Arsenal is the largest arsenal in the United States, and the mission of the Rock Island Arsenal Museum is to tell its story. The museum also boasts one of the best collections of small arms you can find anywhere. Dating to 1905, the museum is one of the U.S. Army's oldest. Its exhibits portray early island history using scale models of Fort Armstrong and the Colonel George Davenport house. Rock Island housed a prison camp during the Civil War, and another exhibit commemorates that time. The arsenal has manufactured ordnance since the 1880s. The museum displays the arsenal's handiwork, which includes leather gear, artillery pieces and rifles. You can see many rare items, such as serial number 1 of the Model 1903 rifle, serial number 2 of the M1 Garand rifle and serial number 1 of the M9 pistol. You can inspect weapons that Sioux and Cheyenne warriors used at the Battle of Little Bighorn. Other exhibits represent the arsenal's people and products in more recent times. The staff at the arsenal today includes more than 250 military and 6,600 civilian personnel. With base closures elsewhere, the Army has moved additional support operations into the arsenal complex, making the arsenal the largest employer in the Quad Cities area. Visit the Rock Island Arsenal Museum, where you can learn about a historic site and view a fascinating collection of small arms.

1 Rock Island Arsenal, Rock Island IL (309) 782-5021
www.riamwr.com/museum.htm

Greater Illinois—Attractions & Recreation   123

Camp Grant Museum and Restaurant

Many people in and around Rockford had forgotten about the site of Camp Grant. Yolanda Weisensel changed that when she opened the Command Post Restaurant in 1996 and the Camp Grant museum in 1997. Originally, Camp Grant was the largest of 16 cantonments built for World War I in 1917. The camp served as an infantry camp, a camp for the Illinois National Guard, a camp for the Civilian Conservation Corp, and as a medical center and prisoner of war camp during World War II. Camp Grant was an obvious choice for the theme of the restaurant since the Command Post was one of the 3 firehouses during World War II. Yolanda is privileged to reintroduce this part of the Rockford history. Now that the museum has rekindled an interest, families, students, veterans and others stop by the museum to share memories while enjoying homemade soups, meatloaf, and biscuits and gravy. Conversations often spread to several tables, and meals usually stretch into the homemade desserts. Apple pie, old-fashioned shortcake and Yolanda's brownie surprise are the big favorites. You will find pictures, postcards, and thousands of pieces of World War I, World War II, and Illinois National Guard memorabilia from the camp lining the walls and filling the display cases. Join friends around a table of homemade meals at the Camp Grant Museum and the Command Post Restaurant, open Monday through Saturday.

1004 Samuelson Road, Rockford IL
(815) 395-0679
www.rockfordsearch.com
www.campgrant.org

Rockford Speedway

Rockford Speedway has been the place to go for racing fans in central Illinois since 1948. The high-banked, quarter-mile oval has hosted Indianapolis 500 stars Johnnie Parsons and Duane Carter, plus such greats as Richard Petty, Mark Martin, Matt Kenseth and Greg Biffle. The year 2007 marked the 60th consecutive year Rockford Speedway has brought great racing to the area. It features stock car racing every Saturday night from April through September and every Wednesday from mid-June through mid-August. Rockford Speedway operates under NASCAR sanction, featuring NASCAR Late Model racing, Winged Women on Wheels, American Short Trackers, Roadrunners, Sportsman Hornets and Figure 8 machines. Hugh and Jody Deery, along with several investors, purchased Rockford Speedway in 1957. Hugh and Jody eventually took over and turned Rockford Speedway into a legendary venue. Hugh has since passed away, but Jody is still on top, assisted by her eight children. In 1994, Jody was honored by her peers in the short-track industry as Promoter of the Year, the only woman to ever receive the award. When it's not hosting races, the speedway's 40-acre grounds are home to events ranging from the circus to concerts. The Deerys also operate the adjacent Forest Hills Lodge, which features a banquet hall and space for group events.

9572 Forest Hills Road, Loves Park IL   (815) 633-1500
www.rockfordspeedway.com

*All photos taken by James Ambruoso
Rockford Speedway Customer Relation Mgr.*

Shenandoah Riding Center

With 40 miles of groomed trails in the Galena Territory, Shenandoah Riding Center is ready to offer variety to even its most frequent visitors. Lindley and Justin Leahy leased the 108-acre riding center in 2005. The couple shares a love of horses and originally met at a horse competition. Justin comes from Ireland, where his family has been breeding horses for many generations. Whether you are just learning to ride or feel confident on challenging terrain, Shenandoah can provide the well-trained mounts and instructors you need. Lessons can accommodate a young child learning the basics or an advanced student learning cross-country jumping. Instruction is available in an English or Western-style of riding. Enjoy a relaxed, 45-minute ride or an all-day romp through woods and valleys, stopping for a picnic lunch. All trail rides are guided. The property includes indoor and outdoor riding arenas, tack rooms and barns for boarding horses. The 35 athletic resident horses include spirited appaloosas, powerful percherons, gentle Tennessee walkers and the popular American quarter horse. The center presents five or six shows a year, including a July rodeo. Get to know the horses, the instructors and the countryside at Shenandoah Riding Center.

200 N Brodrecht Road, Galena IL   (815) 777-2373
www.shenandoahridingcenter.com

Spirit of Peoria

Riverboat Captain Alex Grieves stands at the helm as you tour the scenic Illinois River aboard a majestic sternwheeler called the *Spirit of Peoria*. She is a triple-deck, stern-driven paddlewheel yacht that takes you back in time to a life near forgotten. When you are sick of traffic jams, waiting in line, and the overall hustle and bustle of daily life, this is the way to travel. The *Spirit of Peoria* is an authentic paddle wheeler that cruises with the river at about eight miles per hour. She was built in Paducah, Kentucky in 1988 at the Walker Boat Yard. Her engines are modern, but her styling is authentic, and many of her decorative fixtures were purchased at auction from much older riverboats. You'll be able to watch eagles soar, and depending on when you ride, you can listen to river lore by storyteller Brian "Fox" Ellis, or world-class ragtime piano by Bev Wolf. The *Spirit of Peoria* offers a number of packages, including themed dinner cruises, sightseeing cruises, private charters and overnight excursions. You can view fall colors, take a Christmas Holiday cruise, take mom on a Mother's Day cruise, or do an overnight excursion to Starved Rock State Park. Once you board, you don't have to worry about anything, because they know how to take care of their guests. This is a great way to explore and learn the history of the river. Relax in the lap of luxury in grand 19th century style. Book your next adventure on the *Spirit of Peoria*.

100 Water Street, Peoria IL   (800) 676-8988 or (309) 637-8000
www.spiritofpeoria.com

Greater Illinois—Attractions & Recreation 125

The Farm

The bluffs overlooking the Sangamon River provide a lovely setting for a stroll, even more so when you follow the path from one theme garden to the next at The Farm. A destination for the avid gardener, the herb enthusiast or anyone who simply enjoys being outdoors among such beauty, The Farm features more than 20 gardens in all. The whimsical Fairy Garden and the romantic Lover's Garden are just two of the many that are a delight to behold and to smell. Some, such as the Medicinal and Cook's Gardens, grow useful herbs, while the Pink Garden exists for no other reason than to be pretty. The names of some gardens cleverly reveal the main attraction, such as Ring around the Roses and Mum's the Word. Some celebrate a season, such as the Christmas and Fall Harvest Gardens. All are perfect in their own way. No farm is complete without a barn, and the old-fashioned one at the entrance to The Farm houses a rustic shop full of dried flowers, herbs and gifts. Located halfway between Springfield and Petersburg on Route 97, The Farm holds a spring plant sale as well as fall and winter classes in wreath making and dried flower arrangement. It hosts hayrides, bonfires, garden weddings and there are animals to see, such as the Clydesdales named Samson and Goliath. Visit from mid-April to mid-December and make The Farm your choice for an enchanting day in the country.

21648 Old Farm Avenue, Petersburg IL   (217) 632-2888
www.visit-thefarm.com

Attractions & Recreation—Greater Illinois

Theatre in the Park

There isn't a bad seat in the house at the Theatre in the Park, and there isn't a single show on the schedule that won't have you tapping your feet and wanting to sing along. Located in Lincoln's New Salem Historic Site in Petersburg, the outdoor Theatre in the Park stages musicals throughout its summer season, complemented by symphony performances and other family-oriented concerts. In this land of Lincoln, you can count on shows with a historical bent every summer, including something related to the 16th president himself. With a mix of shows, including new works and Broadway classics, the schedule is sure to feature a performance to please every fan of musical theatre. The theatre holds 500, and all seats provide unobstructed views of the stage. Discounts are given for groups. Since the 1970s, when the curtain rose every weekend on the same show, *The Great American People Show*, the Theatre in the Park has always built its casts with talented individuals from the local area. Performers interested in auditioning should contact the office for information. For a night of enchantment under the stars, catch a performance at the Theatre in the Park.

**225 E Cook Street, Springfield IL
(217) 632-5440 or (800) 710-9290
www.theatreinthepark.net**

Springfield Art Association of Edwards Place

Since its founding in 1913, the Springfield Art Association of Edwards Place has played a very active role in advancing and supporting the visual arts. Appropriately, its Gallery of Art, Michael Victor II Art Library and School of Art share space in a building that is itself a work of art. An architectural masterpiece in the Italianate style, Edwards Place historic home is the oldest home in Springfield on its original foundation. Abraham Lincoln and Stephen Douglas attended social and political events here. Today, visitors may tour Edwards Place to view beautiful examples of Victorian furniture, including many pieces that belonged to Benjamin and Helen Edwards. If you are new to Springfield, you might consider becoming a member of the Springfield Art Association. Membership support such events as the Fine Art Fair, Beaux Arts Ball and Film Festival. You will join an intergenerational force of art patrons, from children who take art classes to senior members who have for decades worked to maintain a thriving art community in Central Illinois. For more information, contact the Springfield Art Association of Edwards Place.

**700 N 4th Street, Springfield IL
(217) 523-2631
www.springfieldart.org**

Greater Illinois—Attractions & Recreation 127

Knight's Action Park

Find something fun and exciting for the entire family to enjoy with a trip to Knight's Action Park, where visitors can play in the sun by day and then enjoy a relaxing drive-in movie by night. This action-packed park is owned and operated by the Knight family and managed by George Knight, Jr., who is the son of founder and former pro golfer George W. Knight, Sr. George Sr. became a professional golfer at the age of 19 after acting as caddie for the famed Willie Anderson, the first person in golf history to win the National Open four times. George Sr. went on to teach the great game; his students included several Vanderbilts, as well as Bob Hope and Judy Rankin, the first woman to win $100,000 on the tour. In 1952, George Sr. started in the recreation business with an archery range at one end of a driving range. His park soon expanded to include a miniature golf course and batting cages. Today Knight's Action Park & Caribbean Water Adventure features fabulous water slides and thrill rides, along with kiddie play areas, bumper boats and a wealth of other fun attractions. End the day at the Route 66 Twin Drive-In Theater, where you can catch great, family-friendly double features and enjoy a snack. When you visit Knight's Action Park, you'll be trusting your family's fun to the Knight family, specialists in safe, wholesome fun for all ages.

1700 Recreation Drive, Springfield IL
(217) 546-8881
www.knightsactionpark.com
www.route66-drivein.com

William M. Staerkel Planetarium at Parkland College

Ever stood awestruck beneath a night sky full of bright stars? If so, you will absolutely love your experience at the William M. Staerkel Planetarium at Parkland College. The second largest planetarium in Illinois, Staerkel's powerful Zeiss M1015 star projector and comfortable seating allow you to sit back and take in the planets, distant galaxies, and 7,600 stars beneath a 50-foot hemispheric projection dome. The planetarium features entertaining public shows for all ages on Friday and Saturday evenings, while its science lectures and school programs throughout the week offer a fascinating knowledge of our world to thousands of students and science enthusiasts annually. Tickets range from three to five dollars and are sold at the door. Check the planetarium's website for a schedule of children's shows, light shows, lectures, workshops and other current events. Take to the sky and stay for awhile at the William M. Staerkel Planetarium at Parkland College.

2400 W Bradley Avenue, Champaign IL
(217) 351-2446
www.parkland.edu/planetarium

Tinker Swiss Cottage Museum

Tinker Swiss Cottage Museum is a virtual time capsule of Victorian life in the 1800s. Owned by the Rockford Park District and Tinker Swiss Cottage Board of Trustees, the museum has existed since 1943 and is listed on the National Register of Historic Places. Robert Hall Tinker came to Rockford in 1856 at the age of 19 and went to work for a wealthy young widow, Mary Dorr Manny. In 1862, Mary supported Robert during a nine-month tour of Europe. Robert came home fully inspired. From 1865 to 1877, he built a Swiss cottage overlooking Kent Creek and put extensive effort into the gardens. There is one Indian burial mound on the property that to this day remains respected and untouched. He linked segments of the property together, crossing the creek with a suspension bridge, and added a three-story Swiss-style barn. Robert and Mary married in 1870 and became one of Rockford's most influential couples. Robert served as mayor in 1875 and was one of the founding members of the Rockford Park District. Robert's second wife, Jessie, left their home to the Park District to share with the community. All tours of the home and gardens are guided. Reservations are required for groups larger than eight. The Museum store, located in the Tinker Barn & Visitor Center, features local history items such as books, reproduction maps of Rockford in 1891, wooden toys, and make-your-own Sock Monkey kits. Take time to appreciate the Tinker's gift with a visit to Tinker Swiss Cottage Museum.

411 Kent Street, Rockford IL
(815) 964-2424
www.tinkercottage.com

Greater Illinois—Attractions & Recreation 129

Statue of Abraham Lincoln in Union Square Park, Springfield.
Photo by Sid Webb

Anderson's Candy Shop

In 1919, Arthur Anderson pressed unraised brittle into patties and called them Peanut Fritters. His candy became a sensation in Chicago when he began dipping it in chocolate. That was the beginning of Anderson's Candy Shop. Over the last hundred years, little has changed but the location. The Peanut Fritters are still popular, handmade every day from the freshest ingredients, and the Anderson family still runs the show. Lars and Leif Anderson, grandsons of the founder, have added truffles and toffee to the offerings. Every new product generates as much excitement as that first candy did so many years ago. Try the chocolate block of caramel and pecans with a layer of tasty white fluff. What is it called? "I developed it, so the employees named it after me," says Lars, waving a Lars Bar in his hand. Acclaim for Anderson's chocolates has come from sources far and wide, including the *Los Angeles Times* in its "America's Best" column and *Consumers Digest* in its feature article, "Rating the World's Finest Chocolate." Bite into a piece of Molasses Sponge Candy or the Buttercream Candy Bar, and you, too, will want to award Anderson's Candy Shop a blue ribbon. If you don't have one handy, a smile of satisfaction will get the message across just fine to Lars and Leif. Drop by and let the chocolate snacking begin.

10301 Main Street, Richmond IL   (815) 678-6000 or (888) 214-7614
www.andersonscandyshop.com

Del's Popcorn Shop

Shellie Jacobs, the owner of Del's Popcorn Shop, has Abe Lincoln to thank for the recent upswing in her shop's business. Business has always been good, but ever since the Abraham Lincoln Presidential Museum opened in downtown Springfield in 2005, she has had to add staff and hours to keep up with the demand for all of her homemade treats. The staff starts early in the morning by dipping 300 caramel apples and popping 100 pounds of popcorn. Del's whips its fudge by hand and roasts its nuts on the premises. If you love popcorn, you will want to taste how the regular butter and salted varieties compare to the best you've eaten, or you may break with tradition by choosing caramel, cheese or a blend of the two called Charmel. Del's has been a Springfield fixture since 1980, though the business itself goes all the way back to 1934. That's not quite as old as President Lincoln, but somehow we think he would have approved. For good things sweet or salty in Springfield, go to Del's Popcorn Shop.

213 S 6th Street, Springfield IL   (217) 544-0037
www.delspopcornshop.com

In Good Taste

Why hand clients a business card when you can give them a chocolate square with your business name and logo on it? Give Marla Brotherton, owner of In Good Taste, credit for this great idea. In fact, it's Marla's trait to keep coming up with new ways of making chocolate even more special than it already is. She began In Good Taste as a home based business specializing in handmade chocolates. She has since taken her recipes for caramel pretzels, cream clusters and other sweet treats to a retail space in Taylorville, where many loyal customers stop by for a piece of candy after lunch each day. When they need something for a birthday or anniversary, Marla is happy to oblige by putting together a gift basket. You never know what she might come up with next. Imagine announcing your new promotion or the birth of your baby with a candy bar that spells out the good news. Marla can make a batch of them for you. She felt not quite up to the challenge when officials from Springfield, Taylorville's neighbor to the north, asked her to make a chocolate bust of Abraham Lincoln for the dedication of the Abraham Lincoln Presidential Museum. To no one's real surprise, however, she eventually produced a remarkably detailed study of her subject. To meet the chocolate wizard and taste her goods, go to In Good Taste.

114 W Market Street, Taylorville IL   (217) 287-1130
www.igtaste.com

Greater Illinois—Bakeries, Treats, Coffee & Tea

Apples Bakery

The motto at Apples Bakery in Peoria is Smiles Made From Scratch. At Apples Bakery, everything is made from scratch. Owner Mary Ardapple watched her business grow out of an O'Leary's restaurant kitchen back in 1989. Mary, who was then the owner of O'Leary's, used her baking as a sideline business. But the sideline became a mainline when customers kept asking for more baked goods. They wanted more pies for Thanksgiving. They wanted more fudge drop cookies. Before long, Apples Bakery was born. Mary firmly believes if you can't pronounce it, or spell it, you probably shouldn't eat it. She incorporates a farm-style of cooking at Apples Bakery that just can't be beat. Soup should feed you like a meal, she believes. Apples are to be peeled. Real butter is to be used. Nothing comes out of a can. These simple values are expressed in every pie, cookie, loaf of bread, cheesecake, and Mississippi mud bar served at Apples Bakery. Even the coffee is locally roasted. Mary and her staff view the bakery as a community home. When you pull up a seat at Apples, it's like pulling up a chair at your own kitchen table, because they make it feel like home. The feeling permeates every baked goody. If you can't make it to the bakery in person, visit Apples online. They will ship their specialties across the country, which is great thing when you want a little of that down-home feeling.

8412 N Knoxville Avenue, Peoria IL
(309) 693-3522 or (866) 9APPLES (927-7537)
www.applesbakery.com

Photos by Michael Anschuetz

Kaladi's .925 Coffee Bar

You may never think of coffee the same way again once you've sampled the blends at Kaladi's .925 Coffee Bar, where the espresso blends come from six different sources and the coffee is freshly ground for each cup. Owner Antonio Morel is from the Dominican Republic, where he picked coffee as a child. He says his grandmother even put coffee in his bottle. With high coffee standards and a desire to fill a niche among Galena's restaurants, Tony and his wife, Carmela, opened the shop in 2000, naming it after the legendary goatherd who first sampled the red coffee berries after watching their invigorating effect on his goats. The couple added .925, a rating for the finest sterling silver, to emphasize the quality of their products and service. Everything at Kaladi's is made in-house. A pastry chef arrives at 5:30 am to prepare scones, muffins and cookies as well as the bread used for the restaurant's creative panini sandwiches. The gelato is another daily creation, made in 50 varieties with 12 flavors available on any summer day. The historical building with its original tile ceiling and bright mural invites lingering. It features comfortable couches, a chess table and free Wi-Fi. Prepare to be spoiled at Kaladi's .925 Coffee Bar.

309 S Main Street, Galena IL (815) 776-0723
www.kaladiscoffeebar.com

Lucile's Tea Room

In a bit of understatement, owners Gene and Cleo Bankord call their thriving business Lucile's Tea Room. In fact, you will find an entire house devoted to the taking of tea, including a room where guests are invited to choose a fancy hat from a box before being seated. The house was built in 1839, and Lucile's is named after the woman who lived in it for 70 years. This tea lovers' haven even features a room just for children, where parties of 10 or more receive a full lunch, learn proper table manners and view a skit. Perhaps best of all, the youngsters get to dress up in hats and costumes. Tea for adults is served in five different rooms during a three-course lunch that lasts about an hour and a half. Lucile's signature food, the cucumber sandwiches, arrives first. For the second course, guests choose from a delicacy tray full of scones, English shortbread and pastries as well as fruit and cheese. A serving of English trifle, complete with a chocolate L on top, concludes the meal. Everything is made fresh at Lucile's, where the décor changes three times a year to reflect such themes as Tea by the Sea, Tea on the Wild Side and Tea in the Garden. For afternoon tea Wednesday through Saturday, try Lucile's Tea Room.

7066 Newburg Road, Rockford IL (815) 484-9906
www.lucilestea.com

Meg's Daily Grind

Meg's Daily Grind is the place to stop for gourmet espressos and light lunch fare. Chris and Jodi Erickson, along with daughters Megan and Leslie, opened the first Meg's Daily Grind in 2001. Now they offer customers five cafés—the Rock Valley College location is an Internet café, and the cafés on North Perryville Road and North Alpine Road both have drive-thrus. A complete line of warm and cold espresso drinks are available, including such specialty brews as the Taffy Apple, made with steamed cider, caramel and whipped cream, and Stu's Macchiato, a caramel and vanilla creation. The house blend whole beans are available by the bag. Meg's offers a full range of smoothies, chai teas and other refreshing drinks as well. Tasty lunch choices include Meg's Special Salad, soup and several sandwich varieties. The cozy colors, eclectic décor and free wireless Internet, make it easy to get comfortable with a cup of espresso at Meg's Daily Grind.

3885 N Perryville Road, Rockford IL (815) 639-0909
1141 N Alpine Road, Rockford IL (815) 316-8785
Rock Valley College (ERC Building), Rockford IL (815) 978-1493
S Alpine Road (Heartland Community Church), Rockford IL
5312 Williams Drive, Roscoe IL (815) 623-5031
www.megs-daily-grind.com

Greater Illinois—Bakeries, Treats, Coffee & Tea 133

Chocolat'

Chocolat' is a European chocolate boutique featuring over 225 flavors of Swiss, German, Belgian, Italian and Venezuelan chocolates. The store was created by owner Bonnie Bellendier and offers only the finest international chocolates. With its sleek chrome, black tile and mirror décor, Chocolat' evokes the deco-style of Paris in downtown Galena. French, German and Italian music add to the store's European ambience. Specialty items exclusive to Chocolat' have been created, including decadent chocolate treats, seasonal drinks and ice cream creations. These artistic delights are a feast for the eyes and the taste buds. Each piece of chocolate is a work of art and a luscious, sinful experience of pleasure. Chocolat's trademark devil says it best, "Let us tempt you."

229 S Main Street, Galena IL
(815) 776-7777
www.letustemptyouwithchocolat.com

Sweet Indulgence

"I have the best customers in the world," says Sue Kirby, "until I run out of sugar cookies." Sue is the baking wizard who owns Sweet Indulgence, a bakery and espresso bar at the Windsor Galleria in Champaign. Sue gives her customers so many treats from which to choose that you would think that they could turn their disappointment at not finding a sugar cookie into an opportunity to explore a different section of the display case, maybe pick out an éclair, cream puff or napolean. The selection of cream and fruit pies is outstanding. The tarts are terrific. Spring and summer bring strawberry shortcakes made with almond biscuits. All of this, and we haven't even mentioned the cakes. Yes, we could go on and on about the cake selection, but we'll just say that if you love chocolate, you must try the Chocolate Indulgence. Still, there's something about those sugar cookies. OK, so Sue was out of them when you dropped by. Would having two dozen with your name on them make you feel better? That's right, Sue hand decorates her wildly popular cookies and will gladly design a batch to complement your special event. For sugar cookies and a world of baked goods beyond, go to Sweet Indulgence.

**1121 W Windsor Road, Champaign IL
(217) 352-2433**
www.asweetindulgence.com

Swiss Maid Bakery

The sweet dough recipe used to make the Swiss Cinnamon Bears and Sticky Pecan Bears at Swiss Maid Bakery has traveled a long way—all the way from Switzerland. Shirley Stricker credits her great grandparents for creating it. Shirley married Anton Stricker in 1950, thus uniting two families whose involvement in the baking business originated in Europe. Their Swiss Maid Bakery, a fixture at its present Harvard location since 1967, produces some 200 different treats, including 18 varieties of bread. From the fancy cinnamon rolls called bears to mouth-watering donuts, muffins and tortes, everything is made by hand and baked individually. Customers are welcome to choose any flavor, any filling for their custom-made wedding cakes, a specialty of Swiss Maid Bakery for many years. The bakery can even add fresh flowers for a finishing touch. During the Christmas season, Swiss Maid Bakery turns out about 3,500 pounds of cookies alone. Shirley and Anton have passed ownership of the business to their six sons, Kurt, Paul, Mark, Eric, John and Todd. Since the death of Eric in January of 2005 at age 39, Paul has continued the Swiss Maid Bakery tradition in Harvard and Woodstock. Pick up a loaf of bread and a few sweet treats at Swiss Maid Bakery.

**104 E Brainard Street, Harvard IL (815) 943-4252
122 N Benton Street, Woodstock IL (815) 338-0414**
www.swissmaidbakery.com

Greater Illinois—Farms, Markets & Delis

Red Barn Farm Market

The Skerke family cut out the middlemen long ago when they decided to market their farm's bounty direct to the public at Red Barn Farm Market. Before building the red barn that folks around Woodstock have come to know as a four-season market, Harvey and Norma Skerke operated a vegetable stand on the side of the highway. They started it as a way to help put their children, Sue and John, through college. Today, Sue and John, together with John's wife, Cathy, find dozens of ways to make the 40-year-old Red Barn worth a visit in every season. They use about 100 acres of their 320-acre farm to raise vegetables, delighting customers with the fresh flavors of sweet corn, tomatoes and such specialties as purple cauliflower and white eggplant. You will also find fruit from Michigan and many gourmet foods, including jams, jellies, salsa, dips and bread mixes. Kitchenware and country style home décor are popular, along with outdoor furniture and garden pottery. In spring, the market sells bedding plants and perennials from the farm's greenhouses. Fall is the farm market's biggest season, a time for enjoying everything from fall produce to such specialty foods as pumpkin pie and chili. Children frolic in the corn maze, pet the farm animals and enjoy hayrides around the farm. During the holidays, Red Barn sells fresh Christmas trees and wreaths along with gifts and decorations. In good weather, customers relax on the back patio of the open-air market with views of the farm's fields. Get closer to the source of your food at Red Barn Farm Market.

3500 S Route 47, Woodstock IL (815) 338-4343

Cobblestones on the Square

Cobblestones on the Square, one of Woodstock's favorite stores, stands out in two ways. One is the striking variety of things you can buy or eat. The other is the beauty of the place. The shop is a cheerful, brightly lit space with hardwood floors and colorful displays. Stop for a cappuccino or enjoy Homer's Gourmet Ice Cream. Take home fine chocolates and bulk candies for the kid in you, plus soups, pastas, sauces, cheeses, dressings and salsas. Cobblestones even has its own private label gourmet food. Current owner Jenny Serritella has added wine to the mix—more than 100 vintages from around the world. Tastings take place on Saturdays. Jenny's great eye and taste yield a fabulous collection of housewares, including linens, kitchenware and calendars. Other wares include infant gifts, candles and jewelry. All these goodies can go into gift baskets in any price range. Jenny's parents started the business back in 1989, and she took it over in 2004. Her mother, Lauren, still helps out. Jenny is involved in multiple community activities and has been named Retailer of the Year three years in a row. Come see Cobblestones on the Square, where gift-giving has never been easier.

111 Van Buren Street, Woodstock IL (815) 337-1750
www.cobblestonesonthesquare.com

DiTullio's

Some of Anthony DiTullio's regular customers come from as far away as 60 miles to buy his cheeses, sausages and pastas. DiTullio's Italian café, market and deli isn't exactly in their own backyard, but it is much closer than Italy. Usually you would have to travel to the Home Country for food this authentic, so a roundtrip of 100 miles or so to Rockford is no big deal. If hungry upon arrival, you could begin your visit to DiTullio's by heading straight to the café and ordering a panini sandwich, featuring DiTullio's own sandwich dressing. Once you start shopping, you won't want to stop until you have loaded your cart with Italian products, including hard-to-find oils, vinegars and chocolates. Stuffed cherry peppers and marinated artichokes are just some of the popular take-home items available at the deli. Growing up, Anthony knew he wanted to be either a fighter pilot or a business owner. You can tell by the way he enjoys sharing his vast knowledge of his products with his customers that he loves what he is doing and that he made the right choice. His sense of customer service even includes occasionally inviting someone with questions into the kitchen for an impromptu cooking lesson. To experience an Italian marketplace, you can go to Italy or you can go to DiTullio's.

1402 20th Street, Rockford IL (815) 399-2080
www.ditullios.com

Grandma's Gourmet Deli

There isn't much difference between Grandma's Gourmet Deli and a deli you would find in, say, Warsaw, Poland. Sure, English speakers will find it easier to order at Grandma's, but the selection of meats, cheeses and baked goods is definitely the real deal. The deli carries such specialty lunch meats as smoked pork loin, German Black Forest ham and blood sausage. The Polish sausage sells briskly, and the duck loaf, unfamiliar to most customers, wins over everyone who gives it a try. Find pierogi in the dairy case, along with farmer's cheese and herring. Offering hot and cold sandwiches, the deli gets busy at lunch time. The signature sandwich, the Big Papa, features grilled Polish sausage with sauerkraut on French bread. When owner Ania Ostrowska Gifford moved to Woodstock from Chicago, she noticed right away that something was missing. Although a sizeable 10 percent of the town's population is Polish, there wasn't a Polish deli or market anywhere to be found. A native of Warsaw, she had adapted easily to Chicago because the city had its own Polish community with many specialty stores. Enlisting her mother, Alfreda Herrick, as her business partner, Ania began bringing the taste of Eastern Europe to Woodstock in 2006. Drop by Grandma's Gourmet Deli to eat as they do in Warsaw.

709 S Eastwood Drive, State Route 47, Woodstock IL (815) 337-4233
www.grandmasgourmetdeli.com

Greater Illinois—Farms, Markets & Delis   137

The Lazy T

For the past two decades, the Lazy T has been active in agriculture production. Recently, it has turned its focus to organic fruit and vegetable production. Joe and Melanne Tarr sell directly to consumers from a roadside stand near Springfield, Illinois. Their stand opens in April with radishes and lettuces, and continues through December with Christmas trees. They also raise free-range poultry, offering fresh turkeys in the fall and fryers in the summer. Egg production continues year-round. Grass-fed beef will soon be added. The next time you're looking for fresh produce and a friendly conversation, stop by the Lazy T where you're only a stranger once.

103 Clear Creek, Dawson IL   (217) 364-9116

Jones Country Meats

The Jones family has been satisfying Woodstock's meat eaters since 1970, when Robert and Darlene Jones purchased a butcher store with already a 30-year history. These days, their daughter Suzy and her husband Jeff Madenis own Jones Country Meats. Unlike most of us, Suzy and Jeff have an intimate understanding of what it takes to prepare a living animal for consumption. All the slaughtering takes place at Jones Packing House in Harvard, a business started by Suzy's grandpa in 1940. Besides traditional cuts of beef and pork, the store carries seafood and such unusual meats as kangaroo, boar, rabbit, elk and buffalo. Beef jerky, brats and frozen or fresh pulled pork are popular. The store has won top state honors from the American Association of Meat Producers for its brats, hams, bacon and summer sausage. Dog treats account for a large portion of sales. Deer hunters rely on the store to process more than 2,000 kills a year. Jeff and Suzy support Sportsmen Against Hunger, a program that donates processed meat to area shelters. For old-fashioned meat preparation and presentation, visit Jones Country Meats.

204 N Seminary Avenue, Woodstock IL   (815) 337-0300
www.jonescountrymeats.com

International House of Wine & Cheese and the American Café

Have you ever paired an Irish cheese with a French wine, or an Australian wine with a Spanish cheese? The possibilities for international flavors to come together on the palate are endless at the International House of Wine & Cheese. A Richmond fixture and family-owned business since 1976, the shop features thousands of wines from all over the world, ranging from everyday favorites to the very rare. You'll also find vodkas, bourbons, scotches and other fine spirits. The selection of cheeses is just as impressive. If you are looking for a delightful gift for somebody with exquisite taste, a gourmet wine basket from the International House of Wine & Cheese might be just the thing. The adjoining American Café serves fluffy oven-baked omelettes for breakfast and thick sandwiches from the deli for lunch. Stick around on Friday nights for the fish fry, featuring all the cod you can eat, plus homemade potato pancakes, cole slaw and applesauce. The American Café is well-known for its superb catering abilities, for which no party is too big or too small. Stop by the International House of Wine & Cheese and check out their monthly schedule of events that includes everything from wine tastings and dinners to the ultimate Oktoberfest.

11302 Highway 12, Richmond IL   (815) 678-2500
www.forwinelovers.net

My Honey

Honey just like the bees make it is the specialty at My Honey, which prides itself on minimal handling of its honey on the way from hive to bottle. The product is natural, completely raw and unpasteurized and contains no additives. My Honey gently strains the honey without the use of industrial microfiltering systems. At the store in Richmond, you'll find shelves of clover, wildflower and cranberry honey, harvested from about 2,000 hives over 100 square miles of Wisconsin. Be sure to check out the observation hive in the back, home to a colony of busy bees that owners Peter and Linda Samorez call their pets. Peter began raising bees and selling honey to market in 1970. He started his own business to maintain the purity of his honey. Other bee products sold at My Honey include beeswax soaps and candles, honey candy and pure bee pollen. For honey that tastes the way nature intended, try a bottle of the sweet stuff from My Honey.

10012 Main Street, Richmond IL (815) 678-4129
www.myhoneyco.com

Strawberry Fields Natural Food Store & Café

Glimpse the changing face of the natural foods industry at Strawberry Fields Natural Food Store & Café in Urbana. You will find young and old here, students as well as families and seniors, shopping for organic produce, freshly baked loaves of bread and food supplements. Once associated with the counterculture, natural foods make sense to everyone concerned with healthful eating and environmentally friendly ways of producing food. Does this include you? If you have never tried natural foods, Strawberry Fields makes taking the plunge easy. First, start with coffee and a muffin in the café to get you ready to cruise the aisles. A nutritionist is on hand to answer questions, and the store is laid out just like a regular supermarket. You'll love the great bargains on granola and spices in the bulk bins. Many of the products come from local suppliers, so you'll know that you are supporting the community when you shop here. Those who are already using natural foods in their diets will find Strawberry Fields a bright, modern and spacious place to shop. "We serve a wide range of people," says co-owner Paul Dohme. When it comes to natural foods, there's room for everyone. See you at Strawberry Fields Natural Food Store & Café.

306 W Springfield Avenue, Urbana IL (217) 328-1655
www.strawberry-fields.com

Massbach Ridge Winery

Peggy Harmston grew up on a dairy farm. When she moved to Elizabeth to raise her children, she rediscovered the rural life. Inspecting the soil and landscape of her new property, she found that it was perfect for grape growing and launched Massbach Ridge Winery in 2003. Three years later, her work paid off with two awards for her homemade wines. Peggy's cherry rosé earned double gold at the Finger Lakes International Wine Competition while her white St. Pepin won a Best of Category at a state competition. Massbach Ridge Winery is a family business, with Peggy's husband, Greg, handling the spraying, pruning and testing. Her three children help with critical jobs, and even the public is invited to help with picking in September. Visitors enjoy strolling through the 18-acre vineyard. A tasting room is open on weekends year-round. The winery holds several special events, including a winter Cabin Fever open house, which pairs wines with cheese and chocolate, and a pre-harvest open house in August. Discover the rural splendors and award-winning wines of Massbach Ridge Winery.

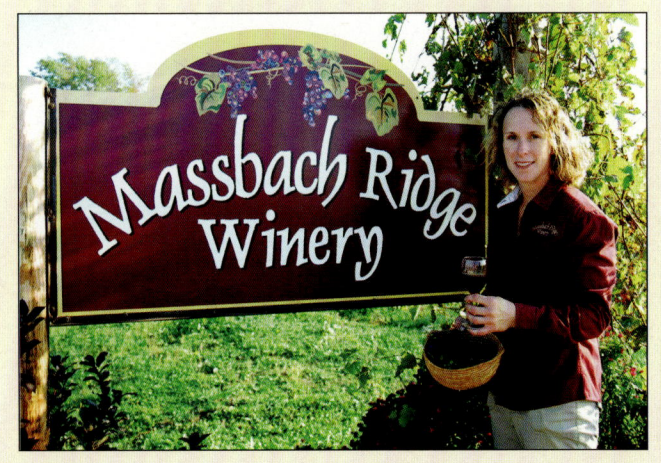

8837 S Massbach Road, Elizabeth IL (815) 291-6700
www.massbachridge.com

Murphy's Gardens

Paul and Lori Murphy both grew up on small farms where they learned a lifelong appreciation for gardening. Now they are passing this heritage on to their son, Kyle, on their own small farm. Since 1995, Murphy's Gardens has grown from a weekend vegetable stand in the garage into a full-time seasonal business with several greenhouses and three acres of vegetable and fruit gardens. An extensive list of over 225 perennials, 40 ornamental grasses, specialty annuals, herbs, native plants, water plants and vegetables include old fashioned heirlooms and the newest cultivars. The boutique garden center also carries garden décor such as birdbaths, birdhouses, pottery and tools. On Mothers Day weekend the Murphys host Plant Addict Weekend, which includes fundraisers for local charities and the opportunity to learn about garden design and care. Patrons are always welcome to grab a complimentary beverage and wander the acres of display gardens. In late summer the vegetable gardens produce a vast selection of fresh produce and fruit that can be purchased in the store. Each fall, one greenhouse is converted into the Pumpkin Palace and is filled to the brim with pumpkins, gourds and squash. Come by Murphy's Gardens to see what's growing.

12550 W Norris Lane, Galena IL (815) 777-4273
www.murphysgardens.com

Sassy Lady

Sassy Lady is a new woman's clothing store in Peoria Heights. Sassy Lady is the creation of four independent business women who in 2001 decided to fly out of Peoria and go shopping. After a four-day shopping bonanza, Pat Drake, Diana Gustin, Lynne Johnson, and Cindy Neal needed to purchase additional luggage to bring all their great deals home. The trip made them acutely aware of what Peoria was lacking, and Sassy Lady was born. The four friends set out to produce a store that featured clothing lines not available in the area. With their business savvy they knew the clothes they offered didn't have to be expensive, and they decided to pass the savings on to their customers. Additionally, they decided the service they offered had to be exceptional. At Sassy Lady, they have been known to take personal shopping trips to find that perfect outfit. If they don't have it, rest assured, they will find it for you. They are honest, and won't let you leave wearing something that doesn't look quite right. Sassy Lady is geared toward a studio-style shopping experience. They teach about body types and discuss fashion personalities. Open to everyone, these ladies don't judge a book by its cover. Sassy Lady carries a wide range of sizes and styles. Have the Sassy Ladies help you with your season colors so you don't have to think when you pull things out of the closet. At Sassy Lady, they welcome you with open arms and will have you feeling like one-in-a-million.

4111 N Prospect, Peoria Heights IL   (309) 688-5680   www.sassyladyclothing.com

August, the Salon

A proud sense of belonging is implied when you say that you are going to *your* salon rather than to *the* salon. Customers have been claiming August, the Salon as theirs since 2002, and owner Andi Sherman is thrilled every time she hears it. For her, it means that she is achieving her goal of offering the highest quality in an upscale yet approachable manner. Andi dreamed of starting her own salon during the many years that she worked in the industry. The skilled team of hair designers, nail technicians and aestheticians that she has assembled perform a full range of services. The massage therapists offer Swedish massage, reflexology and cranialsacral therapy, among other treatments. Many bridal parties have chosen August to get them ready for their big day. Clients enjoy purchasing fine hair care products from American Crew, Biolage, Goldwell and Graham Webb here, as well as nail products from OPI and Creative Nails. Andi chose the name *August* for her business not for its seasonal reference but for the dictionary definition of *marked with greatness, grandeur and dignity*, which describes how you will feel after receiving royal treatment here. August, the Salon is the only salon in Rockford that serves Starbucks coffee and hot chocolate. For a salon that you will love to call yours, come to August, the Salon.

**6785 Weaver Road, #1C, Rockford IL
(815) 637-4600**
www.augustthesalon.com

U Got Purse-onality

What's your purse-onality? Whether you're going for a bohemian look or that out-on-the-town style, you're sure to find it here. Inspired by her fashionable grandmother, owner Carrie Nordbrok had dreamed of opening U Got Purse-onality since she was a young girl. Today, the shop offers a variety of casual, dressy, whimsical and elegant pieces to complement any outfit or occasion. Many of the items are one-of-a-kind, such as the custom bridal line of Swarovski crystal jewelry. Whether you're looking for a classic black handbag to match your professional attire or you want to take a walk on the wild side with a fun animal print, you'll find it here. The store's inventory is updated every two weeks, so it's never hard to find something new and different. In addition to the funky selection of purses, jewelry, belts, wallets and hair accessories, one of the store's most distinctive features comes free of charge. Personalized service by a friendly, down-to-earth staff welcome visitors and regular customers to stop in for a cup of coffee and a piece of chocolate while they shop. For the designer look without the designer price, step into U Got Purse-onality.

511 S Eastwood Drive, Woodstock IL
(815) 338-BAGS (2247)
www.ugotpurseonality.com

Studio Blu Salon & Spa

Sisters Lisa Jimenez and Lauri Brolund shook some weight off their shoulders, and now they invite their guests to do the same at Studio Blu, a full-service salon and spa. They opened Studio Blu out of a desire to do something fun together. Lisa had been in the industry for years, working for other people. Lauri was looking for options to her stressful career in the medical field, so she went back to school to become a licensed aesthetician. Starting Studio Blu was like starting their lives over. Their joyous attitude was so contagious that they quickly took on more clients than anticipated and outgrew their first location. They and their staff currently offer hair, skin and nail care, along with body treatments and massage, at their site in the Edgebrook Shopping Center. Special occasion hair and makeup is a specialty at Studio Blu, where guests are invited to enjoy a glass of wine or beer with their session. Lisa and Lauri are always at the business. They like to keep things loose and friendly while maintaining a comfortably elegant atmosphere. For beauty treatments and enough positive energy to get you through the week, go to Studio Blu Salon & Spa.

1641 N Alpine Road, Rockford IL
(815) 986-1122

Wild Clover Day Spa

As a registered nurse and former hospital administrator for more than 25 years, Mary Rooney Sheahen saw the price people paid for not taking care of themselves. As owner of Wild Clover Day Spa, she enjoys offering therapies that promote wellness. She also gets to work with her husband, Chuck, a retired firefighter who keeps everything working at the spa. Wild Clover provides many signature treatments. The staff can customize services for small groups or cater to the specific needs of very young or very old clients. You will find the spa in the Irish Cottage Hotel in Galena. You can enjoy a hot stone massage, Turkish salt scrub, seaweed bath or sports vapor wrap at this innovative spa. The signature hydrating facial uses aromatic essential oils and a massage of the foot, hand, shoulder and face. Some customers have a special fondness for the wet room with its state-of-the-art hydrotherapy tub and Vichy shower. Others choose sunless tanning, nail services or consultations with master hair stylists on everything from special occasion styling to wig fitting, chemical straightening and human hair extensions. Wild Clover offers professional skin care products by Moiré and Mary Ann G. Galena residents are eligible for discounts. Make spa therapies an essential part of your wellness program with a visit to Wild Clover Day Spa.

9853 U.S. Highway 20, Galena IL
(815) 776-0744 or (877) 3DAYSPA (332-9772)
www.wildcloverdayspa.com

Flower Bin, Etc.

Coming up with innovative floral designs is just part of Denise Carlson's job as owner of the Flower Bin, Etc. Denise and the other designers on her team also manage to listen carefully to customers and respond to their needs, to be consoling when necessary and well organized. It's a challenging business, and Denise wouldn't have it any other way. She knew she wanted to be a floral designer back when she worked in a flower shop during high school and has spent 28 years in the field. She spent 17 of those years working for the Flower Bin Specialty Shop and bought the business, renaming it the Flower Bin, Etc., in 2003. She has expanded the gift and home décor choices to include garden art, candles, metalwork, silk arrangements and plush toys. Her displays change often for interesting browsing. The first Sunday in November finds the whole store transformed for the Christmas open house. Denise takes particular pleasure in decorating customers' homes for special occasions. She also tends to corporate customers, adding cheerful touches to lobbies in nursing homes and offices. You can find a pre-made arrangement or a potted plant, but it's the shop's custom work in fresh and silk flowers that rivets customer attention and makes the shop a favorite for weddings and other special events. Pay a visit to the Flower Bin, Etc. and put an energetic staff to work for you.

1925 N State Street, Belvidere IL
34 N Ayre Street, Harvard IL
(815) 544-2800 or (800) 384-1344
www.flowerbinetc.com

Blossom Basket Florist

Because a gift of roses can make someone feel special, you will always find specials on these beautiful flowers at Blossom Basket Florist. In fact, you could say that Blossom Basket is doing its part, one rose at a time, to make the world a better place. The folks here hand out thousands of roses, many to nursing home residents, during the Good Neighbor Day that the business sponsors. It's one of the ways that Blossom Basket gives back to the community that has supported it for more 50 years. Blossom Basket also sponsors Make Someone Smile Week, which it celebrates by handing out smiley face mugs with flowers in them. You will always find a large inventory of fresh flowers and plants for every occasion when you stop by. The flowers are flown in from South America to Willard Airport and are just two days out of the field when they arrive at the shop. The experienced floral designers at Blossom Basket offer several specialized services, including dish gardens, high-style floral arrangements and silk arrangements. For floral experts with hearts of gold, go to Blossom Basket Florist.

1002 N Cunningham, Urbana IL
(217) 367-8354 or (800) 336-4888
www.blossombasket.com

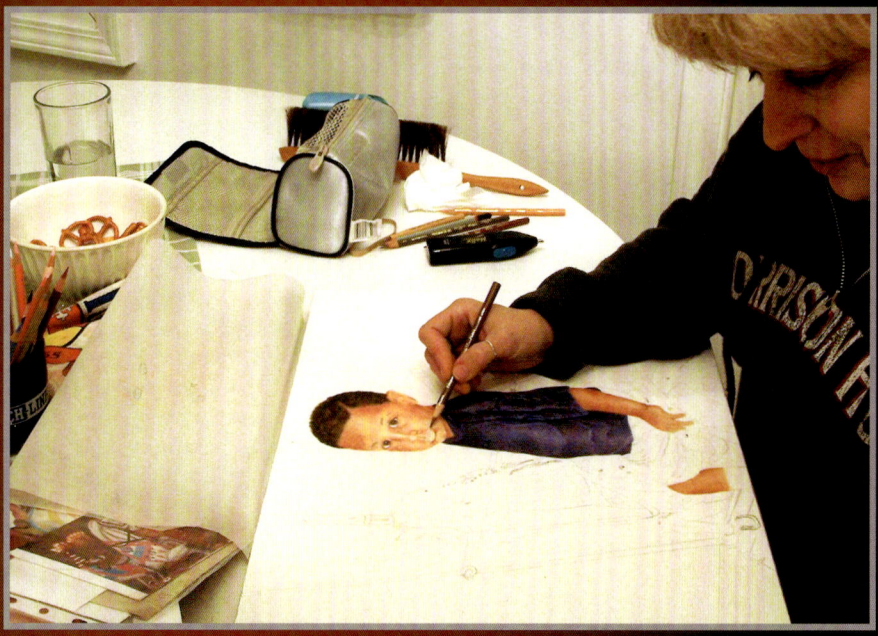

Tiffany Beane Fine Art & Portrait Studio

Portrait artist Tiffany Beane has the ability to bring her subjects to life using colored pencils, acrylic and watercolors. The Tiffany Beane Fine Art & Portrait Studio in Springfield features a choice collection of Tiffany's finest work, which is reminiscent of Rockwell's style and has the same gift of touching your soul. Tiffany's detailed website and email correspondence along with options for in-person or telephone orders help prospective customers understand the portrait process and give Tiffany a feel for individual projects. While she specializes in human portraiture, Tiffany is equally proficient at painting striking portraits of domesticated animals and wildlife, as well as elegant still lifes and *trompe l'oeil* murals that capture architecture and flowers. She belongs to numerous professional organizations, including the Colored Pencil Society of America and the Portrait Society of America. Tiffany holds a Bachelor of Fine Arts degree, with minors in graphic design and commercial illustration, as well as a bachelor's degree from Illinois State University in art education. Her combination of talent and training brings clients from across the country. Many desire to put her talents to use producing artwork with personal significance; others seek to learn her techniques in private or group art lessons for children and adults. Tours of the Tiffany Beane Fine Art & Portrait Studio, classes and meetings to discuss portrait work are available by appointment. For personalized, realistic art that you'll love forever, or to enhance your own art skills through one of the many art classes, make an appointment with Tiffany Beane.

6113 Greenwalt Drive, Springfield IL
(217) 698-3500 (art studio)
www.tiffanybeane.com

Carl Johnson's Gallery

When exploring Galena's historic downtown area, be sure to stop in at Carl Johnson's Gallery, where art and history come together. The gallery is in a beautifully restored drug store built in 1874. Its original tin-covered walls and ceiling are still intact. Carl's representational watercolors instill new life into the historic architecture of Galena. He also paints in Chicago, where he has a condo, and on annual trips throughout the United States. In his gallery you can also find botanical pieces and etchings, which Carl produces on a vintage Howard Etching Press. Carl is the author and illustrator of *The Building of Galena, an Architectural Heritage*, lovingly created with 15 color reproductions and vintage photos, and available for purchase at the gallery. After earning his bachelor of fine arts degree from the University of Illinois, he worked as a graphic designer in Chicago. He and his wife moved to Galena and have operated the gallery since 1971, and continue to be active in the art world. Both originals and prints of Carl's work are available, and you can purchase note cards. To experience art in a historic setting, come to Carl Johnson's gallery; you might even walk away with a painting or two.

202 S Main Street, Galena IL (815) 777-1222
www.cjart.net

Prairie House - Fine Craft Gallery

Prairie House contemporary fine craft gallery opened in 1970 in downtown Springfield. Since then, the gallery has gone through many changes, all under the ownership of Edith Myers. Edith, an Illinois native, received her degree from Northwestern University before marrying James Myers and raising a family of four children and 11 grandchildren. Edith initially traveled from Philadelphia to San Francisco and other locations searching for talented artists. She organized a jury made up of the leaders of Springfield's Art community to ensure high standards of quality. Edith acquires work from the best fine craft artists in the country, including jewelry, glass art, ceramics, wood, metal and fiber arts. One requirement is that all items must be handmade in the US by professional artists in their studio. Edith is especially proud of her rare 19th century and Abraham Lincoln-era prints and maps. Her son David bought the framing section in 1983, opening Prairie House Custom Frames. Needing to expand, Edith moved the gallery in 1994 and again in 1997, when she bought property and built Prairie House in its current location. Her daughter-in-law Gale now manages the gallery and Edith works five days a week taking an active role in the day-to-day operations. Now in her late eighties, Edith still expects the same high quality from the artists and craftspeople that make her store unique. She guarantees you won't find the pieces in her gallery anywhere else in the city. Edith invites everyone with an interest in the Arts and quality crafted unique gifts to visit Prairie House.

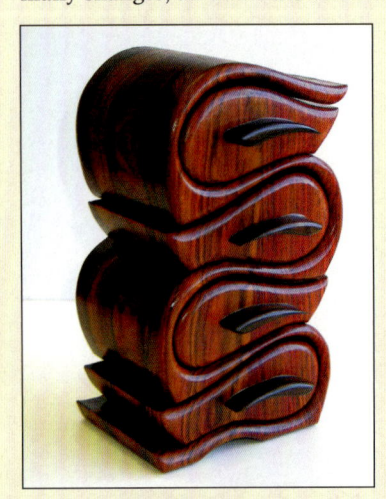

3013 Lindbergh Boulevard, Springfield IL (217) 546-1770

Kortman Gallery

You are likely to get immersed in a conversation about art, design or cultural history during a visit to Kortman Gallery. Kortman is a friendly and inviting space, where owners Doc Slafkosky and Jerry Kortman want their customers to have fun and learn the story behind the artwork here. Doc and Jerry opened the gallery in 1987, making it a key player in the reemergence of historic downtown Rockford. In 2000, the gallery, located on the second floor of the J.R. Kortman Center for Design, underwent a redesign. At Kortman Gallery, everything is about design, from the space itself to the art exhibitions and the quality of the merchandise found in the Kortman store. You'll find jewelry, art books and greeting cards here, along with wine and toys. The gallery store carries limited edition hand painted Rockford Christmas ornaments. Patrons look forward to two new designs, featuring well-known local landmarks, each year. The shop also features artistic housewares and home décor by Michael Aram, Alessi, Robert Eikholt and Philippe Starck, to name a few. The gallery launches six to eight shows a year with an opening reception attended by the artist. Doc and Jerry have chosen select local, regional and international artists to display in this intimate gallery space. Come enjoy a glass of champagne or cocktail at an opening reception or shop for pieces that make design part of everyday life with a visit to Kortman Gallery.

107 N Main Street, Rockford IL (815) 968-0123
www.jrkortman.com

Greater Illinois—Galleries & Fine Art   147

The Studio

In 2002, The Studio first invited folks in Taylorville to tap into their creativity and express themselves through drawing, oil painting and watercolor. The invitation was certainly not ignored. Debby Kiel and Patty Waterman figured that three students would be a good start when they began offering art classes. To their surprise, they had close to 30 people sign up. Although Patty passed away in January of 2006, Debby continues to offer a variety of classes for adults and children at very affordable rates. Debby has a Bachelor of Fine Arts degree and has taught art in the public schools and at the community college. She does the traditional instructing at The Studio. One reason for The Studio's success is that Debby is a natural-born artist who strives to inspire each of her students. Although her best friend Patty is no longer here in person, Debby has resolved to build upon the foundation they began together: to provide a place where people can find peace, relaxation and self-fulfillment through art. If you are seeking a spark to ignite the creative fire in yourself or your child, trust the talent of Debby Kiel at The Studio to provide it.

102 S Main Street, Taylorville IL
(217) 824-4575

Wind Water & Light

If you're thinking that Wind Water & Light sounds like the name of an alternative power company, you wouldn't be totally off track. Everything in this gallery has the power to enchant, delight or soothe. What's more, the unique fine art and fine crafts that you will find here are all handmade either locally or in North America. The artisans bring a fresh look at artistic style, celebrating the beauty and craftsmanship of their functional offerings. They also showcase decorative fine art and crafts that add spirit, originality and beauty to our lives, providing an alternative to mass-produced goods. The artists represent work in many medias, such as jewelry, fiber art, metal work, sculpture, photographs and mixed media, to create distinctive gifts, and accents for the home, office or personal collection. Yes, you can even shop for wind chimes, clothing and accessories at Wind Water & Light, and for nightlights and lamps, too. Owners Mary Tangora and her husband Larry Steinbauer are veterans of the arts and crafts scene, who for years sold their work at art fairs. Their first attempt at bringing local artists together led to a successful gallery in Mahomet. They soon moved to downtown Champaign and now handle a growing roster of 150 artists. Even outside of Champaign, people are noticing. Wind Water & Light was a finalist for *Niche* magazine's 2006 Top New Retailer award. For a gallery that makes a powerful impression, drop by Wind Water & Light.

10 E Main Street, Champaign IL
(217) 378-8565
www.windwaterlight.com

Benson Stone Company

Benson Stone Company has been welcoming friends through its doors for over 75 years. That's why you feel like you've come home the minute you walk through the doors of this 116-year-old restored furniture factory. You're embraced by enticing aromas wafting from the ovens of the HearthRock Café nestled on the first floor. You can shop to your heart's content knowing that the HearthRock awaits you with its hot tempting soups, unique sandwiches and gourmet coffee drinks. While exploring the store, you walk on the original, sometimes creaky, hardwood floors past the massive timbers of the post and beam construction. The many operating fireplace displays cast their glow upon an amazing collection of unique gift and home décor items creatively displayed throughout the store. Benson's truly offers All the Comforts of Home, displayed in ways that will inspire your imagination. You may be surprised to see that this beautiful historic building houses a modern four-story glass elevator. What better way to navigate four floors displaying everything from barbecue grills, kitchen cabinets, granite countertops, landscape stone and brick to floors and floors of furniture—furniture from such industry leaders as Thomasville, Pennsylvania House, Lane, Flexsteel and Kincaid. It quickly becomes apparent why Benson's has become a regional shopping destination. You haven't experienced Rockford if you haven't experienced Benson Stone.

1100 11th Street, Rockford IL (815) 227-2000
www.bensonstone.com

Greater Illinois—Home & Garden 149

Vignettes of Galena & Floral Chic

One family's strong interior design abilities and desire to serve are at the heart of the two Main Street shops in downtown Galena. Lisa Parr, Raechelle Ahmed and Alana Rapp started Floral Chic and later expanded into a second location for Vignettes of Galena. Floral Chic specializes in Floral Design for residential and commercial projects. Whether you want an arrangement while you wait or large scale designs for your hotel or business, Floral Chic has the experience and the materials to make your design one that will get talked about. Vignettes of Galena has the most impressive display of framed art in the area and is filled with the most beautiful furniture, rugs, unique accessories, tapestries, accent lighting and linens. Vignettes of Galena offers full service interior design located in the heart of Galena. Vignettes is open seven days a week and delivers throughout the Tri-States.

Floral Chic:
219 S Main Street, Galena IL
(815) 777-6882
www.floralchic.com

Vignettes of Galena:
105–107 N Main Street, Galena IL
(815) 776-0605
www.vignettesgalena.com

Joseph Layton Antiques and Interior Design

Shopping for home décor should be fun, inspiring and rewarding. At Joseph Layton Antiques and Interior Design, down the street from the historic home of Ulysses S. Grant, owners Phil Eichler and Tim Newman have created a store with an aura of timelessness that makes shoppers want to linger. Maybe it's the blend of old and new, with fine antiques sitting next to attractive new pieces, or perhaps it's the added attraction of an outdoor garden section offering furniture, ornaments and mosaic stone tables. At Joseph Layton, you can start small with light fixtures, area rugs and fine linens by Pine Cone Hill and Yves Delorme, and then move up to upholstered sofas and chairs, tables, chests and armoires. Original art by Nancie King Mertz, and Dash and Albert rugs adorn the walls, making it clear that Eichler and Newman have a passion for beauty. Eichler is a trained architect, and both owners are known for their interior design work. The two started in the garden décor industry then expanded to home décor and design, running a successful business in Chicago for 15 years before moving to Galena in 2006. Whether you're looking for a specific piece to enhance your home or garden or just browsing, Joseph Layton Antiques and Interior Design will put you in the right frame of mind.

525 Bouthillier Street, Galena IL (815) 776-0810
118 S Main Street, Galena IL (815) 776-0810

Greater Illinois—Home & Garden 151

Serendipity

Have you ever walked into a store hoping that someone could direct you to, say, the post office, only to spot the perfect lamp for the antique table you bought a year before at a yard sale? That's serendipity. In downtown Springfield, there's a shop called Serendipity, where people find the unexpected all the time. Owner Justin Kane loves it when someone gets excited over a piece of jewelry, clothing or home décor. With nearly 10,000 products in stock, it happens all the time, and he never tires of it. The ribbons that he ties to his shopping bags are his special way of saying thanks. This dash of flair fits his personality and his store. "Why be average," says Justin, "when you can be exceptional?" While you are visiting Serendipity, talk to Justin about a complimentary home visit. As a professional designer, he can create a plan for your home, featuring the area rugs, custom furniture, florals and window treatments from his store. For everything from wine racks to purses and thousands of pleasant surprises, shop at Serendipity.

221 S 6th Street, Springfield IL
(217) 528-0630
www.serendipityonsixth.com

Village Green Home & Garden

Do you tell your friends that if they knock on your door and you don't answer, then you are probably out back in your garden or on your patio? If, in other words, you seem to live outdoors when the weather is right, then you need Village Green Home & Garden. Since 1965, the six acres of greenhouses and retail space that comprise Village Green have attracted homeowners in search of everything from outdoor tables and chairs to fountains, grills and flowers. Known for its brand name outdoor furniture, Village Green has been ranked among the top 100 patio and garden centers in the country. Everything is displayed in its natural setting, so visitors enjoy just wandering the paths between patios, gazebos and atriums. Inside the greenhouses, you will find what you need to create beauty in your yard. Village Green carries a large selection of annuals in addition to 200 varieties of roses and 1,000 different perennials. Owner Larry Smith delights in hearing customers say how much they love shopping at Village Green. He points out that, with its large selection of indoor furniture and accessories, the store goes beyond enhancing your outdoor living space. For inspiration on how to beautify your home outdoors and in, drop by Village Green Home & Garden.

6101 E Riverside Boulevard, Rockford IL
(815) 877-9559

Biaggi's Ristorante Italiano

Whether it's lunch during a day of shopping, a meal with the family or just because you're hungry, Biaggi's Ristorante Italiano in Bloomington has the answer. The stylish restaurant with a warm, casual atmosphere opened in 1999. The perfect combination of authentic Italian cuisine and affordable pricing proved to be so successful that there are now 21 locations across the country. Corporate Executive Chef Peter Schonman continually changes the menu to keep things fresh, highlighting seasonal ingredients. Enjoy generous portions of pizza, pasta, salad and many other delicious entrées. Diners rave about the Fettuccini with Lobster. The bevy of Italian favorites is sure to please everyone in your party, and even the youngest patrons will find something to tempt their palates from the extensive children's menu. Choose from numerous reasonably priced wines to accompany your meal. The restaurant also offers wine dinners throughout the year for customers who would like to further appreciate the skillful pairing of wine and food. For a fresh, casual Italian meal visit Biaggi's Ristorante Italiano.

1501 N Veterans Parkway, Bloomington IL
(309) 661-8322
www.biaggis.com

The Woodstock Public House

Walk into The Woodstock Public House and you'll see why this is one of the most popular restaurants in town. Its upscale and casual atmosphere will leave you feeling comfortable whether you bring your business partner for a light lunch or your spouse for an elegant dinner. Owners Kathryn and Brian Loprino like to think of the restaurant as a white tablecloth establishment without the price or attitude. The wide choice of menu items reflects the diverse clientele, which ranges from families wanting a fun night out to diners looking for an elegant evening. If you're looking for a light lunch, try one of Woodstock's spicy wraps, such as the New Orleans Wrap, filled with buffalo shrimp and crawfish. Woodstock's signature dishes include a fresh catch of the day and the famous Seafood Diablo, jumbo clear water scallops wrapped in applewood-smoked bacon. Steak lovers can choose a filet mignon or a zesty bleu cheese rib eye. Kids enjoy the name-your-own-burger menu, which allows mixing and matching of toppings. The kitchen makes 95 percent of the food from scratch, right down to the tangy sauces and salad dressings. With so many choices, the menu is more like a book than anything else. The variety of dishes and uncompromised quality make the Woodstock the perfect choice for large groups, whether planned parties or spontaneous lunches. Stop in to taste the Woodstock Public House difference for yourself.

201 Main Street, Woodstock, IL
(815) 337-6060
www.thewoodstockpublichouse.com

Backstreet Steak & Chophouse

The old Galena State Bank building is the stately setting for this steak house with a big, bold vision of dining. Matthew and Sarah Kluesner showcase USDA prime meat at Backstreet Steak & Chophouse, opened in 1997. Their large steaks and chops are hand-cut on the premises and wet-aged at least 28 days for optimum flavor and tenderness. Finally, they are hand-turned on an indoor open-flame charcoal grill. Beyond Midwest corn-fed beef, patrons find pasta and chicken, along with such seafood entrées as King crab legs or the signature Black & White Sesame Ahi Tuna. The bar offers a tantalizing wine selection and traditional drinks, including some fine martinis. It takes a mighty appetite to relish a 38-ounce prime rib along with generous appetizers, freshly baked whole wheat bread and garlic mashed potatoes. Dessert choices include a carrot cake from a recipe belonging to Sarah's grandmother and a locally famous chocolate cake. Backstreet is open for dinner and serves private group lunches by appointment. The restaurant handles off-site catering of everything from picnics to lobster and filet dinners. You can even order meat to take home. Prepare to be wowed at Backstreet Steak & Chophouse, where reservations are mandatory.

216 S Commerce Street, Galena IL (815) 777-4800
www.backstreetgalena.com

Brio Restaurant

At Brio Restaurant in Rockford, small plate dining allows you to choose two, three or four menu options, so you can try a variety of different dishes. The tapas menu is tempting with such choices as seared yellowfin tuna, duck with grilled apples, beef or elk tenderloin, and Colorado lamb porterhouse. Even salads receive delicate and artful presentation. Pizzas made with hand-rolled flatbread offer such imaginative toppings as grilled chicken with Asian sauce or Cajun shrimp with sausage and peppers. Dessert plates include warm chocolate caramel cake and Chambord crepes with fresh raspberries. Wine Sommelier Damien Hunter offers an extensive hand-picked wine selection. Owner and Executive Chef Paul Sletten, who began cooking at age 16, previously operated an independent catering business. One of the things he appreciated most about that setting was his ability to interact with customers. Paul enjoys walking through the whimsically decorated dining areas and seeing people brought together over his food. Another way that Paul shares his love of cooking with customers is through Brio's catering service. Chefs come to your home or event and prepare gourmet food right in your kitchen. For a feast of flavors, come to Brio Restaurant.

515 E State Street, Rockford IL (815) 968-WINE (9463)
www.briorockford.com

Cannova's Pizzeria

While there's no proof that Italians make the best pizza, Cannova's Pizzeria certainly makes a good argument. Cannova's offers Sicilian-style pizza, pasta, sandwiches and desserts. Everything is homemade, from the dough to the desserts. The restaurant's signature classic pizza, a thin crust with spinach, garlic, tomatoes and black olives, is so good that Pizza Today named it Best of the Midwest. Cannova's also came in second in a nationwide competition at the Las Vegas Pizza Expo. Pasta lovers can choose from any of six traditional sauces. The shop has daily pizza specials, weekend steak and seafood specials, and more than 30 wine choices. Sandwiches include the muffuletta, stacked with Italian deli meats, provolone and green olives, and the Chicken Anthony. For dessert, try tiramisu, the classic Italian sweet. Current owners Linda and Patrick Beckman have kept the traditional appeal of the original Cannova's, which Linda's grandfather started in 1921. Brick walls, high ceilings, a huge oak bar and vintage black and white photos of the Cannova family come together to create an ambience that makes you want to cry Viva Italia.

247 N Main Street, Galena IL (815) 777-3735

Greater Illinois—Restaurants & Cafés

Chesapeake Seafood House

Chesapeake Seafood House offers patrons a fine dining environment enhanced by gracious service, vintage surroundings and satisfying cuisine. This popular eatery features hand-cut certified Angus steaks, chicken specialty dishes, pasta, and of course 60 different seafood entrees plus extensive appetizers menu. Don't forget to try the crabmeat stuffed mushrooms! The Chesapeake has been opened since 1983. Owner operators Linda Meiseman and Dan Whitmore handle the day-to-day operations along with the long-term staff, most have been there more than 10 years, and continues to carry on the tradition of excellent service and cuisine to every diner. The elegant vintage home built in 1857 has served as the site of many gala events throughout the years and continues to charm Chesapeake patrons. Bask in the genteel ambience of yesteryear with a visit to Chesapeake Seafood House.

3045 Clear Lake Avenue, Springfield, IL (217) 522-5220
www.chesapeakeseafoodhouse.com

Cozy Dog Drive In

Ed Waldmire, founder of the famous Cozy Dog Drive In, first began experimenting with his tasty hot-dog-on-a-stick in 1945, while serving in the U.S. Army Air Corps in Amarillo, Texas. He concocted a cornmeal-based batter that would stick to hot dogs as they were being deep-fried and then served the well received tidbits on cocktail forks to the GIs. After being discharged in 1946, Ed and his wife, Gin, who changed the delicacy's name from Crusty Curs to Cozy Dogs, began selling the hot commodity at fairs and carnivals across the Midwest. Gin designed the company's logo, two cozies embracing, and Ed opened two *dog houses* before the 1950 opening of his Route 66 location. Today the popular spot is owned and operated by Ed and Gin's daughter-in-law, Sue Waldmire, who continues the family tradition of offering good food at great prices. In addition to the original Cozy Dog, the eatery offers a great breakfast menu full of traditional favorites, like pancakes and cake doughnuts, as well as great lunch and supper dishes, such as pork tenderloin and homemade soups and chili. Cozy Dog Drive In also features its own brand of chili spice and French fry salt. Partake in one of the Mother Road's greatest traditions with a trip to the Cozy Dog Drive In.

2935 S Sixth Street, Springfield IL   (217) 525-1992
www.cozydogdrivein.com

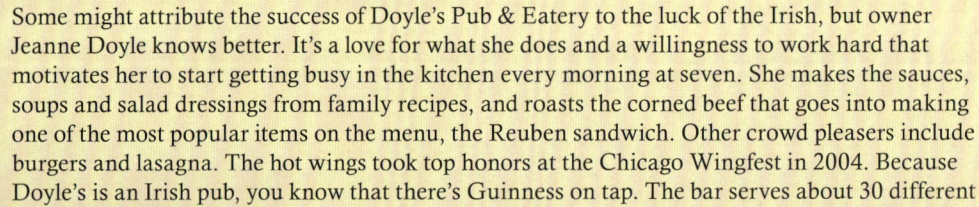

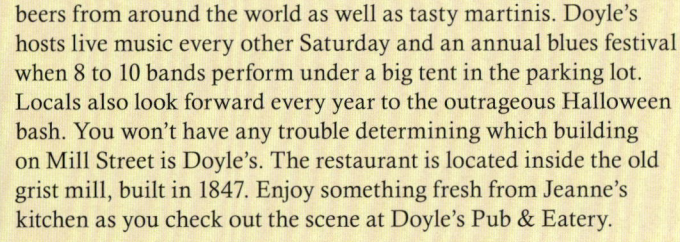

Doyle's Pub & Eatery

Some might attribute the success of Doyle's Pub & Eatery to the luck of the Irish, but owner Jeanne Doyle knows better. It's a love for what she does and a willingness to work hard that motivates her to start getting busy in the kitchen every morning at seven. She makes the sauces, soups and salad dressings from family recipes, and roasts the corned beef that goes into making one of the most popular items on the menu, the Reuben sandwich. Other crowd pleasers include burgers and lasagna. The hot wings took top honors at the Chicago Wingfest in 2004. Because Doyle's is an Irish pub, you know that there's Guinness on tap. The bar serves about 30 different beers from around the world as well as tasty martinis. Doyle's hosts live music every other Saturday and an annual blues festival when 8 to 10 bands perform under a big tent in the parking lot. Locals also look forward every year to the outrageous Halloween bash. You won't have any trouble determining which building on Mill Street is Doyle's. The restaurant is located inside the old grist mill, built in 1847. Enjoy something fresh from Jeanne's kitchen as you check out the scene at Doyle's Pub & Eatery.

5604 Mill Street, Richmond IL   (815) 678-3623
www.doylespubrocks.com

Del Carmen's Pizza East

When Larry Stanley bought his pizza business from Carmen Simone with a credit card and a loan in 1986, he thought he would hold onto the pizzeria until the credit card was paid off. Although he retired his credit card debt a year later, Larry and his wife, Martha, have kept Del Carmen's Pizza East, which now does eight times the business as it did when he bought it. Larry credits consistency with much of their success, and they still use the same specially spiced, homemade sweet sauce, real cheese, meats and spices as they did in the beginning. Homemade pizzas include the Del Carmen's Delight, a flavorful medley of fresh sausage, onion, pepperoni, green pepper and mushroom. Add green or ripe olives and it becomes the La Carmencita, Larry's favorite. He also suggests the stuffed pizza, which has a top and bottom crust, or he'll customize any pizza with anchovies, barbecue chicken or taco meat. Crispy bread sticks and a sweet amd tart French dressing get rave reviews from customers too. Whether you're looking for a family-friendly place to enjoy delicious homemade food or need to grab a pizza on the way home from work, stop in at Del Carmen's Pizza East and see why they call it The Pizza with Pizzazz.

221 N 22nd Street, Decatur IL   (217) 428-5991

Goldmoor Inn Dining

The dining room at Goldmoor Inn offers one of the finest dining experiences in Galena, a gourmet seven-course dinner. The menu changes weekly, offering a carefully balanced symphony of flavors that begins with the *amuse bouche* and ends with something sweet, such as cherry cobbler or mascarpone ice cream. Your entrée might be kobe beef or Cornish game hens. The small courses of soup, sorbet and salad are each carefully executed for your delight. Your waiter will help you select a special wine for each course. The dining room enjoys majestic views of Goldmoor Inn's landscaped grounds and, beyond, the Mississippi River. The setting is perfect for special events. Goldmoor Inn is particularly suited to accommodate weddings. There's a climate-controlled gazebo for intimate gatherings and an outdoor pavilion for groups as large as 125. The pavilion is fully equipped with lighting, sound systems and ceiling fans and looks out on flower gardens and fountains. Goldmoor Inn's on-site wedding coordinator can help with all your arrangements, from photographs to flowers, and you can even make reservations for hairstyling and massages at the inn. After the main event, host your reception in the dining room and let the staff roll out the red carpet. For celebrations that are sheer artistry, dine at Goldmoor Inn.

9001 W Sand Hill Road, Galena IL
(815) 777-3925 or (800) 255-3925
www.goldmoor.com

158 Restaurants & Cafés—Greater Illinois

Photos by Momentum

Greater Illinois—Restaurants & Cafés

Beef-A-Roo

The next time you're in northern Illinois, there's an eatery you really have to try. There's more than one, actually. Beef-A-Roo is a collection of family-owned and operated restaurants that are much beloved in this part of the Midwest. Started 30 years ago by Jean Vitale and Dave DeBruler, Beef-A-Roo is a collection of neighborhood gems that serve good, wholesome food with casual style. The first Beef-A-Roo in Loves Park featured a walk-up counter serving sandwiches and soft-drinks to go. Today, Beef-A-Roo serves wholesome wraps, hot baked potatoes, home-style chili and great salads from restaurants that are as unique as the family that runs them. When Dave and Jean started expanding, they built themes into their restaurants. The original Beef-A-Roo was redesigned as the Engine Company No. 1: Firehouse Beef-A-Roo. When they built a new restaurant on North Alpine Road in 1999, they incorporated a North Woods Lodge theme. The Riverside Beef-A-Roo, built around the nostalgia of the 1950s and '60s, is known as the Rock 'N Roll Beef-A-Roo. As the restaurants have grown, so has the family. Dave and Jean have four adult children working with them, and the entire family is committed to giving back to the community. This is casual, family-friendly dining at its best. Make sure to visit Beef-A-Roo when you're in town. Visit their website to see a list of their locations.

Beef-A-Roo Engine Co. #1
6116 N Second Street, Loves Park IL
(815) 633-6585
www.beefaroo.com

Photos by Momentum

Restaurants & Cafés—Greater Illinois

Gerlinde's Water Street Café

Ask Gerlinde Sampson what she serves at Gerlinde's Water Street Café, and she will tell you emphatically, "No fake food." Her training in the south of France would not allow for such, nor would her career in International cuisine, which has spanned four decades. Her café, she says proudly, "is all about good food," such as sumptuous omelettes for breakfast and her famous goat cheese sandwich for lunch. You will find an ever-changing array of daily specials that delightfully combine American and European cuisine. Orange walnut chicken breast salad, grilled whitefish sandwich on onion ciabatta with asparagus, and a turkey Florentine melt are just some of the recurring favorites. Dessert at the café is extraordinary, featuring Gerlinde's own pastries in addition to imported Italian gelatos, bourbon pecan pie and freshly made soufflés. Gerlinde first made her mark in Rockford with her School of International Cuisine, where she instructed students in the art of pastries, sauces and entrees for three years. She opened Chez Gerlinde, Rockford's first French restaurant, in 1980. Her downtown café on Water Street, her passion since 2003, is open for breakfast and lunch, Monday through Friday, and for fine French five-course meals by reservation only on Saturday evening. For a quaint and cozy restaurant where pride is the key ingredient, try Gerlinde's Water Street Café.

115 N Water Street, Rockford IL   (815) 962-3310

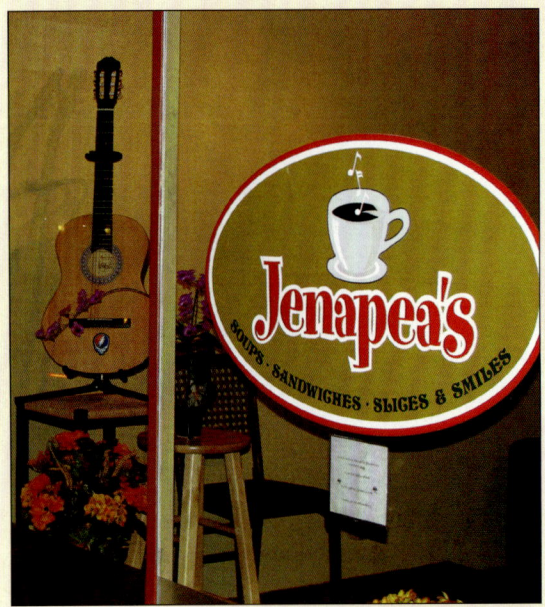

Jenapea's

He always dreamed of owning a pizzeria, while she always wanted to open a coffee shop. For Trey and Jena Rauschenberg, compromise has given rise to one of Woodstock's most popular gathering places. Called Jenapea's, this business on the historic Woodstock Square would need an oversized sign to list everything it serves. Start with award-winning coffee, fruit smoothies, Italian sodas and crèmes, such as the strawberry-vanilla-blackberry-cheesecake concoction. Add soups, such as the Roasted Red Pepper Tomato Bisque. Don't forget Trey's specialties: homemade pizza, of course, plus a very tasty chili. Jenapea's does breakfast and stays open late enough in the afternoon for an early dinner. The signature sandwiches are good any time of day. Try the Apple Harvest, with Black Forest ham, apples slices, raisins and Vermont cheddar on multi-grain bread. The best-selling Chive Turkey gets its kick from a cranberry horseradish cream cheese spread. Jena is adored for her Wild Mushroom & Brie Bisque, which sells out every time it is on the menu. The café hosts live acoustic music every weekend. Creative custom catering is also available, and Jenapea's can be rented out for private parties in the evening. Come and enjoy the ambiance and creative menu at Jenapea's.

109 E Van Buren Street, Woodstock IL   (815) 206-JPEA (5732)
www.jenapeas.com

Photo by Jay H. Polakoff

The Great Impasta

Sometimes a little idea becomes something big or even great, as in the case of the Great Impasta, a popular choice for Italian cuisine in downtown Champaign. Pierantonio Faraci started making his own pasta and selling it to grocery stores nearly 30 years ago. He never imagined that the business would grow into a 150-seat restaurant with four separate dining areas. The homemade freshness of the food is one reason for the success; the variety of Italian delights on the menu, another. The Great Impasta is the place for everything from the basics, such as spaghetti and meatballs, to a seafood lasagna with shrimp, clams and crabmeat that is simply superb. Meat lovers can feast on the meat lasagna, while vegetarians find several delicious options, including the linguini with mushrooms and asparagus. In addition to its pasta, the Great Impasta is known for its trio of fabulous soups: a seafood gumbo, the New England clam chowder and the Marcostrone, which is said to have been Marco Polo's favorite minestrone. The Great Impasta also serves salads and a variety of meat and seafood entrées. Pierantonio has turned the reigns over to Harold Allston, who continues the tradition of offering an atmosphere where you can leave the hustle of today and relax with artful food. For a date with greatness, try the Great Impasta.

114 W Church Street, Champaign IL   (217) 359-7377
www.greatimpastarestaurant.com

Mariah's Restaurant

If you would like to enjoy exquisite five-star cuisine at three-star prices, then try Mariah's Restaurant, where owners Sam and Mary Al-Khayyat have created an Italian eatery worthy of a special occasion. Sam, with more than 20 years of restaurant experience, had long dreamed of owning his own upscale eatery. In 2004, he made his dreams reality by turning a rustic lodge-sized log cabin on the backside of Parkway Point into one of the area's premier dining houses. Mariah's Restaurant, named for Sam and Mary's daughter, features a stately plaque inscribed with Sam's motto, which reads: "Excellence is the result of caring more than others think is wise, risking more than others think is safe, dreaming more than others think is practical and expecting more than others think is possible." All of the restaurant's beef is Black Angus beef, cut on-site, and many of the dishes are prepared completely from scratch, including delicious fresh bread baked to order. The log lodge, which boasts a sweeping, 44-foot cathedral ceiling, features a dining room for 100 with a raised gas fireplace and banquettes of lovely foliage that help to add a sense of intimacy. Experience a relaxing meal with friends or associates at Mariah's Restaurant, where excellence is always the special of the day.

3317 Robbins Road, Springfield IL
(217) 793-1900
www.mariahsrestaurant.com

Jill's on Galena

An exceptional world of fine dining awaits you at Jill's on Galena. This wonderful restaurant has been open for two years, and already it has won the 2005 Best of the Midwest Award for upscale dining. Chef and owner Jill Grube followed a lifelong dream of having her own restaurant. Jill is a graduate of Purdue and The New England Culinary School, and her culinary experience extends from Maui to Cape Cod. When she decided it was time to build her dream restaurant, Jill came home to Peoria. With strict attention to detail, she designed Jill's on Galena. The result is one of the finest dining experiences imaginable. Jill has created a relaxed environment where you can hang out in her favorite place. The Chef's Table is located in the heart of the kitchen, where four to eight guests watch Jill's magic unfold. The ultimate augmenter, Jill thrives at taking traditional dishes and turning them into not-so-traditional masterpieces. Crab stuffed calamari, "Nawlins' Oysters" with Andouille sausage and cornbread stuffing, pan-seared duck with roasted sweet potatoes, grilled herb-marinated filet of beef with blue cheese mashed potatoes and peppercorn hollandaise are just a few of Jill's creations. For the ultimate wine-tasting dinner, you may take a seat near the fireplace in the wine room, where Jill and a local wine expert prepare a five-course dinner accompanied by four wines. The Sunday brunch is exceptional. Private dining rooms and catering are available upon request. Reserve your spot at Jill's on Galena for your next first-rate, five-star meal.

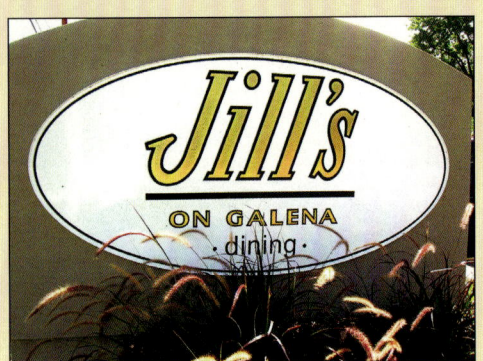

7327 N Galena Road, Peoria IL (309) 692-0200
www.jillsongalena.com

Lunker's

If you want a great fish sandwich, Lunker's in Normal is the place to go. Lunker's is a no-nonsense kind of place. It's a tavern-style restaurant where they know their business. They're famous for their fish sandwiches, and here's why: They're big. They're good. The fish is flaky, and the fillet is bigger than the chucky-sized bun. Lunker's is a casual dining and drinking spot where people feel comfortable hanging out. With seating for about 80 people, they serve lunch and dinner. During the day you'll find working folks and families. At night it's a happening hot spot for the college-age crowd. The walls at Lunker's are covered with fishing décor. Customers even bring in their own stuffed lunkers to hang on the walls. Owner Angel Jaros opened Lunker's eight years ago because she felt the town needed a casual, unpretentious place that served good, honest food. If you want something other than fish, Lunker's has a nice menu of tavern-style favorites, including burgers, sweet corn nuggets, BBQ pork and other goodies. They serve nine different kinds of sandwiches and 14 appetizers. You'll also find 12 beers on tap and a good assortment of bottled brews. The next time you're in Normal, stop by Lunker's and reel in one of their hefty offerings.

104 S Linden, Normal IL (309) 451-3474

Maldaner's

Maldaner's has been a community landmark and a legend in the making since 1886, when it began treating Springfield to premium confections and pastries. John Maldaner, a well-respected Milwaukee confectioner who was formerly with the famed Leland Hotel, founded the restaurant. In the early days John sold only his delicious treats; however, he soon evolved the business into a charming tea room that became a popular locale for ladies-who-lunch. Maldaner's opened for dinner in 1978 and has been a favored destination for special occasions ever since. Chef Michael Higgins began working for Maldaner's in 1982 and purchased the popular eatery in 1995. Caroline Oxtoby owns the building itself and gave the vintage dwelling a much-needed renovation that included attention to the restaurant's high tile ceiling and mahogany wood paneling. The restaurant, which has both dining room and banquet seating, also features a cozy bar with a 6-by-10-foot painting created by local artist and poet Vachel Lindsay. Chef Higgins continues to adhere to Maldaner's high standards by providing an exceptional staff of long-term, professional employees and by offering exquisite cuisine, prepared fresh daily from local, quality ingredients. Popular menu items include the salmon and morel mushroom pie and the sweet corn pancakes, served with creamed chicken. Enjoy an intimate dining experience that is as rich in history as it is in flavor at Maldaner's, a Springfield tradition for more than 120 years.

222 S Sixth Street, Springfield IL (217) 522-4313
www.maldaners.com

Greater Illinois—Restaurants & Cafés

Morning Star Mercantile & Café

More than 20 years of dreaming went into making the cashew chicken salad and other original recipes that you can enjoy today at Morning Star Mercantile & Café. Pat Adamski always wanted to own a café and gift shop, but sometimes life has a way of interfering with one's dreams. First, she went to school, and then she ended up living in Jerusalem for a long time. When she was ready to start her own business, she found an ideal location and a 100-year-old barn that perfectly suited her vision of a little place in the country where people could get away and have a relaxing lunch. The problem was that the barn and the location were miles away from each other. That's when Pat's father and brother sprung into action, dismantled the barn and brought the pieces to Salisbury, a small town just west of Springfield on Route 97. After months of reassembly and renovation, which included adding a fireplace designed to resemble the 19th century fireplaces at New Salem, Morning Star opened in 1998. Pat and her mother came up with a menu of pleasers, such as crepes and the olive nut sandwich. The homemade desserts alone are worth a visit. Try the carrot cake or a slice of tollhouse pie. Celebrate the dreamer in us all at Morning Star Mercantile & Café.

6141 Main Street, Salisbury IL   (217) 626-2022
www.morningstar-cafe.com

Paul's Confectionery

There is nothing fast about the food at Paul's Confectionery, but no one is complaining. It takes time to make good chili, which is what Paul's has been famous for since 1924. Three days gets you one five-gallon pot. Owners Carol and Joe Keller, and their daughter Robin, add their own spices, resulting in what they claim to be the best chili in Decatur. Former owner Paul Dalamas moved his restaurant to its present location in 1945, and few if any of the essentials have changed since then. Chili is still the focus, and you can still get ice cream sodas with phosphates from the fountain. The ice cream and pies are still made on the premises. The milk shakes are and always have been something special. Yes, since Paul and his friend, Pete Metrakos, started the business decades ago, the owners have insisted on making everything themselves. That even goes for the cornmeal mush. The Kellers slice it, fry it and serve it with butter and syrup. They make their own chili tamales, too. Paul's serves a special breakfast called the Trash Plate. Ask about it. For a taste of Decatur from the past, in the present and, we hope, well into the future, eat at Paul's Confectionery.

999 N Water Street, Decatur IL   (217) 428-6665

Perry Street Brasserie

Patrons who dine at the Perry Street Brasserie benefit from the many places Steve and Renée Dowe have lived, and the many interests they have explored. The couple opened the Galena Brasserie in 1999 with Steve as the Executive Chef. Steve attended culinary school in England and worked as a chef in two of the premier resorts in the London area as well as in the Middle East. He met Renée in St. Lucia, the Caribbean island that inspired his St. Lucia dish, a marriage of shrimp, scallops and lobster tail in a reduction sauce of garlic, white wine, curry, mango chutney and coconut milk. Back in the United States, Steve worked in many large resorts and ran a catering business. Today, he uses local, organic products whenever possible, makes all his own sauces and creates a different menu each month with the freshest ingredients available. The Dowes even butcher their own lamb for such dishes as roasted lamb loin served over fresh ratatouille. Dessert offerings change nightly, except for the signature Chocolate Cup, a solid Swiss chocolate bowl filled with two types of chocolate ganache, homemade whipped cream and raspberry sauce. The site of the restaurant is as remarkable as the food. The thick stone walls and wood floors of a 180-year-old former warehouse set off one of the world's largest collections of monumental brass facsimiles. For creative combinations inspired by world travel, visit the Perry Street Brasserie.

Corner of Main and Perry Streets, Galena IL   (815) 777-3773
www.perrystreetbrasserie.com

Pirro's Restaurante

Terry Pirro enjoys taking traditional Italian recipes that he learned from his mother and embellishing them with his own creativity. The results are often spectacular, as anyone who has eaten at Pirro's Restaurante can tell you. Folks who like to get right to the main course will be tempted to think twice at Pirro's. Try the roasted red pepper soup or the bruschetta platter, with its intriguing combination of buffalo milk mozzarella and pesto goat cheese, for an appetizer. Pirro's pastas are zesty and fresh. Consider the spaghetti topped with fresh asparagus, Romano and pancetta sautéed in olive oil with garlic and red pepper flakes. A reviewer for Metromix.com got it exactly right in saying that "somewhere between designer cooking and your mama's kitchen lies a place like Pirro's." The menu is always evolving according to what the customers like. Of course, some dishes have earned a permanent place on the bill. Lasagna is a tremendous favorite, and guests order about 400 pounds of fried calamari a week. The exposed brick walls and tin ceilings of the 1890s building lend plenty of character to the dining experience. For a perfect balance of traditional and nouveau, go to Pirro's Restaurante, located just off of Woodstock's historic square.

228 Main Street, Woodstock IL   (815) 337-9100
www.pirrosrestaurante.com

Saputo's

If you drive into Springfield and ask a local where to eat, chances are the answer will be Saputo's. Frank and Florine Saputo and Frank's twin brother Joe established this community landmark, located just one block north of Abraham Lincoln's historic home, in 1948. Today this distinctive Italian restaurant is owned by third generation daughter Sandy Coffey and her husband, Mike, along with the couple's son Mike Jr. The family works together using old family recipes and fresh ingredients to create your favorite Italian dishes from scratch each day. Saputo's features two elegant dining rooms and a full bar, along with banquet facilities for up to 100 guests, making it the ideal place for family or corporate gatherings, as well as fundraisers and gala events. The restaurant's menu offers a full selection of tempting dishes, such as chicken with peppers, shrimp scampi and homemade ravioli. Luscious desserts include tiramisu and old-fashioned chocolate sundaes. Saputo's also provides a take-out menu, so that you can take generous portions or your family's favorites home for a mid-week dinner or easily cater your next luncheon or company meeting. Enjoy a scrumptious Italian feast, gracious hospitality and a welcoming ambience at Saputo's.

Radio Maria

No, Radio Maria is not the name of a radio station airing out of someone named Maria's basement, though it shares the maverick spirit of such an operation. It's a restaurant in downtown Champaign featuring fine, creative cuisine. Just as someone might want to start their own radio station to play the music that they love and aren't hearing on any other station, David Spears and Sharon Owens opened their restaurant 11 years ago to share a vision of eclectic, unpredictable dining that is uniquely theirs. The menu at Radio Maria typically takes something you thought you knew well, such as a crab cake, and gives it a totally new personality, one defined by avocado and a Jamaican honey glaze. With its interesting twists on tacos and quesadillas, it leads you in a nouveau Mexican direction, only to pull you to the Middle East with the best Lamb Kofta that you'll find away from the Mediterranean. This casserole of potatoes, rice and spiced ground lamb is topped with a tangy tomato sauce and served with onions, yogurt and toasted pita. A decade ago, the owners were told that Radio Maria wouldn't last a month. Downtown had supposedly seen its better days, and the few people who came there certainly weren't looking for a restaurant as unusual as this one. Now that downtown is the place to be, David and Sharon strive to remain creative. For a restaurant that continues to define its own path, try Radio Maria.

119 N Walnut Street, Champaign IL   (217) 398-7729
www.radiomariarestaurant.com

Two Olives and a Pepper

Two Olives and a Pepper offers patrons a delightful dining experience enhanced by artwork and exceptional service. Owners Dean and Marsha Brogdon met while working together at another area restaurant. When the couple discovered the Vinegar Hill Mall location, they jumped at the chance to open their own establishment and soon created a community favorite. Marsha's parents, Keith and Sharon Schroeder, and the Brogdons' friend Meagan Novak worked with the couple to create the restaurant's distinctive hand-painted murals of Italy. Open late into the night seven days a week, Two Olives and a Pepper offers a diverse menu filled with traditional Italian favorites and contemporary treats, many of which are named for friends, family and employees. Sharon and Dean do all of the restaurant's cooking and use old family recipes to create their fabulous soups, sauces and dressings from scratch each day. In addition to favorites, like baked French onion soup and Seth's Swiss Pastrami, Two Olives and a Pepper offers more than 40 different panini sandwiches, each one whimsically served with two olives and a pepper on top. Treat your palate to something extraordinary while delighting in the Italian murals at the delightful Two Olives & a Pepper.

107 W Cook Street, Suite 11, Springfield IL
(217) 241-1027

Cyrus Gifts
& Home Accents

Located on Peoria's riverfront, Cyrus Gifts & Home Accents is a very trendy boutique. Owner Erikka Brookhart has created a fun, swanky shop that is just a pleasure to visit. Cyrus has been located at this address for the past four years and has already been expanded once. Cyrus carries many different lines of fun jewelry from all over the world. You will find the Lolita line of handpainted martini and wine glasses. Each glass comes with its own trademarked recipe on the bottom. Cyrus also has one of the areas largest selections of Robeez footwear for babies and toddlers. You will find beautiful robes and pajamas from Crabtree & Evelyn, along with a huge selection of bath and body products that Crabtree & Evelyn have become famous for. Cyrus also carries The Thymes, Malie Kaua'i and Alba Organics bath a body products as well as artwork, home décor, purses, dishes, serving pieces, greeting cards and the list goes on. Rest assured you will find unique items which you will love to give as gifts as mush as you will want to keep for yourself. Cyrus always has a fresh inventory with new items arriving weekly, if not daily. While you are visiting Cyrus Gifts & Home Accents make sure you don't miss Post & Pillar, their sister store, located right across the hall, and plan to be equally impressed.

401 SW Water Street, Peoria IL
(309) 671-1642
www.cyrusgifts.com

Shopping & Gifts—Greater Illinois

Churchill & Burns

A shared love of fine cigars and spirits inspired father and son team John and Brady Liberg to open Churchill & Burns in 1997. Winston Churchill and George Burns, two famous cigar smokers, would have been quite at home in this downtown Galena shop with its two walk-in humidors that keep the cigars at optimum freshness and flavor. You buy by the box or select cigars singly from 500 open boxes. Among the collection is the store's own label, Lead Mine Cigar, which was last manufactured in downtown Galena a century ago. You can purchase bourbon, cognac, scotch and microbrews to pair with your cigar. You'll also find custom-blended tobaccos and pipes at Churchill & Burns. A smoking lounge on the second floor offers such amenities as a straight razor shave. The store stocks men's shaving and grooming supplies and many classic men's gifts, including pocketknives, money clips, watches, chess games and flasks. Indulge your taste for gentlemanly delights at Churchill & Burns.

301 S Main Street, Galena IL (815) 777-2442
www.galenacigars.com

Fairytale Boutique

When Danielle Gulli buys clothing for Fairytale Boutique, she's using a finely tuned fashion sense to locate children's apparel with heirloom quality. She leans towards designers who understand the magical potential clothes have to transform all sorts of occasions, from days at the beach to formal celebrations. Danielle has noticed that designer clothing tends to develop a child's self-confidence. The store's outfits, in sizes from newborn to 14, will be preserved in family photos and shadow boxes. Danielle opened Fairytale in 2003 as a way to work in the fashion field while staying close to home to raise her children. Her mom, Mary Jane DeCapo, manages the store. At the store, children will find a fanciful playland to amuse them while you shop. A castle mural sets the scene, while walls separate armor for boys from princess crowns for girls. The labels at Fairytale Boutique range from French imports by Catimini and Mini Man to more moderately priced lines from the United States, such as Anita G. and Kissy Kissy. Christening gowns and communion outfits join playwear and such extras as photo frames, hand-painted furniture, chic jewelry and hair accessories. You'll also find clothing, gifts and blankets for newborns. Introduce your children to the enchantment of fashion at Fairytale Boutique.

124 Cass Street, Woodstock IL (815) 337-1995
www.fairytaleboutique.net

Cottage Rose

The comments that Sheila Yost hears from her customers at Cottage Rose, a gourmet food, gift and craft mall, could seem contradictory. "I've never seen anything like this," one might say about the item she just brought to the counter to purchase, while the next person might say, "I knew you'd have this." This must mean that Cottage Rose is a place to shop for both the unexpected and the hoped-for. To cover both categories, Sheila stocks everything from musical tins to sports memorabilia. A few things are certain. For example, you can always count on finding old-fashioned candy here and on being served something good from the 1950s style luncheonette, complete with retro gifts. Gourmet food tasting every Saturday is another constant. The rest you might want to leave to discovery, because Cottage Rose is a place that invites the serious browser to look around. Sheila discovered her own knack for shop keeping only after her kids had left home and her husband decided to start college. She tested the waters with a booth in this store and could have gone home to an empty house when the owners wanted to close it down. Instead, she bought the business in 2003 and has been enjoying a great run ever since. Go to Cottage Rose and see what you can find.

110 S Main Street, Taylorville IL (217) 824-9447

La Mendola

If you remember the days of fine retail shopping with service that truly made you feel like a valued customer, then you will rejoice at finding the tradition alive at La Mendola. Laurie La Mendola Bennett and her business partner, Jim Wojtowicz, opened the store in 2003, filling the need in Rockford for a specialty boutique selling high-end gift and home items. Located in the Edgebrook Center, La Mendola has become a destination for accent furniture, fine glassware and pewter. Italian imports reveal Laurie's connection to Rome, where her uncle was a well known fashion designer. She and Jim keep a line open to France, too, for linens, candles and porcelain. La Mendola also carries a full range of desk accessories and is one of the only dealers in Northern Illinois for fine stationery from Crane & Co. Elegant gift wrapping for any size gift is complimentary at La Mendola. As a symbol of its commitment to old-fashioned service, the staff writes out receipts by hand. La Mendola offers bridal registry and personal home or office consultations. To step back to a time when shopping was a sophisticated pleasure, go to La Mendola.

1651 N Alpine Road, Rockford IL
(815) 877-8014

La Di da

Part clothing boutique, part gift shop and part showroom of vintage treasures, La Di da is anything but predictable. Jeanine Dabson opened the store in 2005. The next year, it was nominated for the most improved business in Rockford's extended River District, a tribute to Jeanine's creative vision, which has transformed this old Ben Franklin store into an enchanting space. The merchandise and eclectic displays are always changing, so the shelf where you find a candelabra today might hold a must-have piece of pottery the next time you visit. Guests are welcome to browse for hours, says Jeanine. Indeed, you might need that long to see everything here. "I'm a very sentimental person," admits Jeanine, "and I love the story that goes with each vintage item." She has collected a delightful assortment of furniture, glassware and linens to mix with such new items as purses, locally made jewelry and candles. Some customers come just for the clothing and shoes, while others come to be surprised. La Di da is located in the North End Commons in the North End Commons area, just north of the downtown River District in Rockford. For eclectic shopping that will intrigue and delight, drop by La Di da.

1416 N Main Street, Rockford IL   (815) 962-1234

Lincoln Souvenir & Gift Shop

Founded by Bess and George King, the Lincoln Souvenir & Gift Shop remains a family-run enterprise. In the summer of 1935, as a way to keep their children George Jr. and Eleanor occupied, Bess bought $3.50 worth of souvenirs, set up a card table in front of their home, and instructed her children to remain until everything sold. Tourists bought everything within hours. Bess purchased more with the profits and George Sr. built shelves on the front porch for the merchandise. In 1938 the King's bought the lot next door and built a log cabin souvenir shop. Since that time, all of the family members have either worked at or owned the business. Current owners, Melissa and Dean King (Bess and George's grandson) have owned the shop since 1998. According to Melissa, the quaint log cabin offers the largest and most reasonably priced Lincoln, Springfield and Route 66 souvenirs in town. T-shirts, coffee mugs, salt and pepper shakers, magnets, shot glasses and key chains line the shelves. The five, original, wooden garage doors remain open to an airy, clean shop. School children on bus trips come to the store annually. Many of them return as adults and recall what they purchased as a child. Some the timeless treasures include big pennies, civil war hats, bows and arrows and pop guns. This is also the best place in town to get directions or local restaurant suggestions. So, while in the Land of Lincoln, stop in, sip a soda from the 1960s soda cooler and shop the incredible selection at the Lincoln Souvenir & Gift Shop.

1407 Monument Avenue, Springfield IL   (217) 523-1106

Paper & Plume

We may live in the electronic age, but some of the most important communications in our lives still begin on paper, whether they be wedding invitations, birth announcements or greeting cards. Owner Catherine Cox offers readymade and custom invitations, programs and greeting cards at Paper & Plume. You will find wrapping paper, fine writing papers and cardstock by Crane, William Arthur and Caspari, plus handcrafted cards. Catherine loves planning for special events and helps clients select the right invitation to fit the theme and budget, and makes sure the invitations follow guidelines of proper etiquette and grammar. Calligraphy is offered in many styles. Also offered is in-house printing for events needing as few as 10 invitations. Catherine carries coordinated paper, plates, napkins and hand towels, plus gift items, such as local artisans' soaps, candles and jewelry. The shop is in a building that dates back to 1891 and the products are showcased in rustic antique cupboards. In childhood, Catherine regularly set up a storefront and resold household items to her parents, a trait that caused her father to predict she would be an entrepreneur one day. Make the most of your communications at Paper & Plume, serving Woodstock since 2002.

132 Cass Street, Woodstock IL   (815) 338-6422
www.paperandplume.com

Photo by David Czuba Photography

Tinsley Dry Goods

Walk in Honest Abe's footsteps and shop where he once shopped with a visit to Tinsley Dry Goods, Springfield's unique purveyor of all things Lincoln. Adjacent to the Lincoln-Herndon Law Office just off the Old Capitol Square, Tinsley Dry Goods first opened up its doors in 1840, and was originally operated by Seth Tinsley. In 1991, the Old State Capitol Foundation reopened the historic landmark. In 2004 the Foundation approached Ron Homann, a Lincoln merchandise sales representative and loyal customer, about buying the shop. As avid Lincoln buffs, Ron and his wife Dana now operate the shop in the historic downtown area. Tinsley Dry Goods underwent a major remodel in 2005 that restored the shop's mid-1800's feel complete with native Illinois white oak wood floors, a tin ceiling and pine beams. The remodel won the shop Downtown Springfield Incorporated's, Best Interior Renovation award for 2005. Stop in to this charming shop to see works from artists Charles Houska, Mike Manning, Gale Myers, and sculptors Tom Clark and John McClarey, as well as a full selection of Lincoln busts, period décor and music, and reproduction civil war weaponry. The shop further stocks exclusive t-shirt, postcard and collector pin designs, a house brand of soy candles, and rustic metal and wood signs with quirky sayings that entertain tourists and local customers alike. Experience *shopping history* at its best at Tinsley Dry Goods.

209 S 6th Street, Springfield IL
(217) 525-1825
tinsleydrygoods@yahoo.com
www.tinsleydrygoods.com

Finials

Karin and Gary Lindberg embrace their Swedish heritage and share it with others at the Scandinavian gift and home store, Finials. The charming 1940s era home offers three floors of goods to delight even the most discerning shopper. Find table and floor lamps, along with more than 2,000 lampshades and a full lamp repair service. The store carries more than 300 finials, including many specialty and hard-to-find pieces, designed to add decorative detailing to any space. Karin and Gary's families are both from Sweden, and much of the space in the store is dedicated to Scandinavian goods, such as pottery, glassware and linens. Each room of the store is devoted to a separate kind of merchandise. In one, find the striking lines of Orrefors crystal. Swedish clogs, including those by Bastad, fill another room. Norwegian sweaters, Dala horses and Royal Copenhagen china are just some of the Scandinavian specialties you'll discover here. Bring the flavors of an authentic Scandinavian meal to your kitchen with Swedish meatballs, *lefse*, *kringle* and other delicious foods. Come to Finials, and take a touch of Sweden home with you.

4626 E State Street, Rockford IL   (815) 398-4428 or (800) 898-4428
www.ifinials.com

HomeElements

Tina Mason, owner of HomeElements, has always enjoyed exploring her creative side. On her way to getting a degree in landscape design, she took many art classes. Now she is in the business of helping people bring creativity into their homes. The wall art and accent pieces on display in her shop represent the work of talented people who strive to express their individuality. Some of it is gorgeous, some kitschy, and it all adds up to a fun and intriguing place to shop. Tina does all the buying for the store and pours her creativity into arranging her merchandise to look just right. She carries many handmade personal items, such as scarves, purses and wallets, in addition to things for the home. Jewelry from Sweet Romance and other American designers sells well for her, as do Beanpod Candles, made of 100 percent soy. A source of positive energy, Tina loves people and loves being on charming and historic Woodstock Square. She offers free gift wrapping and a relaxing environment for browsing. Drop by HomeElements for some creative inspiration.

203 Main Street, Woodstock IL   (815) 337-4707
www.homeelements203.com

The Kilt & Clover

The Kilt & Clover is as much of a cultural center as it is a gift store. Consider it a gateway to Scottish and Irish heritage. Owner Linda Smith-Castree is 100-percent Irish, and she absolutely loves her Celtic roots. A love this grand had to be shared, so Linda created a place where clans, and lovers of clans, can celebrate, research, and take home a little bit of heritage. Listen to live Celtic jams. Pick up a books on the subject. Enjoy Gaelic lessons on demand. Learn the Bagpipe, then see how good you are on open mike night. The Kilt & Clover carries some of the finest Irish and Scottish imports available. You'll find fine Irish linens, Scottish woolens, authentic jewelry, some of Ireland's oldest pottery, along with Beleek china and Heritage crystal. Want to pay tribute to the Royal Highlanders? This is where you'll find Black Watch kilts. Guinness products are here, along with great clothes for all ages to play in, including Barbarian Rugby Wear and Lansdowne Rugby. Linda carries dozens of food items from Ireland and Scotland, including teas, of course. Jacob's, McVitties, Bewley's and Barry's will allow you to savor the flavor of the Isles at home. Visit The Kilt & Clover in Rockford, a store with heart and soul.

1414 N Main Street, Rockford IL   (815) 962-KILT (5458)
www.thekiltandclover.com

Greater Illinois—Shopping & Gifts   173

Poopsie's

Art and Sue Landen roam North America several times each year in search of the 6,000 wacky items that fill their Galena gift store. "It seems the world is populated with lots of folks nearly as crazy as we are," they say. The Landens opened Poopsie's in 1993 on Galena's historic Main Street, the longest surviving 19th century Main Street in America. The large storefront of Poopsie's dates back to the 1850s, but the colors and contents have a contemporary feel. You'll find fine art for walls and tabletops, furniture and jewelry. A kids' corner is filled with toys, games and books. Among gifts as diverse as hand-painted cocktail glasses, cow-patterned socks and glass flowers, you'll find unexpected items that inspire hilarity, mischief or downright puzzlement. The changing merchandise and creative displays have earned Poopsie's a Best Merchandising award from *Niche Magazine*. The shop is named after Sue's grandmother, who solved her problem recalling names by calling everyone Poopsie. The staff, who call themselves *poopettes*, are obviously having a good time, including Casey the English sheepdog. You can shop online, but the whimsical shopping experience is best in person. Tickle your fancy with a visit to Poopsie's and be prepared to be asked, "Where on earth did you find that?"

107 Main Street, Galena IL (815) 777-1999 or (888) GALENA1 (425-3621)
www.poopsies.com

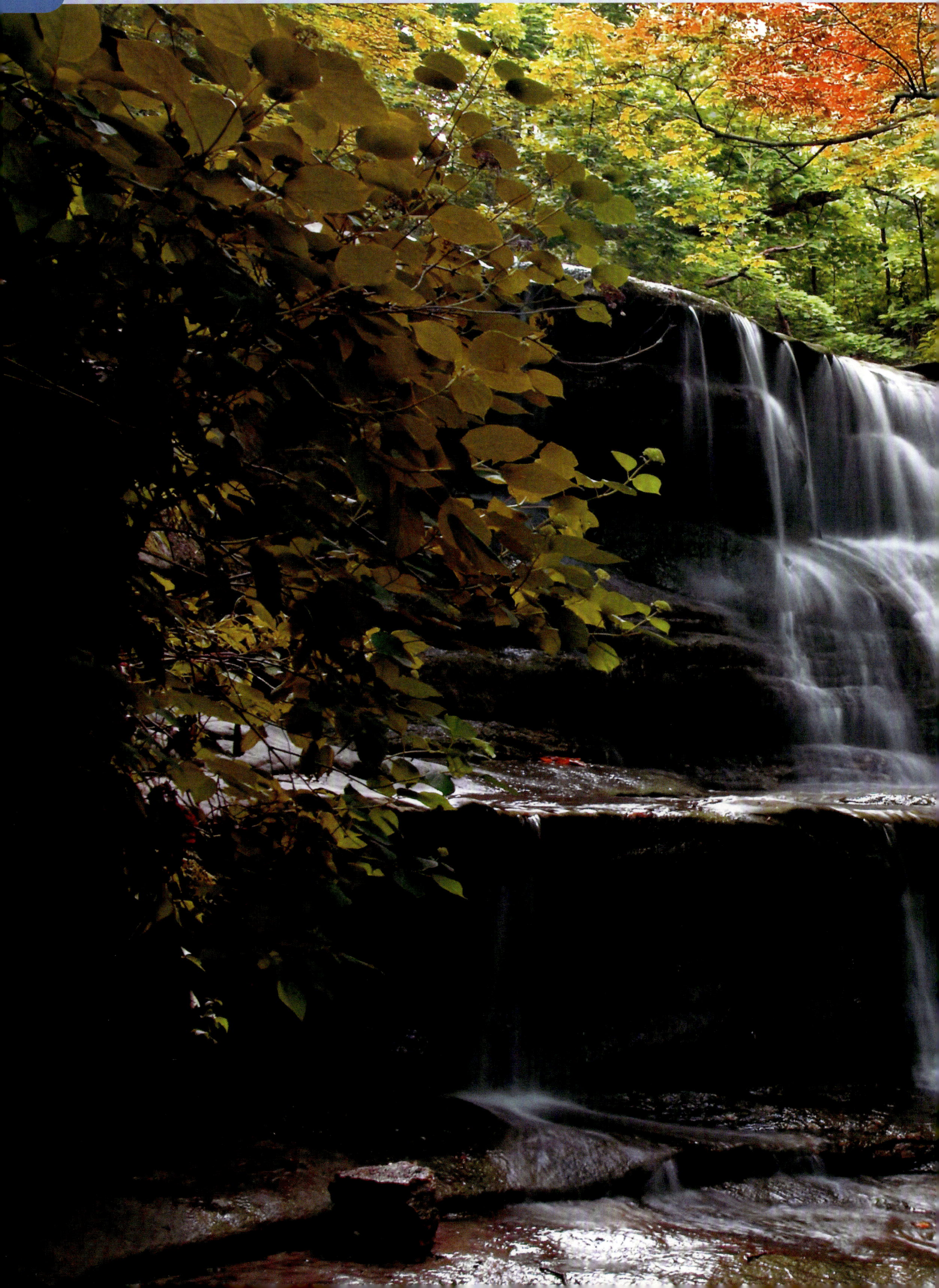

175

Waterfall in autumn at Starved Rock State Park, Utica Illinois

Index by Treasure

#
2 One 7 Skateshop 118

A
Adrienne Clarisse Intimate Boutique 44
Adventure Creek Alpaca Farm 109
Aldeen Golf Club 119
All About Me 48
American Café 137
Anastazia—Treasures for the Home 68
Anderson's Candy Shop 130
Annie Wiggins Guest House 108
Antioch Floral 56
Apples Bakery 131
Around the Clock Restaurant & Bakery 80
Arrowhead Golf Club 22
Art Post Gallery 62
Art Store & Gallery 62
Atrium Garden Center 65
August, the Salon 141
Ayla's Originals 13

B
Backstreet Steak & Chophouse 154
Barrington Flower Shop 54
Barrington Saddlery 89
Beadhive 10
Bearj Antonio Salon & Spa 39
Bears Gone Wild on Third 90
Beaver Creek Pottery 114
Beef-A-Roo 159
Belongings 74
Belvedere Mansion 121
Benson Stone Company 148
Best Art Shop & Gallery 61
Betty Schwartz's Intimate Boutique 41
Beyond the Garden Gate 94
Biaggi's Ristorante Italiano 152
Bloomington Indoor Golf Club 118
Blossom Basket Florist 144
Blue Violet Body Works 45
Brio Restaurant 154
Bristol Renaissance Faire 15
Bundling Board Inn 105

C
Camp Grant Museum and Restaurant 123
Cannova's Pizzeria 154
Canterbury Shoppe 92
Canvasback Ltd. 9
Carl Johnson's Gallery 146
Carrie's Vintage Inn 108
Casteel Coffee 23
Castle Gardens 68
Central Continental Bakery 32
Chalet Nursery & Garden Shops 66
Charmed 92
Chesapeake Seafood House 155
Children's Discovery Museum 118
Chocolat 133
Churchill & Burns 168
Clarice's—Creating Beautiful Looks 50
Cloran Mansion Bed & Breakfast 108
Cobblestones on the Square 136

Coffee Drop Shop 30
Colbert Custom Framing 62
Conscious Cup Coffee Roastery & Café 26
Costello Sandwich & Sides 80
Cottage Rose 168
Country Cobbler 50
Country Naturals 92
Cozy Dog Drive In 156
Cradles & All 94
Craftique and Never Enough Knitting 10
Crocodile Pie, A Children's Bookstore 90
Crystal Cave 91
Cyrus Gifts & Home Accents 167

D
Danny's Tap Room 80
Deb-betts 48
Deerfield Bakery 25
Del's Popcorn Shop 130
Del Carmen's Pizza East 156
Designers Desk, the Complete Needlework Shop 12
Design Toscano 94
Didier Farms 34
DiTullio's 136
Dockside Deli & Custard Shoppe 82
Don Roth's Blackhawk 81
Doyle's Pub & Eatery 156
Dreamwear Shoppe 47

E
Eliza Jane 49

F
Fairytale Boutique 168
Fairy Tales 90
Farm 125
Farmers' Guest House 110
Farmside Country Store & Winery 19
Faye's Attic 96
Fever River Outfitters 120
FiberWild! 114
Fine Line Creative Arts Center 11
Finials 172
Firkin 76
Floral Chic 149
Floral Gardens 53
Flower Bin, Etc. 144
Fold 115
FolkWorks Gallery 64
FoxFire 87
Fresh Flower Market 56

G
Gadjets Galore 96
Galena Beads "serving creativity" 117
Galena Log Cabin Getaway 109
Galena Trolley Tours & Depot Theatre 120
Gardens and Gatherings 68
Genesee Theatre 22
Gerlinde's Water Street Café 160
Gibby's Wine Den 34
Gift Box 96
Goldmoor Inn 107
Goldmoor Inn Dining 157

Good Works Gallery 98
Goose Barn 114
Graham's Fine Chocolates and Ice Cream 24
Grandma's Gourmet Deli 136
Great Impasta 160
Greer 100
Gridley's Grille 79
Grove Banquets 56
Gurnee Antique Center 93

H
Hannah's Home Accents 95
Harrison House Bed & Breakfast 6
Henry Mischler House 111
Henson Robinson Zoo 120
HomeElements 172
Honquest Fine Furnishings 70
Hotel Baker 5
Hotel Père Marquette 113
How Impressive! 88

I
Infini-Tea 29
In Good Taste 130
International House of Wine & Cheese 137
Irish Connoisseur 100

J
Jarosch Bakery 26
Jenapea's 160
Jenny Sweeney Designs 99
Jill's on Galena 162
John Evans Restaurant & Lounge 82
Jones Country Meats 137
Joseph's Floral & Gift Showroom 55
Joseph Layton Antiques and Interior Design 150

K
Kaladi's .925 Coffee Bar 132
Kamp Galleries 63
Kane County Cougars 17
Katherine's Bead Boutique 116
Kernel Fabyan's Gourmet Popcorn Shoppe 26
Kilt & Clover 172
Knight's Action Park 127
Knightsbridge Wine Shoppe 34
Kortman Gallery 146

L
La Di da 170
Lakeside Interiors 72
La Mendola 169
Lazy T 137
Leider Greenhouses 67
Le Petit Marche 36
Libertyville Florist 57
Lincoln Souvenir & Gift Shop 170
Little Havana Cigar Factory 21
Long Grove Apple Haus 18
Long Grove Confectionery 18
Lori's Designer Shoes 52
Lou Malnati's Pizzeria 82
Lucile's Tea Room 132
Lunker's 162
Lynfred Winery 35

Index by Treasure

M
Maclund Gallery 60
Maldaner's 162
Maple Avenue Gallery 60
Maple Crest Bed & Breakfast 110
Mariah's Restaurant 161
Marked for Dessert 28
Massbach Ridge Winery 138
Meg's Daily Grind 132
Mickey Finn's Brewery 83
Midnight Sun Antiques & Design 69
Midwest Cimmaron Archery 122
Mille Fiori! 58
Morkes Chocolates 30
Morning Star Mercantile & Café 163
Motif—Accents for the Home 70
Murphy's Gardens 139
My Honey 138

N
Needle Pointe 10
Neville-Sargent Gallery 64
North Shore Center for the Performing Arts in Skokie 16
Northwoods at Home 70
Nosh 84
Nuts About Nuts 36

O
Oaks Bed & Breakfast 112
Olive Mill 37
Oscar Swan Country Inn 7

P
Paddy's on the Square 99
Painted Cupboard 72
Painted Penguin 13
Paper & Plume 170
Parkview Gourmet 36
Paul's Confectionery 164
Peapod Chinese Restaurant 81
Peggie Robinson Designs 51
Perfect Setting 72
Perlman Fine Jewelry 40
Perry Street Brasserie 164
Persin & Persin Jewelers 52
Peter Daniel Apparel for Men and Women 43
Pick a Cup Coffee Club 24
Pickard China 97
Pine Cone Christmas Shop 19
Piper Glen Golf Club 122
Pirro's Restaurante 164
Plum Blossom 88
Poopsie's 173
Possibilities 98
Prairie House - Fine Craft Gallery 146
Prairie Landing Golf Club 22
Present Moment 98
Proud Fox Gallery 64

Q
Queen Anne Guest House 112

R
Radio Maria 166
Rain Collection 70
Red's Garden Center and Fireplace Logs 73
Red Barn Farm Market 135
River House Bed & Breakfast 104
Riverside Receptions & Conference Center 59
Rockford Speedway 124
Rock Island Arsenal Museum 122
Route 66 Hotel & Conference Center 112
Rustique 75

S
Saputo's 165
Sassy Lady 140
Serendipity 151
Serene Teaz 30
Shadowbrook Farm 16
Shenandoah Riding Center 124
Sheraton Suites Elk Grove 8
Shop 38, For the Love of Shoes 44
Sole Searching 48
Something Sweet and Gourmet 31
Spice House 38
Spirit of Peoria 124
Springfield Art Association of Edwards Place 126
Stained Glass Emporium 12
Stockholm's Vardshus 86
Strawberry Fields Natural Food Store & Café 138
Strawflower Shop & Rug Merchant 74
Studio 147
Studio Blu Salon & Spa 142
Sweet Indulgence 134
Sweet Nostalgia 32
Swiss Maid Bakery 134

T
Tate's Ice Cream 32
Tavern 77
Teddie Kossof Salon, Spa & Wellness Center 52
Thanks for the Memories 9
Theatre in the Park 126
Three Tarts Bakery and Café 27
Tiffany Beane Fine Art & Portrait Studio 145
Tinker Swiss Cottage Museum 128
Tinsley Dry Goods 171
TownePlace Suites Chicago Lombard 4
Trattoria Pomigliano 84
Twinkle Teas & Twinkle Tots Boutique 58
Two Olives and a Pepper 166

U
U Got Purse-onality 142

V
Van Kirk & Co. 71
Victorian Veranda Bed & Breakfast 106
Vignettes of Galena 149
Village Green Home & Garden 151
Villa Verone 84

W
West End Florist & Garden Center 74
Wildberry Pancakes & Café 86
Wild Clover Day Spa 143
Wildwood 85
William M. Staerkel Planetarium at Parkland College 128
Wilmette Jewelers 42
Wind Water & Light 147
Wolfgang Puck Grand Café 78
Woodstock Public House 153
Wool and Company 12

Y
Yaya's Unique Clothing & Accessories 42
Young Tootsies 46

THE ADVENTURE DOESN'T END HERE...

Learn more about our Treasures of America series by visiting
treasuresof.com

▼ Search for a Treasure

▼ Read our testimonials

▼ Purchase a Treasure book

▼ Recommend a Treasure